modern garden design

Janet Waymark

modern garden design

INNOVATION SINCE 1900

With 213 illustrations, 121 in color

Thames & Hudson

For Peter, Chris and Nicky

Acknowledgments

Much kindness was shown by those who lent documents, allowed me access to their gardens and shared their work with me. These include: Julia Sniderman Bachrach, Julian Cotterell, Fridy Duterloo Morgan, Rosie Hunt, Patricia Johanson, Robert McGregor, Sue Parry Davies, Vanessa Fernandes Parry Davies, Michael Stancomb, Isabelle Van Groeningen, and Elisabeth Whittle.

My thanks are also due to Joan Bullock-Anderson, Churchill College, Cambridge; Margaret Owen, Cumbria Record Office, Kendal; Linda Lott, Dumbarton Oaks Garden Library, Washington USA; Sheila Harvey, Landscape Institute, London; Françoise Dierkens-Aubry, Horta Museum, Brussels; Dr Brent Elliott, Lindley Library, London; and Pamela Robertson, Hunterian Museum, University of Glasgow for help with archival material, and to the staff of Dartington Hall Trust Archive, Devon; First Garden City Heritage Foundation, Letchworth Garden City; the Imperial War Museum, London; the Public Record Office, Kew; Somerset Record Office, Taunton; San Diego Historical Society, USA, and West Sussex Record Office, Chichester.

The following were kind enough to lend or take photographs for me: Jonathan Bell, Anthony Blee, Ruth Chivers, Sue Coulbeck, Elizabeth Hingston, Robert McGregor, and Alan Powers.

I am grateful for the wise and kindly guidance of my editor and the staff of Thames & Hudson; especial thanks go to my colleagues Dr Paula Henderson for her helpful comments on two chapters, and Dr Hazel Conway, who read all the text and offered sound advice. My warmest thanks, however, go to my husband Peter, for his encouragement and support throughout.

Title page

Musical Rill, Shute, Wiltshire, England

Geoffrey Jellicoe designed several small cascades at Shute in the 1970s as a celebration of water. There are eight chutes in this musical rill with four outlets shaped to produce an harmonic chord.

First published in hardcover in the United States of America in 2003 by Thames & Hudson Inc., 500 Fifth Avenue, New York, New York 10110

thamesandhudsonusa.com

First paperback edition 2005

Library of Congress Catalog Card Number 2002113178
ISBN-13: 978-0-500-28421-6
ISBN-10: 0-500-28421-0

Printed in Singapore by C. S. Graphics

Contents

Introduction

This book is for those interested in the history of twentieth-century gardens and beyond, who would like to discover the ideas behind their designs. The period has produced a rich variety of talented garden-makers who introduced new styles. Innovation spread rapidly as communications improved, and one of the purposes of this volume is to follow the interaction of ideas between Britain, Europe and the Americas. Using a selection of case studies, gardens are described where they have something to add to the accumulated store of history, or define an attitude to garden-making. The term 'Modern' is used here inclusively, and refers to the present and the recent past. The aim is to acquaint the reader with some of the makers of gardens from 1900, exploring the Modern Movement, and identifying the trends in garden-making to the Postmodern period and beyond. This book seeks to provide a broad context for the history of recent gardens, and to stimulate further research.

While 1900 has been taken as the starting point, historian David Cannadine, discussing the limits of the nineteenth century, has pointed out that a century does not begin until those born in the one before have died.[1] This suggests two things: that a century has no firm boundaries, and that people carry round the historical baggage of the past. The second is particularly true of garden-makers, whose historical baggage can include many past centuries. Garden design has been a very conservative art form, constantly looking backwards, taking its lead from art and architecture, but often lagging thirty years behind.

What is a garden? I take my definition from the International Council on Monuments and Sites (ICOMOS), whose Florence Charter of 1981 described the historic garden (which the Charter sought to preserve) as 'an architectural and horticultural composition of interest to the public from the historical or artistic point of view' (article one), which later makes clear that the term 'garden' could equally well apply to landscaped parkland, cemeteries, allotments, and cultivated and managed green areas in an urban context.

The terms 'garden design' and 'landscape architecture' are sometimes used interchangeably. Although scale may be used as a dividing point beyond which a garden is defined as a landscape, in most cases a landscape is also a garden. The division is also related to the growth of professional training during the twentieth century, which allocated the design of green spaces in urban settings to landscape designers, and private gardens to garden designers. The emergence of Land Art has reversed the separation of 'garden' and 'landscape', and has added a sculptural element to them both.

A garden 'style' is not always so easy to define either. 'Art Nouveau', for instance, had different meanings in different countries. The term 'Modern' was applied across the arts with various interpretations from the end of the nineteenth century onwards. Similarly, ideas do not recognize the boundaries imposed by dates.

Gardens are governed by their physical backgrounds – climate, soil and aspect; but it is the gardener, shaped by his cultural background, who shapes the garden. Garden history is itself a synthesis of different disciplines: the concerns of botanists, climatologists, and soil scientists need to interact with the concerns of geographers, historians and economists to produce a coherent picture of the landscape. If you can't understand the cultural context, you can't understand the garden.

The book begins with gardens at the crossroads of two centuries, re-making the styles of the past. The next three chapters take the reader to the Second World War, identifying themes which will recur. Chapter 2 considers plantsmen's (and plantswomen's) gardens, Chapter 3 architectural gardens, and Chapter 4 gardens associated with the social concerns surrounding the Garden City, which were about providing garden spaces for the working classes. Chapters 5 and 6 cover the period from the Second World War to the 1960s, showing how the Americas pulled away from colonial influences to develop styles of their own, and how continental Europe and Britain emerged from wartime to create distinctive national garden styles.

Chapter 7 takes garden-makers into the Postmodern period and beyond, and unravels a colourful collection of strands, from Parisian parks to gardens of philosophers. Postmodern design has closely allied itself with conservation and the regeneration of degraded landscapes. Designs for the twenty-first century bind together art, sculpture and Land Art at all levels from domestic gardens to larger landscapes. It appears that in this branch of design, gardens have at last caught up, and are looking ahead.

One Foot in the Past: Gardens in Transition

The start of a century, like Janus, always looks two ways: it is a false boundary. There are those who choose to stay with past history, and those who explore their way to the future. At the beginning of the twentieth century, the old social order of aristocratic, rich landowner with large gardens and large workforce still held sway in much of Europe and, with titled connections, the eastern side of the USA. This was to be loosened by the First World War, and still further, as the agriculture on which aristocratic incomes were based was replaced by agriculture in the New World. But for the moment, the nineteenth-century garden mindset lingered on in the revival of past styles. This was true, also, of the new industrial classes who bought themselves country estates. The Arts and Crafts Movement reacted against the advance of industry, mechanization and urbanization, looking to the values of medieval craftsmanship and vernacular materials, whether in plants or local stone. But there were those born in the nineteenth century, including painter Claude Monet, who adopted new ideas in colour and naturalism in gardens, and town and garden planner Thomas Mawson, who used new materials to build gardens, and set the way forward for others.

Revivalism – France

By the end of the nineteenth century France and formality were, as in the seventeenth century, inseparably linked together. Formality dominated the schools of architecture and painting in which garden design originated. Teaching at the Ecole des Beaux-Arts in Paris was based on classical lines, following styles of architecture and decoration adopted by the ancient Greeks and Romans. To ensure success, painters needed to exhibit their works through the Salons. Only as late as 1817 was landscape alone – without classical figures – acceptable for exhibition.

The spirit of Le Nôtre and Versailles still haunted a country shaken by republican revolts and the Franco-Prussian war of 1870–71. Great gardens had been neglected or had fallen into decay; others had been altered into the picturesque and the *jardin anglais* styles. Formality with its axes, allées, grand terraces with grander cascades, and bosquets kept strictly in check by masterful trimming, brought back comfortable memories of an ordered society of the seventeenth century and France triumphant. The landscape designers Duchêne, father Henri (1841–1902) and son Achille (1866–1947),

Opposite
Long Barn, Kent, England
The heart of Harold Nicolson's and Vita Sackville-West's fourteenth-century country home from 1915 near Sevenoaks, Kent. The Nicolsons terraced the sloping site, and here Vita developed her talent for colour and plantsmanship, possibly influenced by a visit to Gertrude Jekyll two years later.

rebuilt and restored gardens from the time of Louis XIV. Their devotion to Le Nôtre brought them a considerable number of commissions, from Vaux-le-Vicomte in 1875 to Courances before the First World War. Their work took them to other parts of the world; Achille designed the circular outdoor ballroom for Nordkirchen park in Westphalia in the early part of the twentieth century, the water parterre for the Duke of Marlborough at Blenheim in England in 1925, and parks and gardens for wealthy Americans. There were other commissions in Australia, Argentina and Russia, town-house gardens for Paris and country-seaside gardens for the flourishing colony of the rich of the Côte d'Azur.

The French landscape designer J.C.N. Forestier (1861–1930) was similarly requested to restore gardens contemporary with Louis XIV, including at the palace of Sceaux. He was also attracted to the sun-loving exiles, and his formal designs took on features of the Moorish garden as he completed commissions in Mediterranean France, Spain and Morocco. The public park of María-Luisa in Seville, opened in 1914, laid out along axes opening into tiled rectangular areas for seating, with low bubbling fountains, tiled alcoves and shady trees, is a good example of Forestier's designs in this genre. Like the Duchênes, Forestier worked widely on park design and eventually on town planning abroad, with commissions in Latin America, North Africa, the United States and the West Indies.

American architects were also trained at the Ecole, taking the tradition of formality back to the United States; as will be seen in Chapter Five, this stifled the advancement of newer ideas until after the Second World War.

Revivalism – England

In England, revivalists looked back more than once to Italy for inspiration. In the 1860s architect Charles Barry (1795–1881) had used terraces, tazzas, staircases, fountains and statuary at Shrubland Park, Suffolk, and painter William Andrews Nesfield (1794–1881) had created parterres at the Royal Horticultural Society's garden, Kensington, to reinvent their ideas of 'Olde England' through Italianate devices.

Edwardian England saw another spell of Italian revivalism, divided between those who continued to see an Italian garden as a collection of small geometrical shapes filled with bedding, tazzas, pots and statuary (as in the gardens of the Earl of Pembroke at Wilton and Earl Brownlow at Belton),[1]

an outdoor museum for sculpture, and those who attempted to move closer to an interpretation of the spirit of the Italian Renaissance.

William Waldorf Astor (1848–1919) was typical of the former group. An educated, rich Anglophile American, prospering on wealth from his German immigrant fur-trader great-grandfather and then from property investments, he became American Minister (ambassador) in Rome in the 1880s. Here he purchased ancient, medieval and Renaissance paintings and artefacts and indulged his interest in sculpture.

He assembled a sizeable collection of classical Roman sarcophagi, many items from the Villa Borghese, other acquisitions made in London and Florence, and later, post-classical sculpture. Many of these were housed in his villa in Sorrento. At the end of his career he took a dislike to his American homeland, considering it unfit for gentlemen to live in, and bought Cliveden in Buckinghamshire in 1893. This was a large house on a cliff above the Thames which, appropriately for Astor, had been remodelled by Charles Barry as an Italian villa. Ten years later he purchased the Tudor Hever Castle in Kent, to which he retired in 1906 after his son Waldorf's wedding, presenting Cliveden to him and his new wife Nancy. At Cliveden he placed the sixteenth-century balustrade from the Villa Borghese – which somehow he had managed to buy after the sale of the villa – below the Barry terrace, but he had been refused the statues which stood on the balustrade. By the 1890s the Italian government had begun to take legal measures to resist the foreign collectors, realizing the historic value of pieces which had been leaving the country. His other Roman

Above
Borghese Balustrade, Cliveden, Buckinghamshire, England
The Borghese Balustrade was bought by William Waldorf Astor from the Villa Borghese in Italy at the end of the nineteenth century. It was installed below Charles Barry's mansion and terrace at Cliveden, where it looks across the grand sweep of lawn and parterre towards the River Thames.

11

Pompeian Wall, Hever Castle, Kent, England

The Pompeian Wall at Hever Castle begins in this rotunda and extends the full length of the garden wall to the lake. Here Astor set out his collection of archaeological artefacts in the early twentieth-century museum fashion, with their backs to the wall.

antiquities and Renaissance pieces were shared between the grounds of Cliveden and Hever.

Astor's Kentish garden displayed his treasures in a much more dramatic manner. Separated from the Castle's immediate environs (and at once breaking the rules of the Italian villa and garden layout) he employed architect Frank Pearson and Cheal's nursery at Crawley in Sussex to construct a long, four-acre walled garden. This ended in a classical loggia overlooking a lake. Leading to the lake loggia with its colonnades and staircases descending to promenades, Pearson made a tall Pompeian wall with embayments and rotundas in which were placed the sarcophagi and statues, Roman and Renaissance artefacts, displaying them, museum fashion, against the sandstone wall. Facing it, across broad lawns, was a matching wall with a long, stone pergola, clothed with climbers which helped to shelter a series of green grottoes complete with gentle fountains modelled on the Villa d'Este near Rome, and which were softened by the planting of tender camellias, roses, and flowering shrubs.

But compatriots of Astor, painter Charles A. Platt (1861–1933) and writer Edith Wharton (1862–1937), had begun to portray Italian gardens in a more perceptive way. Platt had written and illustrated his *Italian Gardens* in 1894; Wharton had been commissioned by *Century* magazine to write a series of articles called *Italian Villas and their Gardens* which appeared in 1904 in book form. She had travelled widely, and her observations in her introduction reflect an understanding of the thinking behind the classical landscape which travellers had rediscovered during the Renaissance. 'The garden must be studied in relation to the house, and both in relation to the landscape', she wrote. The garden 'must be adapted to the architectural lines of the house it adjoined; it must be adapted to the requirements of the inmates of the house, in the sense of providing shady walks, sunny bowling-greens, parterres and orchards, all conveniently accessible; and lastly it must be adapted to the landscape around it.'[2] In this she could have been summarizing the younger Pliny's (*c.* AD 61–113) description of his villa near Rome.[3] Equally significant is the link forward to the modernists, in Wharton's emphasis on the Roman principles of utility of purpose and the designing of house and garden together.

Harold Peto – Italian Revival in Edwardian England

In England Harold Ainsworth Peto (1845–1933) was the architect who most
nearly approached the spirit of the Italian villa in his own garden at Iford in
Wiltshire. He was the son of Sir Samuel Morton Peto (1809–89), a Suffolk
landowner, Member of Parliament and builder, whose railway contracting had
bankrupted him in 1866. Harold was articled locally and became a partner of
Ernest George between 1871 and 1892. After this the terms of his partnership
precluded him from practising as an architect in England; but since he had
become drawn towards garden design this had little effect on his career
and he was able to work as an architect abroad. Most of his best-known
commissions date from after the termination of his contract with George.
Peto travelled widely in Europe. His diaries show a preference for the
Mediterranean countries and, in particular, for Italy; he also travelled to the
USA in 1887 and the Far East in 1898. But Peto's most fruitful years are
sparsely recorded in first-hand documentation, and there are no planting
plans for Iford.[4]

He became owner of an Elizabethan manor house near Bradford-on-Avon
in 1899, set on the lower part of a tree-fringed slope descending to the river
Frome. *The Boke of Iford* is an account written by Peto in 1917 describing his
uncovering of the hidden layers of architecture in the house and his careful
moulding of the landscape, until he felt he had reached the spirit of the house
and had matched it with an Italianate garden in sympathy. The *Boke* explains
the provenance and placing of Peto's collection of architectural treasures from
Italy and elsewhere.

The bones of the garden were formed by the main stone staircase with
pillars surmounted by urns, ascending at right angles to the house, rising to

Iford, Wiltshire, England
The Venetian-style Casita
(left) contains some of
Peto's collection of Italian
marble. Peto believed that
a green Italianate garden
should not be overcome
by colourful flowers.
The stone staircase (right)
formed the main vertical
axis, crossed by terraces
leading to small enclosed
garden rooms.

a series of crossing terraces. The staircase replaced a grassy bank, and was to form the core of Peto's 'hanging garden'. Off the terraces lay small, enclosed spaces and garden buildings. At the end of the main terrace an existing Georgian stone summerhouse was re-sited to close the vista in a pleasing manner. Giving length to the paved terrace was a colonnade of local stone especially made for Peto, which was joined by chains which supported trailing plants. The view was opened by the placing of a lily pond, over which the distant countryside could be admired. Water was brought into the garden from springs in the woods, and the house end of the main terrace was marked by a well-head. Above the well-head, facing the sun, stood the casita or garden house with its Venetian-style shallow-pitched roof, which displayed 'many of my pieces of old Italian marble'.[5]

An arcaded loggia was made for sitting out of the sun at the foot of the stairs. Here Peto took his meals when it was fine. Hidden on the east side of the Georgian summerhouse was the Cloister, a small, arcaded building dedicated for Christian worship, its dim peacefulness evoking a monkish retreat, and at the same time the arcades remind the visitor of Peto's pleasure in the Court of the Lions in Granada, which he mentions in his travel diaries. Here Peto placed the rest of his collection, remarking 'old buildings or fragments of Masonry carry one's mind back to the past in a way that a garden of flowers cannot do'. Peto was more at home with 'broad walks with seats and statues and tall cypresses' than 'English Gardens… running riot in masses of colour irrespective of form'.[6] Judging from contemporary photographs, Peto used plants such as nepeta and bergenia, jasmine and lavender, ferns and erigeron which merged in natural masses, edged paths and steps, and never became dominant. Plant form was enhanced by the use of acanthus and agapanthus; taller structures by roses and wisteria. His use of evergreen juniper, cypress and yew, bay and phillyrea, enclosing peaceful walks and giving intimate spaces within an ordered architectural framework, brought him closer to the Italian villa at Iford than was achieved by many contemporary Italianate gardens.

There were other notable Peto Italian gardens in England; at Buscot Park in Oxfordshire, he made an exceptionally fine water garden for Alexander Henderson, Lord Faringdon, in 1904, with further work between 1911 and 1913. The eighteenth-century house, designed on the top of a rise for Edward Loveden Loveden (c. 1749–1822) and built by James Darley (1744–1821), came into Henderson's hands in 1889. He asked the Ernest George Partnership to make changes and additions to the house and estate, and Peto designed a link between the house and a large lake in the park. Following the line through a Victorian arboretum, Peto used the gradual fall in height to design a series of 'incidents' along a green corridor leading to the lake. Below stone steps and a

lawn, which accommodate most of the fall in height, begins a narrow canal. On the journey to the canal the eye is held by Peto's temple on the far side of the lake, and suddenly on the edge of the lawn, a quatrefoil pool opens at the walker's feet. In the middle of the pool is a bronze fountain of a boy with a dolphin. From here the water is channelled into its canal, then enters a tranquil, rectangular pool, and exits under a hump-backed, balustraded bridge into the final section before quietly entering the lake. The green corridor along the canal opens into a series of clipped box-edged rooms in which there are marble seats and Italian statues, including herms representing Roman gods.

Peto's 1912 plan to build a pergola as a horizontal element across a new stairway in the upper part of the water garden, with low stone walls flanked by pencil cypresses, was never implemented.[7] However as it stands, the elegance of the simple stairway and canal with its quiet waters running through the green walls of trees and shrubs, provides Buscot with a satisfying example of the Italianate garden in England.

Peto's love for the Mediterranean brought him into contact with wealthy clients for whom he was able to design house and garden together, in true Italianate style, in the years before the First World War. Of these, the Villa Maryland in the Alpes Maritimes was made for Mrs Arthur Wilson (c. 1904) as a Renaissance villa on a sloping site, which Peto used to create terraces and cross-axes. One axis led southwards down a long staircase to a garden house built as a temple overlooking a pool, replicating the Villa Lante near Rome

Water Garden, Buscot, Oxfordshire, England
Harold Peto was asked by the first Lord Faringdon to connect his eighteenth-century hilltop house in Buscot Park to a lake in the grounds. In 1904 Peto made an elegant stone stairway below which opened an Italianate water garden, in sympathy with the age of the house.

Villa Maryland, Alpes Maritimes, France
Harold Peto designed villas and gardens for the wealthy inhabitants of the French Riviera. The Villa Maryland, made for Mrs Arthur Wilson, was one of a series in which he borrowed the shape of the loggia of the sixteenth-century Villa Lante at Bagnaia as a model for a cool pavilion in a sun-drenched garden.

with its round-headed central arch flanked by rectangular openings. Citrus trees in pots, olive trees and slim pencil cypresses stood above the reflections of the pillars in the round pool. As at Iford, erigeron massed against the stairs. The cross axis above the pool was marked by single columns crowned with figures; squared, topiary columns topped with clipped balls edged the path; and a pergola-like arched walk was fashioned from timber and clipped cypresses.

More than any other Italian revivalist of the time, Harold Peto appreciated the importance of the connection between house and garden. But it was the elegance of his stairways, terraces, colonnades, garden buildings and the placing of pieces of Roman sculpture and statuary which caught the

imagination of those who loved Italian gardens, and made him one of the most sought after architects of his time.

The Arts and Crafts Movement: William Morris (1834–96)

It was perhaps the social concern of William Morris which encouraged the evolution of the philosophy known as the Arts and Crafts Movement, though, ironically, it was the income from shares held by his stockbroker father in Devon Great Consols copper mine, near Tavistock, which enabled him to move between various spheres of influence – architecture, painting, design, writing – and which made his life secure in his different enterprises.

In 1853 Morris went to Oxford to read medieval history. There, he read John Ruskin's *The Stones of Venice*, which had just been published. Ruskin's philosophy condemned the industrialists' drive towards capitalism, mass production, and machine-made goods, with its implied rejection of the value of craftsmanship. Both Ruskin and Morris believed this gave poor-quality products, and lost the ennobling character of work lovingly produced by hand. All products should be beautiful as well as having functional application, and decoration should be based on natural forms. Followers of the Arts and Crafts Movement valued the vernacular – local materials, and, in gardens, local plants. Unfortunately this philosophy led to expensive goods which only a few could afford, and a further encouragement to their mass production.

Morris commissioned Philip Webb (1831–1915), who had supervised his work at architect G. E. Street's practice, to build him the Red House at Bexleyheath in Kent. This gave him the opportunity to construct the surroundings which he could fill with furniture, wallpaper, and fabrics for curtains made by his new foundation of Morris, Marshall, Faulkener and Co. along the lines of honest craftsmanship. 'The Firm' was set up in Red Lion Square in London in 1861.

The Red House was a considerable departure from what was being designed at the time. It had the air of a medieval manor with its steep gabled roof, mixture of round and Gothic windows and deep porches; but it was

**Kelmscott Manor,
Lechlade, Oxfordshire,
England**

William Morris and
Dante Gabriel Rossetti
leased Kelmscott Manor,
a peaceful sixteenth-
century stone house,
where the willows and
wild flowers in the water
meadows surrounding the
house found their way into
the fabrics and wallpapers
designed for 'The Firm'.
Morris wrote about
Kelmscott in *News From
Nowhere*, in which a
woodcut immortalized
this view of the front
garden of the house.

notable that Morris employed local craftsmen, local materials, and local
methods of construction, and the house and garden were expressly
designed as one.

It was to be expected that Morris would have a preference for the enclosed
garden, given his early interests in the church and medievalism, and he
divided the space of the inner garden with hedges and wattle fences. The
L-shaped house was built within the site of an orchard, leaving the old trees
intact. Trellis was used to train honeysuckle, roses and jasmine, and enclose
a well which had a conical tiled roof. Morris's delight in wild flowers was
displayed as he and his colleagues – Webb, painter Edward Burne-Jones and
poet Dante Gabriel Rossetti – designed wallpaper and fabrics. Morris's first
pattern for cotton fabric was called *Jasmine Trellis*, and depicts the flower
winding its way through tied, cut sticks in the same way that it would have
grown in his garden. 'The Firm' produced *Daisy* wallpaper in 1864, with red
campion and aquilegia in the design, *Strawberry Thief*, a cotton fabric based on
the wild strawberry in 1883, *Pink and Hawthorn* tiles in 1887, and many others.
Not only does this illustrate Morris's concern to preserve wild flowers from the
invasion of exotics, but it echoed his use of local flora as a vernacular 'raw
material' in gardens, matching the vernacular use of local building materials.

William Morris moved from the Red House after only five years, after illness
aggravated by daily commuting to London. In 1871 he leased Kelmscott

Manor at Lechlade in Oxfordshire with Rossetti; this was a typical gabled, grey stone Cotswold building dating from the sixteenth century. It had an established garden which Morris appears to have maintained and enriched with cottage garden flowers. His writings describe the buttercups and heartsease in the wild meadows beyond the walls, the snowdrops, cherry, crab-apple and hawthorn blossom in the spring. Wild flower designs continued to be depicted in the furnishings made by 'The Firm'. On the frontispiece of *News from Nowhere*, which Morris wrote in 1891, is a woodcut of the front garden of his Oxfordshire house, with standard roses lining the short stone path to the door, and ramblers climbing over the porch.

William Morris's lifelong concern for working men was displayed in the last garden he made. Finding his premises for making furnishings in Queen Square, London, too cramped, in 1881 he took over an old textile factory at Merton Abbey on the banks of the River Wandle. Here he set out a garden with spring bulbs, lilies, wallflowers, hollyhocks and the like, where the men could enjoy the view of the willows and poplars by the river, and the colour of the cottage flowers, while the fabrics they had been making dried in the sun on the grass. Factory gardens were provided by other philanthropic employers, together with allotments and gardens (a theme explored in Chapter Four).

Morris's legacy for the Arts and Crafts garden may be seen in his use of craft skills, local materials and local plants. However, he did not make the step between floral design inside the house to actual floral design on the ground.

Impressionism:
Claude Monet (1840–1926)

Claude Monet was a grocer's son, born in 1840 in Paris. Although he lacked the financial security enjoyed by Morris, his father supported his painting lessons with academician Charles Gleyre. To succeed, he needed to exhibit in the Paris Salons, which were notoriously conservative. Instead, he created a form of painting which inspired those who were moving towards naturalism in both form and colour in their gardens (discussed in Chapter Two).

Monet's circle included like-minded painters: Alfred Sisley (1839–99), Pierre-Auguste Renoir (1841–1919), Gustave Courbet (1819–77) and Camille Pissarro (1830–1903). These men painted *en plein air* (out of doors), greatly helped by the invention of tubes for oil paint in 1840, though their canvases were often finished in the studio. Of the dealers who helped to promote and sell Impressionist paintings in France, possibly Paul Durand-Ruel was one of the most influential. Despite Monet's original misgivings, Durand-Ruel sold many paintings in the United States, and in the 1920s found buyers in Japan. Not only did this help to keep Monet solvent; it promoted the Impressionist ideas of colour and naturalism in landscape and the garden abroad, and brought a trickle of would-be Impressionist painters from the United States to settle at Giverny.

Monet frequently referred to his search for 'the personal experience of nature'.[8] This he achieved by concentrating not on the subject itself, but on the light and atmosphere around it which were constantly changing. These were challenging attitudes for a would-be exhibitor at the Paris Salon to adopt at the time. But for the garden historian, they explain the warmth and richness of colour which emerge in the paintings of Monet's own gardens and the landscapes of the villages along the Seine; more especially in the depiction of flowers and water at Giverny which Monet had created for his own delight at the turn of the century. For those with eyes to see, they marked the end of formality in planting, they opened up new ways of using colourful plants, and they underlined the value of the middle-class garden in a world that had been dominated by images of grand estates.

Monet's gardening friends included painter Gustave Caillebotte (1848–94), who bought many of his paintings, and with whom he discussed theories of colour which were circulating at that time in the works of Michel-Eugène Chevreul (1786–1889). Chevreul's book *De la loi du contraste simultané des couleurs* (1839, published in English as *The Principles of Harmony and Contrast of Colours,* 1854) aroused considerable interest. Chevreul, who was a chemist working on dyes for the Gobelin tapestries, claimed that complementary colours – that is, those which were opposite each other on a wheel of the three primary colours and the three secondary colours with their linking intermediaries – suited each other. The implication for the gardener was that flowers with these colours could be planted together.

Monet's knowledge of plants was extended by his visits to horticultural shows and the reading of horticultural journals. Though no gardening notes survive, contemporary photographs, his paintings and the writings of visitors have helped to clarify how the garden at Giverny was laid out. Today's planting, however, may have drifted away from Monet's time. His friend Caillebotte's garden at Petit-Gennevilliers has been lost to industrial development.[9] With the help of his family (Monet planted, and the eight children weeded and watered), and then a gardener and five assistants when he was financially secure enough to buy the property in 1890, the garden took shape.

The walled flower garden, bisected by a gravelled *grande allée*, which disappears in summer under a mass of scarlet nasturtiums as they snake their way to the centre, is bordered by two sets of small beds which, despite the neat regularity of their disposition, give the impression of informality because of the way their contents are laid out. The smaller, paint-box beds to the east of the allée and the north-south rectangular beds to the west of the allée and a

long lawn, are the key to the 'vernacular raw materials' of Giverny. Each bed
was filled with flowers of the same colour and near-colour, and it seems that
Monet used these as his own experimental flower-spectrum, adding and
changing to gain the effect that he wanted. The western beds, and the lawn,
contained many different shades of iris, which Monet loved, and tall elements
were introduced by wild cherries, crab apples and clematis trellis. Plants which
he used include the Asiatic varieties of lily, penstemon, the deep blue *Salvia
patens*, Japanese anemones, sweet peas, gladioli, asters, and larkspur. He
preferred single forms of flower for their more natural effect. What is
important here is that Monet appears to have created and planted his
garden with painting in mind.

From 1853, Japan had begun to open up trading relations with the West,
after two centuries of isolation. Monet, like others of his time, was fascinated
by all things Japanese, and this theme was developed in his own style in a new
part of the garden which he began in 1893. He bought two acres of land to the
south of the railway line (now a road), diverting the River Epte to make a lake
in which he could grow waterlilies, and develop an Asiatic theme. Monet's
house is still full of prints from the East, illustrating flowering cherries,
nasturtiums, and bamboos. He never went to Japan, but invited a Japanese
gardener to advise him on planting, and he imported yet more iris, azaleas,
peonies, and a wisteria which was trained over a wooden bridge.

The garden was not a truly 'authentic' Japanese one, for the bridge was
painted green, not red, there was no cutting back of shrubs, there were no
stone ornaments, and there was no symbolic meaning to the layout or
contents of the water-garden. It was a French version of the 'stroll garden',
where visitors walk around the edge of the lake, admire views through the
planting, and move through a bamboo tunnel. Although Japanese gardens
are regarded as highly formal, the prints in Monet's house show that there was
a great deal of humour and informality in the depictions of everyday people:
three ladies with parasols battle their way around a lake in the snow (Utagawa
Kunisada); a group takes tea under the flowering cherries (Hiroshige).[10] The
gardens in which Monet was interested and which he painted were not those
of the aristocrats.

In this water garden, with its blue iris and reflected lilies, Monet painted
steadily and obsessively, despite suffering cataracts, turning his back on the
First World War and many of the American settlers in Giverny who wanted to
paint as he did. He continued to buy irises, and European and North American
water lilies from a grower in Bordeaux.

Of the French Impressionist garden makers perhaps Caillebotte was the
closest to Monet in enthusiasm. He painted cabbages in his more formally laid
out estate at Yerres as Renoir painted still life in his greenhouse, Pissarro a

peasant's wheelbarrow and Sisley market garden land. All painted colourful, everyday flowers and scenes, which exerted a notable influence on garden-makers.

Arts and Crafts:
Gertrude Jekyll (1843–1932) and Edwin Lutyens (1869–1944)

The partnership of Gertrude Jekyll and Edwin Lutyens has had lasting influence in England and elsewhere. Jekyll had met Monet and Morris, she had a copy of Descaisne and Naudin's *Manuel de l'Amateur de Jardin* (Manual for the Amateur Gardener), and knew of Chevreul's *Principles of Harmony and Contrast of Colours*. In England journals such as the *Gardeners' Chronicle* created a forum for debate for head gardeners, who pompously denounced Chevreul's ideas as unworkable in the garden, but appear not to have been given the benefit of further comment on the subject by two French garden writers who claimed to have put Chevreul's theories into practice.[11] From a prosperous middle-class background in Surrey, Jekyll studied painting at the Kensington School of Art from 1861, soon after travelling to Greece, Rome and to Constantinople, and took lessons on watercolour from Impressionist Hercules Brabazon Brabazon.

Through her father's friends at the British Museum, Jekyll made contacts with Ruskin, Burne-Jones and Rossetti, absorbing their dedication to high quality craftsmanship and its perceived sources in the work of the Middle Ages. She gained craft skills herself, learning carpentry, embroidery, carving and metalwork. Two other acquired crafts accompanied her career in garden design. One was photography, with which she recorded her work, and the other was writing. These two spread the concept of the Jekyll garden beyond Britain. She wrote steadily between 1899, when *Wood and Garden* was published, and 1908, when *Colour in the Flower Garden* brought together her accumulated wisdom on planting. This was all the more remarkable because Jekyll had become severely shortsighted. By the 1880s she had had to abandon the intricate work required by embroidery and jewelry, and had become drawn to work more with plants.

Her family's move to Munstead in Surrey in 1878 following her father's death seems to have marked her point of arrival as a garden designer. Needing more space for herself and more peace for her mother, Jekyll bought land nearby and invited the young Edwin Lutyens to design her a house. Munstead Wood, which was begun in 1895, marked the start of a most productive partnership. After 1912, Lutyens had commissions abroad, and Jekyll's poor sight kept her bound to Munstead. But throughout, she demonstrated an ability to visualize: she would send long letters to clients to discuss all aspects of her proposed designs, and soil samples would be sent for Jekyll to assess.

Edwin Lutyens, whose father had retired from the army and had become a
successful painter, also lived in Surrey and enjoyed a comfortable upbringing.
Having been educated at home because of ill-health, Lutyens did not take
kindly to formal training and abandoned both a course in architecture at the
South Kensington School of Art and architect's articles in the office of George
and Peto. At the age of twenty he had the courage to set up in a London office
on his own, relying on commissions from family friends in Surrey.

Munstead Wood was Jekyll's apprenticeship in garden-making; she
began to plan and lay out the design before the house was built. Though
from childhood she had taken delight in wild flowers, and observed the
planting in the cottage gardens round about, she also had friends in the Royal
Horticultural Society who could tell her of the introductions of plants from
abroad. Jekyll has often been wrongly described as a designer of cottage
gardens because of her use of wild flowers and perennials grown by cottagers.
Cottagers grew vegetables alongside flowers in their gardens, and Jekyll's
middle-class clients did not want humble plots. The colleague and mentor
who shared her views on the value of indigenous flora was the irascible but
knowledgeable Irish gardener and writer William Robinson (1838–1935).
(Robinson's ideas on the 'natural' garden are explored further in Chapter Two.)

Jekyll conceived of her garden at Munstead as one for all seasons, with
areas for spring, summer and autumn, just as the modernists made houses
where the sun could be followed from room to room. Owners of Arts and
Crafts houses and gardens appreciated the use of the spaces provided for
sitting and the growing of fruit and vegetables, as well as good planting. Often
they had tennis courts and lawns for croquet or bowling. However, Edwardian
country houses built by Lutyens were made from local stone and brick, not
steel and concrete, materials which were beginning to be used by the
modernists in France and Germany.

The design of the house at Munstead, with its deep roofline, recalls Morris's
Red House at Bexleyheath; but there were no Gothic windows or porches.
Instead, tall chimneys and long vertical accents in rectangular windows
under the roofline established the Lutyens trademarks. The house then gave
gracefully on to the garden in a series of gentle changes of level, with a north
court emerging from an overhanging gallery, and the sandstone of the paving
relating to the brick of the house wall. Leading from the north court was a nut
walk and a pergola, long borders and, beyond a wall, the spring and kitchen
gardens, establishing features which, with the wild and woodland garden,
were to recur in Jekyll's other garden designs. The borders became the trial
grounds for the colour schemes for which she became known.

On the other side of the house, the ground rises gently to grass and
ordered woodland. The planting here supplied material for her first book, and

Munstead Wood, Surrey, England

Two views of the recently restored borders at Gertrude Jekyll's 1895 house, with its drift planting of perennials. Jekyll massed the hottest reds and oranges towards the centre, grading through blues to grey at the ends; white was used to ease a change of colour sequence.

illustrates a masterly blend of wildness and order. The acidic sandy soil lent itself to the cultivation of rhododendrons, gaultheria, heathers and azaleas, and the trees which thrived there included silver birch and Scots pine, oak and chestnut. Bulbs were planted along some paths, ferns encouraged along others, and perennials such as lilies and lupins emerged on the woodland edges.

Munstead's summer border was built up by placing drifts of strong reds, oranges and yellows in the centre of the bed with plants such as cannas, coreopsis, African marigolds and day lilies, and moved down the spectrum on each side. Next to the hot colours came paler yellows such as those of verbascum or foxgloves, then perhaps white sweet peas. On the other side of the red shades, pink flowers such as antirrhinums might give way to pale blue such as hydrangea, and end in darker blue delphiniums. Grey and silver foliage plants such as stachys, *Artemisia stelleriana* and *Phlomis fruticosa* planted along the edge helped to set off the colours behind and lead the eye from greys to yellows and then reds; architectural plants such as the yuccas *filamentosa* and *recurvata* marked the ends of the colour drifts. The border was constructed with a depth of fourteen feet so that tall shrubs could be placed at the back to form a strong foil to the plants in front, and to leave space to attend to weeding, pruning back, and replacing flowers past their best, or disguising them by covering them with stronger flowering neighbours such as *Crambe maritima*. Jekyll had a reserve garden which she used to refurbish holes in the border. Jekyll gardens were not low-maintenance gardens.

Jekyll used bedding plants such as calceolarias, zonal pelargoniums, cannas and dahlias for the end of the season, though she disliked the way they had been used by the Victorians, with their emphasis on straight rows in borders and strong colour contrasts.[11] Jekyll's drift planting with its colour sequences delighted English tastes and was copied widely, though not always in the same way, in Europe and America.

Occasionally Jekyll worked with other Arts and Crafts architects such as Baillie Scott and Sidney Barnsley. In 1906 Robert Weir Schultz (1860–1951), a Scots architect trained in Edinburgh, asked Jekyll to design a wild garden for Tylney Hall, at Rotherwick in Hampshire, where Schultz was employed by African millionaire Lionel Phillips to landscape the grounds.

In 1908 the founder of the Arts and Crafts journal *The Studio,* Charles Holme, asked Jekyll to design a garden for the Manor House he had commissioned from architect Ernest Newton (1856–1922) at Upton Grey in Hampshire. On five acres the characteristic Jekyll features unfold; the tennis lawn contained by its dry stone wall rises to a bowling lawn. Steps lead up to a geometrical rose lawn and then to a pergola and terrace to the house. The dry stone walls which contain each terrace level are planted with *Armeria maritima*, aubretia, thrift, valerian, and *Nepeta mussinii.* A nuttery encloses the garden on the southwest and an orchard and kitchen garden on the southeast. Rosamund Wallinger, the present owner, obtained the archival material on her garden from the Reef Point collection,[12] and has used Jekyll's plant lists to stock the borders with

Upton Grey, Hampshire, England
The tops and crevices of dry stone walls (top) are packed with cascading plants; terraces provide spaces for flowers and sport. A courtyard divides the front of the house from its wild garden (above); low walls and gates frame the view and invite further investigation.

25

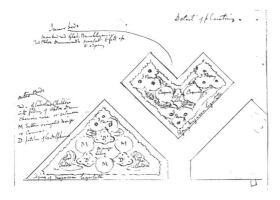

Hestercombe, Somerset, England

The Grand Plat, the focus of Jekyll's garden. The view south from a balustraded terrace (top) displays the planting within geometric beds and looks towards Lutyens's pergola which divided the orderly garden from the meadows, orchard and canal beyond. Jekyll's neat planting plan (above) shows a repeating segment of the Grand Plat.

Bergenia cordifolia, rudbeckia, gypsophila, lavandula and helianthus as she has the roses in the formal bed – Mmes 'Caroline Testout', 'Lombard', 'Laurette Messimy' and 'Abel Chatenay'. 'Blush Rambler' and 'The Garland' have been planted along the pergola, but not Jekyll's 'Kitchener', which was too poor a survivor to reach the commercial market.[13] The wild garden is entered via a metal gateway in front of the house, and a series of gentle semi-circular turf steps rise to mown grass paths which lead through islands of roses and bamboo to a pond; in the spring the grass is full of bulbs – daffodils, cyclamen, and leucojum. Chestnut trees line the drive.

The talents of Jekyll and Lutyens were combined in Hestercombe, Somerset, where the Hon. E. W. Portman asked them to design a garden at the back of his large and rather ugly Victorian mansion in 1904. Using the warm golden Ham limestone from nearby quarries, Lutyens built an orangery which marked the top of the slope, from which a path led through a paved Dutch garden towards Coplestone Warre Bampfylde's earlier eighteenth-century landscaping. On the other side of the Orangery, a terrace leads to an enclosure with a round pool, the Rotunda, echoing the millstones set in the path of the East or 'Dutch' garden. From here, steps descend past earlier Victorian formal bedding towards a terrace overlooking the Grand Plat. This, the showpiece, is a square flower parterre planted on the diagonal which fills the centre of the garden, flanked by water rills issuing from below shell-shaped fountain enclosures. The Grand Plat looks inwards, with steps leading down to grassy paths from which the planting can be admired. The garden is divided from the countryside beyond by short stone canals and a stone pergola clad with roses and clematis.

Hestercombe is lucky in having a set of Jekyll plans of its own, discovered in a drawer in the potting shed in the 1970s. Dating from between 1904 and 1907, they supplement the Reef Point collection and help to clarify the Jekyll planting. On the south-facing wall of the Grand Plat, drifts of santolina, rosemary and phlomis were punctuated by the globe thistle, echinops, with nepeta and cistus breaking through to the path. A rill with its circular pools was planted with *Myosotis palustris* (now *M. scorpioides*), *Alisma plantago* and *Calla aethiopica*. The geometric east garden in 1907 was planned with centrally planted china roses or *Fuchsia gracilis*, surrounded by rosemary, nepeta, *Funkia sieboldi* (now hosta), and with all its beds edged with stachys. Stronger colour is shown in 1904 plans for the Plat or Square Garden, where gladioli are placed in a bed with delphiniums, orange lilies and variegated maize, cannas are set out with white lilies, and there is a direction for inner beds to be given a filling of *Phlox drummondii*, scarlet or salmon or chamois rose – 'not the dwarf kinds'. However, not all of the recommended planting was implemented, as shown by illustrations in *Country Life* magazine in 1908.

There is also a 1907 plan for naturalistic planting along a sinuous stretch of water made from an eighteenth-century canal, with clumps of willow, quince and water elder interspersed with spiraea, *Iris sibirica* and *orientalis*, and *Geranium ibericum*. At the time this wilder area lay to the south of the house beyond an orchard and a meadow.[14]

In France, Lutyens built a house for Guillaume Mallet between 1898 and 1904. Le Bois des Moutiers at Varengeville stands on a slope looking towards the Normandy seashore, and contains the hallmarks of the Arts and Crafts interior designers – handmade window catches, furniture by William Lethaby, tapestry wall hangings, and a gallery overlooking the library. Outside, the house has tall chimneys, a low roof, rectangular and elongated oriel windows.

Lutyens planned the garden space next to the house as a series of geometrically designed courtyards behind brick walls, opening from one to the other. Planting here was proposed by Jekyll. Today, white roses fill the square beds in the first, stone-flagged courtyard; the entrance courtyard is paved with bricks set in a circle, with flowerbeds around the edge. Colours are gentle; a pergola leads the visitor to the rest of the garden behind the house, which is a woodland park dropping towards the sea. Though it is claimed that Mallet planted the parkland entirely on his own, there is a strong feeling of the gardens of the Surrey heathlands. Mallet collected a

Le Bois des Moutiers, Varengeville, France
Edwin Lutyens's landscaping close to Guillaume Mallet's home at Varengeville. The planting design at Le Bois des Moutiers was Jekyll's, though she did not visit this garden in Normandy. A series of courtyards define the formal garden, and lead to the parkland with its colourful shrubs on the slope to the sea.

Great Maytham,
Kent, England
Lutyens built the austere
Great Maytham in Kent
for H. J. Tennant, 1907–9,
matched by an equally
austere garden – Jekyll
had no part in the planting
here. However the walled
garden with its pergola
and terraces close to the
house create a dignified
architectural link to the
wide lawns beyond.

considerable number of rare Chinese azaleas, rhododendrons from the
Himalayas and eucryphias from Chile, as well as Japanese maples, which have
developed remarkably well on this pocket of sandy soil.

Some gardens were designed by Lutyens on his own, for instance the
steps and paving at Great Dixter, Sussex, the home of Nathaniel Lloyd and
his son Christopher, the Dutch garden at Long Barn, Kent, owned by Harold
Nicolson and Victoria Sackville-West, and the terrace and walled garden
at Great Maytham, Kent. Here Frances Hodgson Burnett wrote *The Secret
Garden* in 1909.

Lutyens and Jekyll's successful partnership put an end to the long-running
and heated argument between two bombastic Edwardians, Sir Reginald
Blomfield (1856–1942), and William Robinson, and their supporters. Put
simply, Blomfield, the architect, argued that gardeners knew nothing of
design, and should keep away from planning gardens. Robinson, the
plantsman, riposted that architects knew nothing about plants, and should
leave garden designing to those who did. The harmonious relationship of
house and garden achieved by Jekyll and Lutyens speaks for itself.

Godinton, Kent, England
Architect Reginald
Blomfield created this
idiosyncratic Italian secret
garden with its entrance
through a long wall which
divides the formal from the
bulb-filled wild gardens at
Godinton. Near the house,
Blomfield's massive yew
hedges enclose topiary, a
pool, and a hedged garden
presided over by a statue
of Pan, and exemplify the
designs he favoured in his
*The Formal Garden in
England*, written in 1892.

Secondly, by example Jekyll clarified the use of
colour in planting. She used the full spectrum of the
colour wheel, Chevreul's complementary colours, and
toned down effects by interspersing them with white.
She would have liked to create single-colour gardens.
Jekyll broke from the Victorian system of bedding out
rather gaudy annuals in regimental fashion and
planting in lines; in its place she introduced drift
planting with a concentration on perennials,

which had been somewhat neglected by the Victorians. What she did not create was a version of the cottage garden; she used wild flowers and ferns, and perennials which cottagers planted in their gardens around their vegetables.

The English have continued to create superb gardens in this genre, and some find it difficult to think in any other. American-born landscape architect Madeline Agar planted the now restored walled flower garden, with its moated pergola made by Arts and Crafts architect C. F. A. Voysey (1857–1941) for philanthropist tea merchant Emslie Horniman's Pleasance in North Kensington in 1913. Agar's student Brenda Colvin (1897–1981) set out Steeple Manor garden in Dorset for Major Holland Swan in 1923–24, matching the seventeenth-century house to a tulip parterre, and enclosed small gardens. She made a fountain pool, and planted sloping borders by a sunken grass tennis court. Victoria Sackville-West (1892–1962) made gardens at Long Barn (1915–30) and Sissinghurst (1931–62) in Kent. Sissinghurst is arguably the best of its kind, with clouds of flowers making themed colour garden rooms round the red brick of the towers, walls and cottages of the sixteenth-century castle, with Italianate green enclosures, and wilderness-orchard beyond.

The English garden, with its delight in flowers, colour and informal planting, was envied abroad. Many continental gardens had attached

Above
The Pool Garden, Steeple Manor, Dorset, England
Brenda Colvin's series of small gardens respected the spirit of the seventeenth-century house.

Below, upper right
Long Barn, Kent, England
Vita Sackville-West designed a series of terraced enclosures dropping to a lawn with long borders. In the foreground is part of Lutyens's Dutch garden.

Below, bottom left and right
Sissinghurst, Kent, England
Two views of the garden rooms from Vita Sackville-West's tower, made by the Nicolsons from 1930 at Sissinghurst, which dates from the sixteenth century. To the left, the hedged rondel opens to colourful beds, contained by a wall. To the right, the red border of the tower lawn hides the wall behind which the Priest's House is surrounded by its own garden.

The gardens at Ninfa, near Rome, Italy
Two views of the romantic garden made in the 1920s by the Caetani family. The medieval ruins play host to English clematis and climbing roses, streams reflect the wisteria and flowering shrubs, whilst Mediterranean conifers remind visitors that they are still in Italy.

themselves to the English landscape movement or remained wedded to the Baroque, having had no Capability Brown to remove them. One of the most beautiful English gardens abroad is Ninfa, south of Rome, made by three generations of the Caetani family who had married English or American wives. Italy has few twentieth-century gardens, and this one has no formal elements at all.

Ninfa was made around the ruins of a village which was burned in the fourteenth century, and developed after the malarial Pontine marshes were drained in 1922. Springs have been channelled so that many streams run through the grounds; the ruins are home to wisteria, clematis, climbing roses and bougainvillea, and the garden opens as a series of romantic pictures rather than Sissinghurst 'rooms'. There is a wide spectrum of plants, native and exotic, peonies and bamboo, honeysuckle and oleander.

Arts and Crafts in America:
Beatrix Farrand (1872–1959)

In the United States, Jekyll's influence was strong among the many wealthy middle-class women who wanted to make gardens.[15] As Jekyll's books became available in America in the first part of the twentieth century, English flower gardens began to supersede the French parterres and Italian green gardens which had been the accepted style until then, especially on the wetter northeastern side of the continent, where there was ready contact with Europe.

Beatrix Farrand was a respected member of the body of skilled American women garden-makers, whose clients emerged from their wealthy circle of friends. Farrand had visited Jekyll in 1895, and had toured Europe, making notes, sketches and photographs of plants and sites. Most of her commissions were in Maine, where she made a series of small gardens with cottage flower planting in Bar Harbor, including those at Mildred McCormick's The Farm House, and The Haven for the Milliken family at Northeast Harbor. As her skills developed, she obtained many influential commissions from universities, botanic gardens and arboreta, and from prominent individuals such as Mr and Mrs John D. Rockefeller Jr in Seal Harbor in Maine (1926–35), and Mrs Woodrow Wilson for the White House (designed in 1913 but not executed until 1916, after Mrs Wilson's death, by the second Mrs Wilson). Her only commission in England was for the Elmhirst family at Dartington in Devon in the 1930s (discussed in Chapter Five).

Farrand's style suited her clients, in that it was conservative, influenced by Europe, and generally reflected the Arts and Crafts philosophy of vernacular materials and planting ('vernacular' extended to English garden flowers). She also had a strong feeling for Italian gardens. Farrand was Edith Wharton's niece, and stayed with her while Wharton was compiling *Italian Villas and their Gardens*. One of her best known designs for gardens and woodlands is that for Dumbarton Oaks, Washington, D. C., for Mr and Mrs Robert Woods Bliss, made between 1922 and 1940.

The correspondence between Farrand and Mildred Bliss shows the development of a firm friendship between the two women as they realized a common purpose in design. Married to an American diplomat, Bliss travelled frequently with her husband, and needed to be sure that she had left her garden in good hands. The Blisses were cultured people with a large and varied collection of Greek, Roman and early medieval antiquities, and pre-Columbian art, and it was intended that this should be housed in the large house in Georgetown.

Farrand made a thorough investigation of the site, realizing that plans could not give a good impression of relief. Her long, preliminary reports of June 1922 suggested that the sloping site should be terraced at the back of the house, making a series of enclosures with pots, urns, mosaic and pebble pavement and planting, opening from one to the other just under house level, dropping to a geometric rose garden. The slope fell further to a stream which Farrand suggested should form a romantic pool surrounded by greenery; this became an amphitheatre commanding a glade. The rise beyond was eventually planted with forsythia.[16] Farrand's report and planting lists were greeted with delight by the Blisses: 'Your letter and its enclosure have made us purr with contentment. You have got it exactly!' Farrand opined, 'As for the colors of the rose garden I should quite frankly cut out almost all of the pinks… But, like you, I see a medley of soft yellows, oranges and orange-salmon colors, blacks and creamy whites, and none of that horrid shade

**Dumbarton Oaks,
Washington, D.C., USA**
Beatrix Farrand created this
sunken rose garden for
American diplomat Robert
Bliss and his wife Mildred in
the 1920s. It is an eclectic
but very satisfying design,
with its seventeenth-
century-style stone
ornamentation defining
the boundaries. Farrand
herself referred to 'the
familiar Italian and
eighteenth-century
English design of the
rectangle with the circle in
the center' (letter dated
11 September 1922).
English standard and
hybrid tea roses are
mixed with older varieties
in formal, geometric beds.

known as "cerise" by the milliners. I should also mix in some boxbushes and yew as there is nothing that makes a better background for rose coloring. Jasmine and honeysuckle with lilies and a general floppy tangle of plants… will make the garden look used and lived in as quickly as possible.'[17]

This was a very eclectic garden, with seventeenth century-style stone ornamentation around the rose garden, its 1930s English standard and hybrid tea varieties mixed with older names. The enclosed gardens near the house seem to relate to an Italian garden, as does the arcaded changing pavilion next to the swimming pool, and the little loggia by a paved garden below the rose terrace. All these were blended into a unique 'Italianate Arts and Crafts' style. As Jekyll commented in her preface to American Wilhelm Miller's book on *The Charm of English Gardens*, 'the author wisely deprecates any exact imitation of English or Italian gardens. The important thing is to get hold of a comprehension of the spirit in which they are planned.'[18]

The proximity of the Orient was more marked in the use of the vernacular in gardens in the Southwest, where Charles and Henry Greene designed Japanese-style bungalows in Pasadena, and branched evergreens were pruned into cloud-shapes beside gravel paths. Planting in California was gradually moving away from imported western European species, due to the state's dry climate and its mountainous terrain. Irving Gill's houses and gardens also reflected the patio designs of the Spanish settlements in California. Charles Greene's large garden for Mortimer and Bella Fleischhacker at Green Gables, Woodside (1911–28), used local live oaks, poplars and cedars, to link and enhance the landscape near the house with its brick terracing and stairs, to a balustraded pool in the middle distance, and then to the natural landscape of the Santa Cruz Mountains beyond.

The Arts and Crafts philosophy, embraced by a country as varied in its climatic zones and immigrant populations as the USA, was bound to result in different styles of garden. However, Farrand's East coast gardens in Maine, drawing inspiration from Britain and Europe, and the Spanish- and Japanese-influenced Californian gardens of Gill and the Greenes, used local materials and climatically appropriate planting in a true Arts and Crafts manner.

Steps Towards Modernism:
Thomas Mawson (1861–1933)

The arguments between architects and plantsmen had become old currency by the first decade of the twentieth century. But few possessed the rare combination of architectural and horticultural skills, and could take them forward towards modernist designs using new materials. Thomas Mawson fitted this role admirably and bridges old and new. His early designs are adaptations of sixteenth- and seventeenth-century gardens and relate to the contemporary delight in 'Olde England'. Later he was one of the first to use concrete and asphalt in his hard landscaping.

Thomas Hayton Mawson was born in 1861 in Yorkshire to a Lancashire cotton warper who had been forced to turn to fruit farming following the downturn in textile manufacturing.[19] Thomas was sent to work at the age of twelve in the office of an uncle in Lancaster who allowed him time to study drawing. After his father's death, Thomas's mother decided to take her family to London to start a new life and find work for her sons. After short spells of work with a garden designer, nurserymen Kelways in Somerset, and a nurseryman in Tottenham, he set up on his own in 1884 in Windermere, where the railway brought demand from the new industrially enriched middle classes in the northwest who wanted to build villas near the lake. Thomas Mawson set up Mawson and Partners – the Lakeland Nursery – with his brothers Robert and Isaac, until in about 1889 he separated his garden architect's practice from the contracting firm.

Seeing a growing demand, Thomas Mawson was prepared to branch out in new directions. His early entries in competitions for town planning, in which he had no training, and park design, show Mawson's realization that 'those judging were seldom professionals with any knowledge of the subject'.[20] Mawson campaigned tirelessly for the education of town planners and for the university education of landscape gardeners. Eventually he wrote *Civic Art* in 1911, which addressed the aesthetics and practicalities of town planning. He lectured on the first course established at Liverpool University, from 1910 to 1924, helped to set up the Institute of Town Planning in 1914 and the Society of Garden Architects (later the Institute of Landscape Architects) in 1929.

Mawson admired the work of Edward Kemp (1817–91), who had said: 'It is much to be regretted that architects and landscape-gardeners do not more usually work together, in complete unison'.[21] Mawson regarded garden-making as both a fine art and a craft; and in 1900, and with Kemp in mind, he set out his own principles in *The Art and Craft of Garden Making*. In this he distanced himself from the eighteenth century and set out his interest in formality.[22] He sent his sons Edward Prentice and James Radcliffe to the Ecole des Beaux-Arts in Paris. Edward was previously trained in architecture and James (who was killed in the First World War in 1916) was first given a horticultural training.

Mawson's gardens were often made on sloping sites, giving him the opportunity to design terracing, with the topmost level anchoring the house to its setting. There were often geometrically planned 'panel' gardens, in room-like enclosures off the top terrace. Mawson valued 'velvety lawns' and 'well placed stately trees' to give the serenity he sought to impart. All was strongly axial; canals, long, architectural pergolas with domes at the turn of an angle, flights of steps linking the terraces, walls or hedges lining herbaceous borders, and carefully placed gazebos and summer houses continued the straight lines throughout the garden.

But Mawson looked beyond the Arts and Crafts period. He used wood and stone for some of his pergolas, but for others he used concrete and metal. Though he made paths with gravel and then paving, he was one of the first to use asphalt. His commissions for gardens and town plans in Europe and North America reinforced his recognition of the 'modern' garden as an outside room, with its lawns for entertainment and sport, and its purpose as a provider of fresh air for healthy living.

Most of Mawson's garden clients, in Britain, Europe and America, were businessmen. For several years he had an office in Conduit Street, London, and another in Vancouver. His sons Edward and James proved able partners and often prepared the way for their father's preliminary plans, and in Britain Thomas had the back-up of his brothers' nurseries and contracting works in Lakeland, which also supplied garden furniture and ornaments.[23]

In 1905 Mawson was commissioned to design a garden for Reginald Cory at Duffryn, Saint Nicholas, Cardiff. The house had been built in 1893 for his father, John Cory, a wealthy ship-owner dealing with coal and iron through some twenty-seven ports round the Empire – a useful connection for his son Reginald, who collected plants. Mawson described the house as 'reminiscent of an Italian villa as interpreted by English architects some forty years ago'.[24] Cory commissioned Mawson in 1905 after his father's death. Cory, a solicitor who went plant hunting with Ernest Wilson, was also a member of the Royal Horticultural Society, helped to set up the Chelsea Flower Show, and was himself a gold medallist. Unfortunately he left instructions that all his papers should be burned after his death, which probably included planting plans. However, watercolours of 1923 by Royal Academician Edith Helena Adie give an insight into the colours and plants used, and Mawson commented that Cory had some six hundred varieties of dahlia for trials in his garden.[25]

Duffryn's 55-acre (22-hectare) garden was part of an unbroken estate of 2,000 acres (810 hectares), and the flat site looked towards its own parkland, pasture and woodlands. Mawson planned a straight drive to the front, flanked by a double avenue of trees. Here there are still a number of his 'mushrooms', shaped by grafting golden yew onto a darker green yew base. On the south front the house was set off by a shallow terrace with balustrading above a narrow border, which descended to a croquet and tennis lawn. A wide semi-circle of stone steps then led gently down to a great lawn whose level had been excavated, the spoil contributing to surrounding embanking from which could be viewed, in seventeenth-century style, the whole garden.

Duffryn, Wales
Thomas Mawson designed this Pompeian Garden (above) for plantsman and landowner Reginald Cory from 1909, after they had visited Italy together, and this view painted by Edith Helena Adie in 1923 shows an English interpretation of an Italian garden, with vigorous climbers clothing the pillars and pediments. Mawson's formal canal (below) provides an imposing centre in the long expanse of lawn. At the crossing Cory planted lilies. Beyond the evergreens a shallow grass terrace rises towards bright bedding in front of the house.

At right angles to the house, Mawson made a long canal in the great lawn, reflecting the house, and a crossing which held Cory's collection of recently introduced *Nymphaea* hybrids. Further south a change of mood was indicated by a horizontal line of balustrading with pots and pavilions, more small gardens enclosed by trimmed yew hedging, and then a lake. This was hidden from view behind one of Mawson's more monumental features – an arched brick wall with ramparts and an observation tower looking over both garden and lake, with plans for a chamber below the tower to watch the fish. But as the lake filled, so did the cellars at Duffryn house; the flooding and the First World War ended further work here.

Inspiration for the small panel gardens near the house came from a visit to southern Europe by Cory and Mawson early in their partnership. The Edwardian taste for a collection of Moorish, Dutch, Mediterranean, Italian and other themes revealed separately in enclosed gardens, opening one to another, was replicated at Duffryn. From the terrace, a long herbaceous border, lined by Mawson's concrete pillars joined with iron half-hoops at the top, led into a series of surprises. A green theatre garden, repository for Cory's collection of bonsai trees, opened into a yew allée known as the Cloister garden. Mawson was also responsible for the Pompeian garden,

begun in 1909, its slim concrete colonnades topped with flower troughs round a fountain court. Unfortunately Mawson's concrete pillars lacked proper metal reinforcement, and suffered badly until their recent restoration.

At the same time as Duffryn was being made, Mawson wrote to industrialist William Hesketh Lever (1851–1925), as one non-conformist to another, asking for a donation for a chapel screen at Hest Bank in Lancashire where Mawson lived. Thus in 1905 began a fruitful relationship between the two men, Mawson making gardens for Lever at Thornton Manor in Cheshire where Lever famously demanded long walks in which he could pace up and down,[26] and Roynton Cottage at Rivington in Lancashire, with its millstone grit pergola defying the winds of its Pennine site. In the same year, the garden of The Hill, Hampstead was made for Lever, as a place in which he could entertain guests in his London town house. The site was indeed hilly, formed from the only remnants of the glaciers which had made their way southwards to London. Mawson worked on this with his sons, achieving a considerable feat of landscape engineering with the spoil from the newly excavated Hampstead underground railway – which Lever, business acumen to the fore, was paid to remove. The site, as Mawson explained, had an adjacent overlooking hillock which made 'any sort of a fête or garden party quite out of the question unless something was done to give shelter and seclusion; and secondly, this seclusion must be obtained without obstructing the unique view in the direction of Harrow-on-the-Hill'.[27]

Lever had purchased The Hill in 1904 and had employed architect E. A. Ould to enlarge the house. Mawson needed to provide a setting in which Lever could entertain between the newly-built wings of The Hill. He therefore joined the south-facing house to a lawn with a loggia, and using the natural slope of the site, placed central stone steps down to another lawn which was split by the central axis of a rectangular lily-pond, with its lead fountain and its paved enclosure. Paved paths outlined the rectangles made by the lawns; narrow flower borders made edges to the loggia and the paths. But the pièce de résistance was undoubtedly the raised terrace which Mawson built, using Mawson Brothers as contractors, on the south and east sides of the garden. On top he made a massive pergola, whose structure with its terrace wall resembled medieval ramparts from ground level, and made a clear line of definition between the garden and the heath beyond. The entrance to the lawns to the north was beneath a wooden dome which joined and divided the pergola walks from a trellis screening the house and framing the entrance towards the lily pond. Here guests could stroll between the Portland stone pillars and rambling roses and admire the views towards Windsor, at the same time being sheltered from the gaze of outsiders from below. Later plans to extend the garden further after Lever's 1911 purchase and demolition of the

adjoining Heath Lodge, progressed no further than the building of a bridge across the lane which divided the territories, and the extension southwards of the raised pergola walk to a belvedere. The First World War interrupted the now Lord Leverhulme's plans for expansion.

Mawson managed to meet Lever's demands for an instantly flowering garden, and an economical use of space, placing the necessary 'utilitarian' requirements for potting sheds, frames, and propagating houses below the terrace on the southern side.

The Hill garden, with its simple but bold plan contained within the massive geometry of the pergola, with its wooden temple domes marking change of axis and the entrance to the house from the south, its terracing and belvederes, matched the spirit of enterprise and hard work which bound Leverhulme and Mawson together, and reflected the ruggedness of the northern landscapes from which they had sprung.

This chapter has shown that the beginning of the twentieth century was unwilling to relinquish the garden designs of the nineteenth, albeit that some of those looked even further into the past. Revivalism was not a British invention, but the Arts and Crafts movement certainly was. It began its outward progress often with garden-makers' visits to Gertrude Jekyll, and their importation of its philosophy across Europe and the United States. Architects such as Hermann Muthesius (1861–1927) and Frank Lloyd Wright (1867–1959) helped to spread distinctive German and American concepts of Arts and Crafts building and landscaping. Gradually the adoption of new materials such as concrete for hard landscaping, and a recognition of the healthy outside lifestyle with its new requirements in gardens, announced the arrival of the Modern Movement.

The Hill, Hampstead, London, England
From 1904 onwards Thomas Mawson made gardens and this massive pergola as part of a raised terrace, separating William Hesketh Lever's London house from the eyes of the public on the Heath down below. Lever's guests could promenade and look down at the gardens which surrounded the pergola, and enjoy the shade provided by climbing plants.

The Natural Garden:
Plant-centred garden-making to the 1930s

The concept of the 'natural' garden raises some of the most interesting issues concerning the making of recent landscapes. What began in England at the beginning of the twentieth century as a rejection of bedding-out schemes and the reworking of old styles, and the realization that perennial plants were disappearing, was developed variously by designers in different countries. To Kate Sessions in southern California, 'natural' meant putting a plant in a setting to which it was ecologically best suited. To Jac Thjisse in the Netherlands, conservation of the 'natural' was essential to save a countryside fast disappearing under the pressure of urbanization. And for Willy Lange in Germany, the definition of the 'natural' appeared to lead to a search for an exclusive national identity in the landscape.

While artists and architects explored ways of moving towards new styles, a similar momentum was quietly building amongst plantsmen and women at the end of the nineteenth century. This momentum led towards the creation of a 'natural' garden; but 'natural', 'nature garden' and 'native' meant very different things to different people.

The growing interest in plants, fuelled by their continuing importation from every part of the globe, underlined the division between plantsmen's gardens and gardens made by architects. The division was widened by the growth of the separately trained professions of horticulture, landscape architecture, landscape design, garden architecture or similar titles. A strong interest in horticulture emerged in the Netherlands and Germany, while more architectural forms of design tended to predominate in France and Spain. Though some differences emerged from climate, soil and landscape form, much of it was to do with the variations in the institutions from which garden design emerged – that is, in the university or institute departments of agriculture or horticulture in some countries or in departments of architecture in others; and many differences were made according to cultural background.

What was articulated – though not begun – by William Robinson in 1870 was the divergence of plant-centred landscape-making into many different expressions. Robinson's influence on the gardens of Gertrude Jekyll was considerable, and his *Wild Garden*

Opposite
Gravetye Manor, near East Grinstead, England
William Robinson's home from 1885, where he set out his ideas on natural planting.

Below
Bedding in the form of shoes, published by W. Hampel, Berlin, 1891
Extraordinary designs appeared in pattern books, causing derision amongst critics such as Robinson.

Bottom
Waddesdon, England
High Victorian formal bedding was criticized for brash colours and the bare spaces left after flowering.

of 1870 affected thinking on garden-making far outside Britain. In the Netherlands, where there was growing debate on the scientific background to the physical grouping of plants, Jacobus P. Thijsse encouraged the education of the Dutch through the concept of the natural in wild parks which became called *heem* (natural or wild) parks. In the United States, Danish-born Jens Jensen became perhaps the first to develop a 'natural American' style, working in parks and then on public sites and private homes with architects such as Frank Lloyd Wright, Howard Van Doren Shaw and George W. Maher; the recently overlooked Kate Sessions, however, has a strong claim to be first with the promotion of climatically appropriate flora to the sunny and arid southwest of the USA. In Germany, Willy Lange's promotion of 'native' flora has been associated with the eugenics policies pursued by the National Socialist Party.

Many of these people had plant nurseries, most wrote about their ideas, and many had worked in parks or had helped to create parks as well as private gardens. Some were not the first to broach their views, but became important for articulating such views in their own cultural context. All were significant plantsmen and influenced succeeding generations.

William Robinson (1838–1935)

William Robinson was typical of a group of gardeners of the Victorian era who rose from poverty through the ranks by hard work, self-education and training at the 'big house'. Beginning as the boy in charge of watering the garden, living in a bothy on the Marquess of Waterford's estate at Curraghmore in Ireland, he progressed to the estate of the Reverend Sir Hunt Johnson-Walsh at Ballykilcavan, where apocryphal tales have him putting out the stove-house fires to kill off his hated bedding-out plants before storming off to Dublin. From there he went to the Royal Society's garden at Regent's Park, London, on whose behalf he collected plants and toured nurseries and botanical gardens. He wrote for *The Gardeners' Chronicle*, later leaving employment at Regent's Park to cover the horticultural aspects of the French International Exhibition of 1867 for *The Times*, the *Field*, and the *Gardeners' Chronicle*.

Robinson's knowledge of gardens and plants and his writing skills brought him contacts and funding to travel; this enabled him to found eight gardening periodicals between 1871 and 1903, including *La Semaine Française* which ran for five years. He took his brother James to America in 1870 in search of their father, who had deserted their mother and run away from Ireland when William was ten. The visit, aided by newly established railway links, took the brothers to New York, Chicago, and then California. They encountered great climatic variety, from temperate east coast to western hot desert, collecting plants with leading botanists. This, together with his experiences gained from

travelling in Europe, especially amongst the mountains of the Mediterranean countries, enriched Robinson's understanding of the distributions of plants in different climatic zones. Books flowed from him, and were popular. He wrote nineteen between 1868 and 1924 including a volume on French gardens and another on French parks. *The English Flower Garden* went through fifteen editions in Robinson's lifetime, from 1883. His books were influential in America and Europe, especially in Germany, where they resonated with the ideas expressed by Hermann Jaeger in his *Illustriertes Allgemeines Gartenbuch* (General Illustrated Garden Book) of 1864, six years before Robinson wrote *The Wild Garden*, and were taken up in the garden journal *Gartenzeitung* (Garden Magazine) in 1882 and 1883. Here, a writer under the pseudonym 'Dendrophilus' recognized that he was gardening in the same way that Robinson had suggested, so he adopted *The Wild Garden* to set out his own.[2] Graduates from the garden architects' school in Berlin came to England to work in nurseries and for landscape architects, and must have come into contact with Robinson's ideas. Frederick Law Olmsted acknowledged his influence in the making of Central Park, New York. Robinson was widely (but not universally) admired in the northeastern states of the USA.

Throughout, he was refining his ideas on the composition of the English garden, which came to personal fruition when in 1885 he bought himself a 360-acre (146-hectare) estate at Gravetye in Sussex, with its dilapidated Elizabethan manor house. He enjoyed robust exchanges with Reginald Blomfield, John Dando Sedding and their followers, on the merits of

Above
**The West Garden,
Gravetye Manor, near
East Grinstead, England**
This engraving shows the early stages of Robinson's garden; in the foreground, a rich mixture of English and imported plants, growing informally together. Robinson commented,'Any one who thinks of the culture of such beautiful things can only smile at the bare idea of enjoying their life in anything but the natural and picturesque way.'[1]

Above

Moat Farm, Gravetye
Robinson's farmhouse
on the Gravetye estate
became a refuge while
the manor was being
repaired. At the end of
the nineteenth century
he planted several
thousand narcissus
to naturalize under the
trees by the lake.

Above right

**The West Garden,
Gravetye**
A path between beds
of perennials leads to
Robinson's garden pavilion.

Opposite

**Lake and alpine meadow,
Gravetye**
On the east side of the
house the ground falls
steeply to the lake. Wild
flowers were encouraged
on the sloping meadow
by restricting the cutting
of the grass, reminding
Robinson of plants he
had seen growing in the
Alps. Lilies were grown
in the lake.

plantsmen creating gardens rather than architects. He promoted the use of perennials, which he claimed (as did the German horticulturists) had all but disappeared in favour of seasonal bedding. But he is now as well known for his development of the theme of the natural, which appears in *The Wild Garden*, published in 1870.

The Wild Garden was in part a revolt – though a quiet one, by Robinson's standards – on bedding out. This system, helped by the advance in glasshouse technology, had gradually taken hold from the 1840s, using tender plants coming in from the colonies and elsewhere. The emphasis was on seasonal planting with high colour contrast – typically, for example, yellow calceolarias, blue lobelia and red salvias in tight and regimented patterns. Later, foliage plant and subtropical plant bedding were to follow, with carpet bedding achieving the ingenious and the grotesque in its quest for new patterns, as plants were assembled in shapes resembling family crests, coronets, and even shoes. All the plants were dependent upon the glasshouse until the weather was suitable for the new residents to take up their appointed places. Robinson complained that 'the dreadful practice of tearing up the flower beds and leaving them like new-dug graves'[3] meant that the garden was partially bare when the plants were changed; but just as important, many of the old perennial favourites which had been resident in English gardens, were being lost – plants such as lilies, hepaticas, larkspurs and winter aconites. Though he did not want a return to the old mixed borders with their 'bundles of decayed stems tied to sticks'[4] at the end of the season, or the dreary current manner of planting in rows, he planned another approach to the garden which would add variety to both planting and plants.

Whilst not advocating the removal of 'formal' beds near the house[5] or even some seasonal planting here, Robinson felt that English gardeners were wasting areas of their gardens by overlooking the value of wild plants, and hardy plants from other countries which would adapt very well to the English climate. Neglected ground under copses, at the edges of woodlands, and zones presently left for weeds, could be homes for lily of the valley, bluebells, foxgloves, anemones and violets. Hedges could encourage honeysuckle and briar rose. Rambling roses, hops and vines could climb into trees. Bulbs could be allowed to naturalize in the grass; and by reducing the cutting, meadows would produce 'a world of lovely flowers'.[6] If the garden-maker was unsure how to proceed, all he needed to do was to look for 'lessons in grouping [which] are to be had in woods, copses, heaths, and meadows, by those who look about them as they go'.[7] Robinson's descriptions of the mingling of plants in different settings evoke strong pictorial images. He had a large collection of paintings, which underlines his artistic view of the landscape, and commissioned Alfred Parsons, who also designed gardens, to illustrate his books.[8]

Robinson's travels had introduced him to the wide variety of hardy plants which grew in temperate climates such as his own, and in mountainous parts of the Mediterranean such as northern Greece and Italy. In addition he had gathered a wide knowledge of alpines and suggested their uses on walls, in rock-gardens, and on ruins. He suggested that 'exotic' plants and seeds – meaning those from any other locations, whether English, European, American – could be planted into English flower beds and amongst woodland drives and grassland walks in a loose and informal manner, where they could spread and naturalize with a minimum of management. Robinson was happy to mix garden varieties with wild flowers. Peonies could bloom in grasses; evening primroses could complement the shade under pine trees. There could be a spring garden, using bulbs in lawns and meadows, bog and water gardens could be planted with day lilies, iris, and loosestrife, supplemented by yuccas and American lilies. In this way, argued Robinson, the plant palette available would be enlarged.

For Robinson, 'natural' meant an informal way of planting, with minimum management, and an eclectic mix of wild and garden plants, exotics which came from many countries, and which blended with each other in appropriate geographical settings. The garden would have seasonal colour without formal bedding. Of course he had in mind the country house garden, which was big enough to accommodate the seasonal variations suggested by his varied planting. At no point did Robinson consider fostering 'English' plants for 'English' settings; however it could be said that his handling of the planting produced recognizably 'English' pictures in the landscape.

Kate Sessions, 1923
The feisty plantswoman, Kate Sessions, promoting Californian Lilac (*Ceanothus cyaneus*), as part of her attempt to gain recognition for indigenous plants in the gardens of Californians.

Kate Olivia Sessions (1857–1940)

Kate Sessions met William Robinson in 1925, when, at the age of sixty-seven, she took a tour of Europe and went to see him at Gravetye Manor. It is likely that she had corresponded with him for some time, as she corresponded with many leading botanists and horticulturists in England, France, and South Africa. Robinson had visited California in 1870 when he was beginning to make a name for himself, and his visit may have left a mark amongst older residents who later relayed details to Sessions.

Representative of the nurserymen who pioneered the planting of new territories and who are sometimes forgotten by historians, Kate Sessions came into horticulture as much by accident as by choice.[9] She went to the State University of California at Berkeley in 1877, becoming one of the first women graduates in science in any country. Her course included agriculture, botany, horticulture and mathematics. She wrote a paper entitled *The Natural Sciences as a Field for Women's Labors*; at this time female graduates were expected to go into teaching.

In 1885 she abandoned teaching and joined the Blaisdell family who were about to take over the first nursery in San Diego. With the spread of the railway

into the southwest in the 1880s and the introduction of irrigation, the small
pioneer settlement was growing fast, and shaking off the colonial landscape
of the Spanish missions.

The Blaisdells put her in charge of their city florist's shop where she
supplemented the nursery's supplies by taking short-term leases on building
plots to grow cut flowers. Gradually these plots were developed for houses,
shops or offices, and Sessions had to move on. The drive, focus and success of
this young woman was remarkable, especially as she was the only woman to
be running a nursery business at the time. She made contact with growers in
the north of California, in Hawaii which she had earlier visited, and with David
Fairchild in the newly formed Federal Office of Seed and Plant Introduction in
the Department of Agriculture in Washington, D.C. She had realized that the
warm climate of San Diego could accommodate plants outside which were
raised under glass in cooler areas, and that there were many plants from
similar climatic zones to San Diego which would be worth cultivating for the
avid garden market created by the land boom in southern California. Her
contacts sent her cuttings, seeds and plants with which she experimented.

The Blaisdells moved their activity on to the Coronado peninsula which
faces San Diego. This area was developing fast, not least because of its long
Pacific beach and the luxurious Hotel del Coronado being built at one end. San
Diego is a seaport, and many plants, seeds and cuttings were off-loaded here,
to find their way to the thriving nursery trade. In 1887 Sessions decided to set
up on her own, borrowing money or selling property to build an office, florist's
shop, glasshouses for propagating, and rose houses. She sold young trees and
shrubs to the developers to plant along the front of their lots, and obtained a
contract to landscape and supply plants, shrubs and trees for the courtyard of
the Hotel del Coronado.

**Tree planting in
San Diego**
Land development in
California increased
rapidly in the early part
of the twentieth century,
and Sessions advised
on the landscaping of
roads, sometimes selling
young trees from her
nursery to developers.
She recommended the
Queen's Palm (*Arecastrum
Romanzoffianum* –
shown here) as a good
street tree which needed
no trimming.

**Arbor Day, City Park,
San Diego, California,
USA, 1904**
In 1904 Sessions
supervised the planting
of the barren slopes of
San Diego's City Park
(later renamed Balboa
Park). Nursery stocks of
pines, cypress and firs were
augmented by Sessions's
corralling of men, women
and children to plant as
many tree cuttings as
could be mustered from
the city gardens.

An expanding streetcar network in San Diego and the arrival of the motor car widened demand for cut flowers, gardens, plants, and advice on how to garden. Sessions's activities were reported in the *San Diego Union*, where she wrote a column between 1891 and 1893 called *Notes on Planting*. Interest in gardening was reflected in the growth of horticultural societies; in 1906 San Diego's Floral Association held its first meeting, and in 1909 it began to publish the *California Garden*, to which Sessions was to contribute regularly until her death.

By the end of the 1890s the peninsula nursery had become inconvenient, and Sessions saw an opportunity to do a deal with the City of San Diego Council whereby she could use a part of the 1,400 acre City Park for her nursery. The lease, negotiated in 1892, gave Sessions the right to some thirty acres of land for ten years rent-free to establish 'an experimental nursery and garden', in return for planting 'one hundred choice and varied sorts of trees' and for provision to the City of 'three hundred ornamental trees… to be used… in park, street, plaza or school ground planting'. The City promised to supply water if Sessions paid for the pipelines; she had to maintain the trees, provide fencing, and the park had to remain open to the public.[10]

Sessions planted Monterey cypress, torrey pines, cork oak, acacia, pepper trees, palms and eucalyptus – all well adapted to local conditions – on the western side of the Park, with no landscape plan, as she objected to the grid system used so frequently in the United States. In response to the San Diego Park Improvement Committee's decision to plant a 'forest' in 1903, Sessions and her colleagues drove round the city in a horse and buggy, collecting as many cuttings as they could muster to supplement those of the Californian nurseries.[11] 'Arbor Day', first instituted by San Diego in 1904, saw several thousand adults and children, supervised by Sessions, planting pines, cypress and firs in City Park. At the beginning of the twentieth century there were moves to fill in the canyons which cut into the hillsides, blocking them with dams and filling the spaces with lakes. This Sessions vigorously opposed on the grounds that it would destroy the natural landscape.[12] San Diegans decided to celebrate their Spanish colonial roots by re-naming City Park 'Balboa Park' in 1910; by then, Sessions had moved her nursery again to the Mission Hills. In the early 1930s she promoted an agave and aloe garden within the Park, forming a collection well suited to the climate and terrain.[13]

San Diego's natural flora was sparse until the Franciscan missionaries brought in food crops such as citrus and stone fruit trees, vines, nuts, dates, soft fruit, vegetables, cereals, and various conifers and palms for shade. Many of these arrived as cuttings from Spain or Spanish-settled territories. Trading ships, settlers after the gold rush of the mid-nineteenth century and others who migrated across from the east brought in trees, shrubs and garden flowers to soften the San Diegan flat-topped mesa landscape which was home to sage and scrub with few indigenous trees. Sessions saw the need to widen the palette by adding plants from other semi-desert and Mediterranean climatic zones, so that they adapted to a 'natural' background to which they were suited. She often gave plants, seedlings or cuttings to her clients to try out for her, with frequent checks on local conditions. She found that of the many palms which were often used as street trees, the *Arecastrum Romanzoffianum* (*Cocos plumosa* or Queen's palm) was best as it was tall and needed no trimming.[14]

Sessions promoted plants which were already indigenous but needed better recognition, including the showy Matilija poppy (*Romneya coulteri*),[15] the bougainvillea, which had been imported in 1884,[16] and the *Ceanothus cyaneus* (Californian lilac).[17] She advocated the widespread scattering of the seed of the golden eschscholtzia as the state flower of California, promoted lesser-known trees such as the *Eucalyptus citriodora* (lemon-scented gum), *Eucalyptus ficifolia* (red flowering gum), and *Grevillea robusta* (silk oak),[18] and hunted for better adapted species with botanist T. S. Brandegee, such as *Fremontia mexicana* (Californian flannel bush or Fremontedendron), and the dwarf fan palm, *Erythea brandegeei,* in 1903.[19]

Sessions was in a good position to offer plants from her nursery and advice to new homeowners, as there were very few trained landscape architects available at this period. A sketch would be made on site, after an appraisal of the conditions. Once the client had agreed, the garden would be marked out by Sessions's boot, and a nurseryman would follow behind to dig holes for the

The E. F. Chase House, San Diego, California, USA, 1911
This modern Spanish-American house was designed by architect Irving Gill, with harmonious planting by Kate Sessions. The picture, taken in 1933, shows the site-appropriate, drought-resistant shrubs, cypress, eucalyptus and banana trees, all typical of a variety of Mediterranean regions.

plants. Though apparently rough and ready, her methods ensured that the tree or shrub suited its soil, site and setting.[20]

Sessions sometimes worked with architect Irving Gill and his assistants. Gill embraced a modernism suited to California's legacy of Spanish settlement, and his gardens were linked to the houses by colonnaded patio features; Sessions advised on the planting of these spaces. In 1911 Gill built a canyon-side house later occupied by E. F. Chase (now the Katherine Teats house), whose hillside garden was landscaped with low walls and low, drought-resistant shrubs such as cotoneaster. The concrete house, in a Spanish/cubist style, was complemented and given shade by tall cypress, eucalyptus and banana trees.[21]

It was difficult to persuade settlers from the eastern side of the USA to accept that they would not be able to grow plants with which they were familiar. Throughout her career, Sessions ignored European styles and planting. A smaller garden made for Mrs Robert at Coronado in 1918 illustrates how colour and texture were combined to create a new, Californian style, where the overriding consideration was adaptation to habitat. In this way plants from New Zealand, South Africa and the Mediterranean could exist side by side. Louisa Yeomans King's account of the garden in 1921 dazzles the inner eye.[22] The house walls were covered with orange trumpet vine (*Campsis radicans*) and the equally orange Marmalade bush (*Streptosolen jamesonii*). More streptosolen lined the path, beside which there were massed blue-purple *Convolvulus sabatius* (syn. *C. mauritanicus*), violet *Verbena rigida* (syn. *V. venosa*), *Centaurea maritima,* and the Californian poppy, *Eschscholzia californica*. These bright colours were complemented by grey succulents and cacti, and contrasted with tall balls of leaf-spears from the Dragon trees (*Dracaena draco*), New Zealand flax (*Phormium tenax*), and yuccas. Sessions banished the lawn. In the Robert garden sparkling mesembryanthemums replaced it; other low-growing succulents were used elsewhere.

Sessions's plants suited their sites, and her landscapes in streets, gardens and Balboa Park reflected a new, southern Californian character. She gives us an example of how pioneer landscapes were developed by nurserymen who were not afraid to mix the indigenous (cheaply available in the wild) with appropriate exotics to satisfy popular demand. Yet Sessions had an equally strong mission to educate Californians in the value of their natural landscapes, which she achieved in her popular writing, the teaching of children in their school gardens, and at the University of California Extension Department where she taught a class about garden and landscape design in 1939, the year before she died.[23]

Jens Jensen (1860–1951)

Jens Peter Jensen believed that creating gardens was a skill born of man's combination of art and nature, where natural landscapes should be appreciated for what they were, and where planting should reflect the indigenous plants of the region. This was somewhat at odds with the first American university course in landscape architecture, taught at Harvard in 1900, a year after the foundation of the American Society of Landscape Architects. Jensen emerged, with O. C. Simonds, as leading proponents of what Wilhelm Miller called the Prairie Style of Landscape Gardening.[24] Ossian Cole Simonds (1855–1931) designed and developed Graceland Cemetery, which became one of the best-known park cemeteries in the United States. Though the two men shared common views on planting and design, they appear not to have worked together or corresponded, and Jensen seems to have reached a wider public than Simonds.[25]

For Jensen, there was a strong streak of peaceful patriotism, freedom and democracy in what he valued in the landscape. Born in the Schleswig region of southern Denmark, in 1884 he emigrated to the United States, taking his Danish bride-to-be with him. As a child he had witnessed his homeland being taken over by Prussian invaders and his family's farm being burned, and he was later conscripted for military service with the army of united Germany. It is possible that these early experiences, coupled with current criticism of influential architectural gardens, may have coloured Jensen's approach to landscapes. He equated highly formalized landscape with profligate spending.[26] Not only were architectural gardens seen as 'unnatural', but architects and landscape gardeners were at odds with each other about the responsibility for garden-making, particularly in England and America. However Jensen's *Siftings*, a slim volume of reminiscences produced in 1939, suggests there was an anti-military reason for his love of the natural. 'The study of curves is the study of life itself. Curves represent the unchained mind full of mystery and beauty. Straight lines belong to militant thought. No mind can be free in a concept of limitations. Straight lines spell autocracy, of which most European gardens are an expression, and their course points to intellectual decay, which soon develops a prison from which the mind can never escape. The free thought that produces the free curve can never be strangled'.[27]

Jensen's early education in local culture and history at a Danish Folk High School, and then as a young adult at an agricultural college in Denmark where art and agriculture were given equal value in the curriculum, made him a plantsman with a strong sense of place. 'Art must come from within', he said, 'and the only source from which the art of landscaping can come is our native landscape'.[28] The area he eventually settled in was not so very different from Denmark. The northern Midwest (particularly Illinois and Indiana, south of Lakes Michigan and Erie) also has landscape formed by retreating glaciers and glacial lakes – rolling low hills, swampy areas of ill-drained moraine and sandy soils, with dunes on the shores around Lake Michigan reminiscent of the coastline of Jutland.

Despite his lack of landscaping qualifications, Jensen worked his way through employment in a nursery in Chicago, and benefited from the prospects offered by the rapid growth of the city. Created by twenty-odd railways carrying timber products and bringing in grain and meat from the agricultural midwest for shipping via the Great Lakes, Chicago fast became an industrial centre making agricultural machinery, cement and cars. By 1890 it was the USA's second largest city. This growth created rich industrialists, wanting estates, grand houses, and landscaping, especially along the lakeshore. It also attracted immigrants from Europe, which led to poor housing, pollution, a lack of park space, and the destruction of the natural environment.

Conservation became an issue dear to Jensen's heart. He fought hard, for instance, to rescue the Indiana sand dunes along the shore of Lake Michigan from the threat of development by industry, and to establish a Forest Preserve System to prevent developers from clearing woodlands. He was also concerned that historical landscapes – including American Indian settlements and old trails and log cabins used in the days of exploration – should not be destroyed.

Geographically the 'prairie' in the USA is a vague term corresponding to the equally vague term 'midwest', taking in the grassy plains at the foot of the Rocky Mountains to the grass and woodland of the lands to the south of the Great Lakes and into the upper reaches of the Mississippi. Visually the 'prairie' means low, rolling hills or long horizons seen over flat meadows, with shrubs and short trees windblown into horizontal shapes matching the horizontal outcrops of rocks, with winding rivers, and a recognizable palette of flowers and trees. The Prairie School of landscape gardeners identified the twofold problem facing the prairies: imported trees and flowers unsuited to the ecology were swamping indigenous varieties, and imported European revivalist designs were unsympathetic to the landscape. These were matched by the fears of the Prairie School of Architects including Walter Burley Griffin and Frank Lloyd Wright, who saw imported European Beaux-Arts thinking as negating any attempt to pursue an American style of their own. In short, the Prairie School – both landscape gardeners and architects – wanted to celebrate the prairie landscape, not disguise it. 'The plains speak of freedom – earth and sky meet on the far horizon', Jensen wrote in *Siftings*.[29]

Jensen's design for an American Garden in part of Chicago's Union Park in 1888 set him off towards 'natural' landscaping, at first in the parks where he was employed, but after 1910, in private estates, the grounds of schools, hospitals and corporate buildings, and along highways. He was delighted to observe the evolution of his American Garden, which was made up of indigenous trees, shrubs and perennials, and with wild flowers that he had had to collect from the woods 'with a team and waggon' – similar to Sessions's attempts to clothe Balboa Park. Local nurserymen had never before had requests for wild stock. 'This was the first natural garden in Chicago, and as far as I know, the first natural garden in any large park in the country'.[30]

Union Park was one of a group forming the West Parks District of Chicago, of which Jensen was to become Superintendent and Landscape Architect, and then Consulting Landscape Architect in 1909. He described his 1917–20 work in Columbus Park as 'an attempt to realize a complete interpretation of the native landscape of Illinois', and his best work in a park.[31] By diverting a road Jensen was able to open the centre of this site as a prairie-meadow, enclosing it from housing and industry with groves of trees, planting low-growing

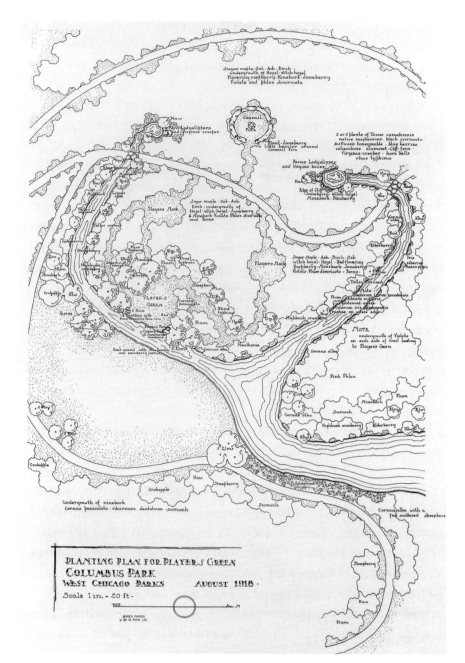

Players Green, Columbus Park, Illinois, USA
Jens Jensen made his best park for Chicagoans on farmland outside the city, striving for a landscape appropriate for the prairies. He harnessed two natural springs, leading them south to become a prairie river. Where the streams joined, Jensen made a raised players' green for outdoor performances, the audience sitting on the grass beyond the stream.

shrubs, especially hawthorn, to break the line between trees and grass. He used natural springs, as he often did, together with an old beach-line which marked the retreat of a lake at the end of the glacial period, joining them together in a serpentine evocation of a prairie river. He planted the edges with arrowhead, sweet flag, waterlilies and rushes, iris, swamp mallow, swamp rose, and marsh marigold. There was a playground and a 'swimming hole'. This was a place where children could swim recalling pioneer days, when adults and youngsters splashed about in river pools. Horizontal layers of rock were laid

at the edge, the mortar protected by recessing the
stone. Alder and dogwood were planted round
the pool, wild vines over the rocks, and ferns by the
pool's edge.

The rapid growth of the city created sufficient
civic concern for a Special Park Commission to be set
up in 1899 to plan a series of interlocking parks and
green spaces, recreation and conservation areas for
the city. Jensen produced *A Greater West Park System*
in 1920, and though few of his suggestions were

implemented, the report embodied many of his concepts of the importance of
community, and the healthgiving and spiritual values of parks in urban areas.
Parks cultivated and preserved a love of nature, he claimed. They were
'practical schools of horticulture and the bone and sinew of art out-of-doors',[32]
whose grounds should have a school of agriculture and a school of art.[33]
Jensen suggested municipal kitchen gardens where nearby residents without
gardens could grow food for themselves and sell off the surplus in a Market
Hall. There are many analogies here with the allotments which emerged in the
European 'back to the land' movement from the 1880s. Jensen wanted parks
to be neighbourhood centres around schools, with provision for school
gardens, games, and council rings. In *Siftings*, he described these as circles
made of seats in a clearing round a camp-fire reflecting 'the beginnings of a
new social life in the gardens of the America of tomorrow', where all are equal,
and friendship is demonstrated.[34] Jensen refers to the fire in the centre of the
circle as a link with the past, around which America's forebears first gathered.
Many such circles were made, as simple stone benches supported by stone
pillars, and they provided a focus in the wild for singing, story-telling and the
production of plays and pageants. Acting took place also in players' greens,
where audiences could watch performances in clearings in the trees.

Lincoln Memorial Garden, on which Jensen worked in Springfield, Illinois
between 1935 and 1936, continued the natural park concept.[35] This long, well
maintained park is on the shoreline of Lake Springfield, along whose inlets
were planted Jensen's favoured prairie river species. Trees such as *Cercis
canadensis*, and indigenous small trees and shrubs such as the dogwood
Cornus florida, the prairie crabapple *Malus ioensis*, and hawthorn, were planted
in same-species stands, with sumach, plum, and hazel, along the edges of
trails. Jensen planned groves of oak, sugar maple, honey locust and many
others, separated by clearings filled with prairie flowers such as purple
coneflower, phlox, rudbeckia and evening primrose.[36] Children gathered
acorns to plant, and wild flowers were brought in from the surrounding
countryside which was under threat from urbanization and industrialization.

Columbus Park Pool
Meant to resemble a
country swimming hole,
Jensen's pool was
contained by walls of stone
laid in layers, mimicking
the local rock stratification
of the prairies. Shrubs were
planted that were native
to the area, such as alder
and dogwood.

Above

Lincoln Memorial Garden Council Ring, Lake Springfield, Illinois, USA
Jensen's deep sense of democracy and history is a repeated feature of his work. The Council Ring, a circular raised stone bench, allows people to sit around a bonfire, singing or telling stories. Jensen saw the ring as a way of bringing people together socially and binding them to the past.

Opposite, top

Prairie River, Humboldt Park, Illinois, 1941
Part of Jensen's vision for his prairie landscapes included the illusion of a lazily meandering river, winding through banks of waterlilies, iris, arrowhead and marsh marigold. Here in Humboldt Park, west of Chicago, this prairie river came from constructed water sources, and Jensen planted indigenous plants along its edges.

Opposite, bottom

Prairie Meadow, Highland Park, Illinois, 1926
Jensen skilfully opened out spaces in woodland without allowing the full view to be seen at once. Irregular edges, planted with hawthorn and crabapple, fringed the grassland, with the end of the meadow oriented towards the setting sun.

Jensen planned a grove of white oak, *Quercus alba*, in the middle of which was placed the Lincoln Council Ring, a ring of seats in memory of President Abraham Lincoln (1809–65).

Jensen's private work began in the first decade of the twentieth century. He ruefully admitted that many of his clients, including the new wealthy Midwesterners, did not appreciate his work. 'Those with a real understanding of landscaping are the very, very, few'.[37] But Harry Rubens, on whose estate at Glencoe in Illinois Jensen worked between 1903 and 1906, became one of the converts. The next buyer of the Rubens estate was sufficiently impressed to vow 'I shall not allow any showy geraniums or other foreign flowers to spoil the composition made for the previous owner of my place'.[38]

Discord was a strong element in Jensen's relationship with the Ford family, though through Henry he obtained many commissions. Henry Ford (1863–1947), creator of the Ford Motor Company in Dearborn, Michigan, one of the region's new rich, built a large mansion on the banks of the Rouge River. He engaged Jensen in 1914 to landscape the 1,240 acres (502 hectares) around Fair Lane which once had been farmland. Formal gardens were made for his wife Clara Ford, next to the house – a course of action rarely followed by Jensen. Ford shared Jensen's concerns over conservation, and was happy with his reforestation of the major part of the property. In the forest were clearings or trail gardens leading to a council ring, beside three long meadows which were to form a key element in the design. The river, which was sufficiently deep to allow the passage of motor boats, was enhanced by a cascade made from horizontal layers of vernacular limestone, into which was crafted a boathouse.

The discord arose over the meadows. Clara Ford, a strong-minded woman with firm views about gardens and 'all of them bad', did not appreciate the beauty of the natural garden.[39] Similar to a long forest glade, with gentle, unclipped edges of hawthorn ending in a group of silver birch, the Great Meadow had an element which was repeated in many Jensen commissions: it was oriented towards the path of the setting sun.

In 1920, piqued because Jensen refused to alter his landscape for her, Clara brought in another designer who placed a formal rose garden the full length of the second meadow. Jensen was angry at the failure of the American Society of Landscape Architects to discipline the designer for breaking Jensen's contract with the Fords, and resigned his membership. He never worked again at Fair Lawn; and from then on the Jensen design was altered by Clara. The rock work along the river was dismantled, and the trail gardens filled with bright flowers.[40]

Jensen fared better with Henry's only child Edsel and his wife Eleanor. They acquired from Henry 125 acres (50 hectares) of Grosse Pointe on the American side of Lake St Clair, Michigan, away from urban Detroit. Here they achieved a paradox – the European house, looking to past styles and cultures – with grounds landscaped by Jensen. Following his father as president of the Ford Motor Company, from 1921 to 1943, Edsel could afford to visit Europe with his architect Albert Kahn and collect artefacts which appealed to him. 'Gaukler Pointe' was begun by Kahn in 1926; it is a pastiche of a large sixteenth-century Cotswold mansion. Stone for the roof tiles was imported from England, and English craftsmen were hired to work on the house, which contained panelling, staircases and chimney-pieces from English country houses.

The grounds reflected Jensen's concern to integrate prairie and settled landscape on the lake shore. The house was set in a meadow which flowed up to the house. Only later were trees planted here. Circling the meadow, and connecting with the road out, was a drive shaded by trees along the lake edge. Jensen enlarged a lagoon between the lake and a free-form swimming pool, using the soil to create a peninsula sheltering the northern shore. The peninsula was planted with shrubs which produced berries, as Edsel Ford was concerned to protect birds. Wild flowers were left to proliferate. In the meadow a grove of maples was planted, and birches by the swimming pool. Trees enclosed other more formal areas, including a rose garden full of yellow and white hybrid tea roses. This was made by Jensen for Eleanor by special request; more to his taste were the paths he made through hemerocallis, phlox, cornus and trillium.

After his wife's death in 1934 Jensen moved from Chicago to 'The Clearing', the family's summer home at Ellison Bay, Wisconsin. It became a school for the teaching of landscape design, and a place for American youth to learn about themselves through studying horticulture and the landscape around them. Jensen's influence waned after his death in 1951, despite his involvement in some 700 commissions; his reputation had spread little until a chance discovery of records in 1987 in the vaults of the Chicago Park District rekindled interest and led to conservation of his work.

J. P. Thijsse (1865–1945)

Unlike Jens Jensen, Jacobus Pieter Thijsse was raised in a country which lacked the luxury of space. The Netherlands became the most crowded country in Europe as its population grew rapidly from the middle of the nineteenth century, and Thijsse's landscaping philosophy reflected the need to protect the fast vanishing countryside. The geological structure of the Netherlands is composed of heavy clays, sands and gravels left by retreating glaciers, fringed by dunes along the coastline, and crossed by the Maas and the Rhine. The substantial deltas of these rivers occupy much of the land space, and nearly half of the country is below sea level. More recent times have seen peat formation on the land surface. The grid-like canal and dyke network began to appear as early as the seventeenth century, as attempts were made to raise land for cultivation above the level of waterlogging. Drainage was helped by the use of the steam pump from the middle of the nineteenth century, and the competitive advances in agriculture overseas intensified food-production and horticulture, and encouraged industrialization.

The intensive use of space alerted garden designers, naturalists and writers to the loss of natural habitats such as the forests, the heathlands of the eastern border, the dunes along the coast, and the wetlands. This began to focus attention on the need for conservation, and stimulated more scientifically based discussion about how plants should be grown together. There was also the need for a professional body of landscape gardeners and for planning for green spaces in the built environment. Recent garden design in the Netherlands has emerged from the plantsmen, rather than the architects, from an agricultural rather than an architectural education. The Society of Dutch Landscape, Park and Garden Architects (BNT) was founded in 1921.

The son of a military officer, Thijsse was trained as a primary school teacher in Amsterdam. He was interested in nature, and like Jensen, saw the value to young people of a knowledge of the wild environment. Unlike Jensen, Thijsse explored the background of plant biology. With a teaching colleague, Eli Heimans, he prepared a number of books for children, aimed at raising awareness of nature and the need for its conservation. Together with a magazine called *Living Nature* (1896) and the first *Illustrated Flora of the Netherlands* (1899), his books also helped to introduce the concept of different environments or biospheres inhabited by plants. Many Dutch designers followed German ideas such as those advocated by Willy Lange in *Gartengestaltung der Neuzeit* (Garden Design for Modern Times, 1906), including placing plants according to their natural habitats. There were also divisions amongst those who favoured the use of native plants. In the early part of the twentieth century, traditional landscape architects argued for a managed wildness, using cultivated garden species, in a style representing the natural. Others considered that native species, not cultivars, should be used.[41] Jac Thijsse, and later, the curator of the Amsterdam Hortus Botanicus, A. J. Van Laren, advocated phytogeographical grouping, or planting areas by country of origin – a convention followed by many botanical gardens.[42]

**Jac P. Thijssepark,
Amsterdam,
The Netherlands**
Jac P. Thijsse created a
series of managed wild
parks to conserve natural
flora in the Netherlands,
called *heemparken* (wild
parks). In the Westelijk
Bovenland area of
Amsterdam, a number of
environments support
woodland, waterloving
and heath plants, such as
meadowsweet along the
streamside (top), and
bog asphodel in the
watermeadow (bottom
right). The park features
a wild flower nursery
(bottom left).

Thijsse's social concern expressed itself most often in the provision of
public parks. He would have liked to see nature parks in every city, and became
involved in a committee looking at the requirements for parks in Amsterdam.
The town's setting had become increasingly urbanized. How would a
proposed series of green spaces best be organized?

Over thirty years Thijsse contributed a variety of ideas to newspapers
and took part in the development plan for parkland around Nieuwe Meer,
southwest of Amsterdam, which eventually became the Bos Park, opened
in 1937. He envisaged a series of green spaces linked with public gardens
in the city, similar to Ebenezer Howard's policy as set out in *Garden Cities of
To-morrow* (1902); he also visited other European cities to see how they
dealt with similar needs for the provision of green spaces.

There was further debate on how plants should be used in the Bos Park.
The concept of planting according to country of origin became complicated
by considering whether plants should also be grouped together in their
natural habitats – for instance, plants that would occur together in dunes or
wetlands. Thijsse rightly pointed out that 'plant sociology' might be a better
term to use, as the public would not understand these 'phytogeographical

principles',[43] and the awkward terms eventually disappeared, to be replaced by 'plant ecology'. Both Thijsse and Van Laren urged the protection of the character of native planting in the parks, as 'foreign plants are intended for the garden'.[44] However, Thijsse chose plants for 'ecological rather than political and nationalistic reasons'.[45] Though the Dutch understood the message implicit in Lange's writings, they did not follow suit.

Thijsse promoted his desire for conservation practically, with a 5-acre (2 hectare) garden for all the plants that grew in the dunes, at Bloemendaal, to the west of Amsterdam which he opened to the public in 1925. Known as Thijsse's Hof, the garden was set out very simply with a central pool encircled by a path, the whole surrounded by sheltering planting. To encourage others to make similar plant reserves without removing natural stock from the wild, he set up a nursery to supply wild plants. The idea proved popular, and over one hundred and fifty other educational wild parks had been made in the Netherlands by the 1990s. In 1939 and 1940 the landscape architect C. P. Broerse designed the De Braak and Westelijk Bovenland wild parks, as green havens within urban areas, shaped by plants rather than architecture, and intended to be educational as well as pleasing to the eye. Both parks were made in Amstelveen to the south of Amsterdam; and it was Broerse who suggested calling them *heemparken* (wild parks), as the term aptly implied the reasons for their construction.

Westelijk Bovenland was later renamed the Jac P. Thijssepark. It was made in a wedge of land between buildings and the Amsterdamse Bos, on an area verging on wetland, with an acid soil low in nutrients and thus well suited to many wild plants. Here is a series of environments providing homes for different plant communities – waterside, heathland, woodland – set in a design of winding paths and waterways which contrasts strongly with the straight lines and grid patterns of the canals and buildings of urban Amsterdam. Over time, a system of managed wildness has evolved, with gardeners deciding which species should be allowed to dominate. Much of the area would revert to woodland if left to itself, and seedling trees are removed along with other rampant species. However, trees and shrubs divide this *heempark* into recognizable zones including juniper heathland, bog asphodel wetland and alder marsh woodland, but the whole has landscaping which includes long vistas along waterways and colourful flower borders along paths. The planting is made up of wild species, and Amstelveen has its own wild plant nursery. By managing species in this manner it has been possible to encourage and conserve rare plants such as dianthus, marsh gentian, geum, and wild lilies.

Thijsse was able to realize much of his aim for conservation before he died in 1945. He was instrumental in setting up the Dutch conservation body

Vereniging to Behoud van Natuurmonumenten (Society for the Protection of Natural Landscapes). Children were taken on instructed nature walks in his wild parks. The value of wild vegetation was recognized. Areas of the Netherlands such as Amstelveen had *heemparks* and the wild areas were linked by public gardens and fingers of green planting or *heemgroen*. The parks need careful maintenance to preserve a chosen natural balance, but this is not so far from the original concept.

Willy Lange (1864–1941)

At the end of the nineteenth century Germany was becoming bored with past garden styles. Garden historian Marie Luise Gothein quotes the journal *Der Kunstwart* which refers to rather absurd examples of bedding as 'pipsqueak gardens' (*Piepenbrinkgärten*) and 'a child's twisted cake' (*brezel*),[46] and it was time to bring 'fresh air' into what landscape gardeners were doing.[47] Much of this vulgarization of design accompanied the increased demand for small gardens by the expanding German middle class, whose growth and prosperity came from industrialization and the trickle-down effect of reparation money paid by the French for the Franco-Prussian War of 1870–71, but whose knowledge of garden styles was perhaps less discriminating than that of their forebears.[48]

At the beginning of the twentieth century German gardening journals were concerned that English gardens, from where many of the ideas on garden styles had been garnered, were 'suffering disfigurement from the clipping shears', a reference to the revivalism of the Edwardian era.[49] The lack of interest in modernism with its concentration on 'functionalism' was more marked in England than in Germany, where architects such as Hermann Muthesius (1861–1927) had begun to promote gardens as open air rooms, as part of the total concept of house and garden combined.[50] However, German gardeners continued their admiration of the English landscape movement long after it disappeared in England; and perhaps because of this, and the absence of any significant designer in Germany, plantsmen were

Frühling in Gartenheim (Spring at Gartenheim): **Willy Lange's garden, from** *Gartengestaltung der Neuzeit***, Germany, 1907**
Lange's idea of the nature garden on first sight was similar to that of William Robinson, with indigenous flowers and shrubs and a loose, unbounded shape, as seen in his own garden near Berlin in 1928. But Lange attached his use of German plants to the ugly nationalistic ideology of the National Socialist Party.

experimenting with 'natural' gardens before William Robinson.[51] Writers such as Hermann Jaeger, in his *Illustriertes Allgemeines Gartenbuch* of 1864 and 'Dendrophilus' in 'Der Wilde Garten' in *Gartenzeitung* of 1882 and 1883, discussed gardening along the *Wild Garden*'s lines. Dendrophilus identified himself closely with Robinson. There was common cause with the English concern for the neglect and disappearance of old-established perennial plants, with writer and magazine publisher Theodor Ruempler (1817–91) producing *Die Stauden* (the perennials) in 1889; there was discussion of colour, borders, and the placing of flower gardens near the house, or in enclosed areas in the grounds. Unlike the English, Germans continued to use bedding out into the twentieth century, and for both annuals and perennials. The Association of German Garden Architects was founded in 1913, much earlier than the British Institute of Landscape Architects in 1929.

The German garden architect Willy Lange explored different realms of the German psyche as he formulated his concept of the nature garden in the journals *Gartenwelt* (garden world) and *Gartenkunst* (garden art) from 1900 onwards. In the 1980s, two German garden historians – Joachim Wolschke-Bulmahn and Gert Gröning – saw that Lange's work on the nature garden was being reinstated by historians without sufficient understanding of the blatant racist ideology to which it originally gave rise.[52] They then stirred up controversy in the *Journal of Garden History* and elsewhere by analyzing Lange's work.

Lange's *Gartengestaltung der Neuzeit* (Modern Garden Design, 1907) borrowed ideas from Jekyll and Robinson.[53] He incorporated parts of *The English Flower Garden* and *The Wild Garden*, placing them in his own version of the 'nature garden', a landscape with trees and shrubs and some flowers but little imposed shape; but in order to distance himself from the current practice of architects, Lange claimed that his philosophy was built upon another discipline which had gained ground in the nineteenth century – science.

Darwin's *Origin of Species* was well known in Germany, but its tenet of the survival of the fittest was adopted by Lange to justify the selection of certain types of plant for his garden. The work of the phytogeographers, who grouped plants in communities to which they were best suited geographically, could also be used to argue that certain plants should be placed in certain communities. The analogy between plants and human beings, at first implied, later became overt.

Lange also drew on the work of the German biologist Ernst Haeckel, who claimed that nature was the equal of man, and therefore that man should not dominate nature.[54] From this, Lange decreed that a garden should be part of the landscape, from which it should be almost indistinguishable on its boundaries. Trees and shrubs should not be cut. It followed that gardens should be neither geometric nor architectural, as these gardens were anthropocentric – i.e., man-centred. Lange's gardens had indistinct boundaries, trees, shrubs and flowering plants loosely placed, bulbs naturalized beneath trees and few paths, in a manner reminiscent of a mix between the English landscape garden and Robinson's wild garden.

Lange's natural garden became mixed up in a very nationalistic

In Germany under the ruling National Socialist Party, *Die Land-Baufibel* (The Rural Primer) denounced any form of modernity or departure from the characteristic rural village scene surrounding the deep-roofed, timber-framed cottages. Disapproval is shown here of the use of concrete pillars and metal fences and gates, instead of hedges and wooden fences. Intrusive petrol stations, modern script on signs, warehouses and wires carrying electricity were all unwelcome forms of landscaping.

Die deutschen Gaue haben mannigfaltige heimatgebundene Umfriedungen gestaltet, von denen viele für Dorf und Flur zu erhalten und weiterzuentwickeln sind: so z. B. Wallhecken in Schleswig-Holstein und im westfälischen Münsterland, Bruchsteinmauern in Gebirgsgegenden, Findlingsmauern in Pommern, Flechtzäune in Niedersachsen, Sodenwälle in Friesland und andere mehr.

Gut gepflegte Hecken sind von langer Lebensdauer. Als Abgrenzung zur Straße bieten sie dem Garten Staub-, Wind- und Sonnenschutz und Nistgelegenheit für viele nützliche Singvögel.

Nach heimischer Art hergerichtete, einfache Holzzäune sind in waldreichen Gebieten noch heute geeignete Umfriedungen. Entstandene Schäden können vom Hofbesitzer leicht ausgebessert werden.

Drahtzäune mit Eisenstützen, Betonpfeilern und Gittertoren in kümmerlicher Gestaltung, spielerischen Aufbauten und Zutaten sind teuer und häßlich und zerstören das einheitliche Dorfbild.

Weltanschauung or ideology which suited the national mood after German unification in 1871, and which continued during the Weimar Republic (1918–33). The German Romantic painters had looked forward to national unity, as architect Karl Friedrich Schinkel (1781–1841) depicted a new dawn behind ancient trees and Gothic churches, and Caspar David Friedrich (1774–1840) chose moonlit scenes as a prelude to a new day. Their images of figures in medieval costume, old trees as symbols of noble longevity, and looming Christian architecture were suggestive of continuity into a new age. The same images can be seen more blatantly in some German Expressionist painting and are discernible in the music of Wagner. There was a nostalgia for the vanishing countryside – a common phenomenon in all countries where dislike of the urban spread was matched by dislike of the sprawl of industry with its smoke, dirt and ugliness. This metamorphosed into nature worship, where all that was rural was good, and all that came from the town was bad.

Willy Lange's 'nature' became linked with ancient, anti-Christian *völkisch* mythology which claimed that the true German/Nordic peasant races were 'rooted in the soil' and were superior, and that those who were foreign were inferior. The link between 'nature and exotic plants, indigenous and foreign populations' has been traced to F. K. H. Günther's *Rassenkunde des Deutschen Volkes* (Racial Handbook of the German People, 1922), which inspired Lange's attacks in the *Gartenbilder* (Garden Images) of 1922 and *Gartenpläne* (Garden Designs) of 1927.[55] The highest form of garden culture, said Lange, was the nature garden, which was only attainable by the German/Nordic races.[56] Therefore only German plants should be used in gardens. In a further, confused attack on the architectural garden (which had flourished in German states in the seventeenth and eighteenth centuries), Lange claimed in 1933 that in the formal garden, the Nordic race 'spiritually perished in the race-morass of the south'.[57]

Through Richard Walther Darré, the Minister of Agriculture between 1933 and 1942, the Nazi party which came to power in 1933 adopted the 'Blood and Soil' ideology of superior cultural groups closely allied to the earth. It followed that any nomadic or homeless group – for instance, Gypsies or Jews – was inferior. Translated into garden terms, this meant that plants from other countries should be rejected or destroyed. Garden architects who wished to keep their jobs also professed this ideology. Many architects, though proportionately fewer garden architects, left Germany. The ideology was all-pervasive; of its many exponents, the leading National Socialist garden architect Alwin Seifert (1890–1972) is remembered for banning foreign plants and trees from the planting of the autobahn in the 1930s. English landscape architects, including Sylvia Crowe, visited Germany and were impressed by the autobahn systems. Crowe illustrates her book *The Landscape of Roads* with five photographs of the work of Seifert, with, it seems, no inkling of the darker implication behind his choice of 'native plants and trees'.[58]

Karl Foerster (1874–1970)

Karl Foerster was a nurseryman and plant breeder rather than a garden designer. But it was through the breeding and testing of plants, his garden design service and his twenty-eight books and other writings – especially between 1920 and 1941 in the magazine which he founded, *Die Gartenschönheit* (the beauty of the garden) – that he helped to promote a natural style of planting. However, Robinson had no influence on his work; although he was respected elsewhere in Germany, Robinson's ideas had not penetrated this far. Foerster's father was a director of Berlin's Royal Observatory, but rather than follow an academic path, Karl took up an apprenticeship as a gardener and then trained in horticulture in Potsdam's Wildpark. He opened a nursery in Berlin-Westend in 1903 and was successful enough to move, some seven years later, to a larger area in Bornim, Potsdam. He built a house and made a garden which also served as a showcase for his

plants. Foerster's aim was to produce hardy plants which would be easy
to cultivate for the ordinary man in the street, and were not intended for
privileged clients such as those of Jekyll and Robinson in England, with
large old houses and large numbers of gardeners.[59]

There are photographs of the Bornim garden in 1917 in Foerster's *Vom
Blütengarten der Zukunft* (From The Flowergarden of the Future), and a plan
of 1925 in *Die Gartenschönheit*[60] shows that within the rectangular layout
there was an ornate and geometric sunk garden facing east. A nature garden
with winding paths was reached from the sunk garden on the north, which
led to a rock garden on the northwest corner of the plot. There was a circular
trial garden, with separate small beds. On the south side of the sunk garden
was a spring path. The trial garden and nature garden no longer exist.

The rectangular sunk garden, with woodland beyond, was enclosed by a
wooden pergola, painted blue, on its three sides. The pergola has gone, but the
photographs of 1917 show it was clothed with small-flowered rambling roses,
Russian vine, and honeysuckle, and it sheltered wooden benches which faced
the sun. In the centre of the pergola, facing the house, was a curved wooden
arbour. The sunk garden may have been designed with the help of Willy
Lange, and was possibly the first in Germany.[61] Leading down from the pergola
level to the central, oval lily pool from the four sides were solid, stone steps
which linked the surrounding shallow planting terraces, edged by dry stone
walls. The terracing was put in by Hermann Mattern in the 1930s, replacing
sloping banks. The 1925 plan published in *Die Gartenschönheit* shows a very
intricate pattern of geometric beds in the central space of the sunken garden,
which was simplified by Mattern. The paths around the pool and leading into
the garden were gravelled. The garden was reshaped in the 1960s, as the
growth of trees and shrubs had begun to change the overall balance – this
was partly addressed by the landscape architect Hermann Goeritz.

The 1917 illustrations of the garden in summer show the sunken garden
displayed Foerster's favourite phlox, which filled the beds nearest the house.[62]
At the four corners of the lily pool were planted large mop-like clumps of
grasses, which Foerster recognized for their form in winter and their
movement and texture in summer. Lining the pool edges were gladioli and
day lilies. Bearded irises flanked the steps leading to the arbour, in front of
which played a small fountain, now gone. The terraces were planted with
alpines, and yet more phlox. Vertical elements were provided by clipped
ball-headed shrubs in pots on the paths facing the pool, tall lilies, *Eremurus
robustus*, verbascum and seed-head globes – possibly alliums – rising from
low-planted beds nearer the house. Aromatics such as lavender, thyme and
the curry plant enjoyed the sun under the house windows. Close to the house
walls were hollyhocks, and delphiniums, also well loved by Foerster.

To the side of the house in the nature garden was an area planted with species common to Germany's ecological zones of heathland, mountain and beechwood; Foerster's planting according to ecological grouping became influential in German parks. Behind the house is a rock garden, which has become shaded over time by the growth of large trees. Foerster's garden was a showcase for his nursery. The plant material that it contained represented the end-product of a rigorous system of five-year plant-trialling in the nursery at Bornim and elsewhere in Germany.[63] Foerster introduced over 650 new plants, which were all thoroughly tested. Only a few were chosen for sale in the nursery from several thousand seedlings. The qualities he sought were long life and manageability, resistance to drought, cold and pests. He introduced

Karl Foerster's garden, Potsdam, Germany
Foerster's house and sunk garden in 1917 show his pergola and arch with climbers, features now no longer practicable as the surrounding trees have grown too close to the garden. The borders are filled with sturdy, colourful perennials which Foerster trialled – asters, phlox, coneflowers and hollyhocks.

Top and bottom right
Freundschaftinsel
(Friendship Island),
Berlin, with Foerster's lily
pool and planting
Recent restoration
has returned Foerster's
planting to the Friendship
park in Berlin, especially
the lilies in the long ponds
and bright perennials in
the beds.

Middle left and right
Foerster's garden at
Bornim, Potsdam
September sun streams
through the garden,
dissolving shapes, and
lighting the colours of the
perennials and grasses,
and the woodland garden
(middle right) from within.
In the dry and cold east
German winter, the forms
of the plants will give
interest to the garden.
Foerster's daughter
Marianne admires the
scene with a friend
(bottom left).

sturdy cultivars of the delphinium, phlox, helenium and aster, philadelphus,
spiraea and dahlia, amongst many others. He was the first to use grasses as a
complement to other flowering plants and as an important component which
had all-year colour and form. *Carex pendula maxima*, *Festuca glauca*, *Stipa
pennata*, and *Molinia coerulea silvatica* are among varieties recommended by
Foerster.[64] By developing a colourful range of manageable plants from native,
exotic, and well established garden species, Foerster was able to produce
continuity of interest for what he called an extended range of 'seven seasons'
in the year.

Foerster's plantsmanship has influenced many including Mien Ruys in the
Netherlands, Rosemary Weisse and Ernst Pagel in Germany, and Wolfgang

Oehme in the United States. The garden and plant development at Bornim are maintained today by Foerster's daughter Marianne, who continues her father's tradition of the massed planting of colourful perennials which soften the edges of paths, and grasses which play their part during the summer, and produce seed-heads and interesting shapes in winter. In 1927, Foerster began a garden design service with Hermann Mattern (1902–71) and Herta Hammerbacher (1890–1985) which led, in 1935, to the creation of three separate services – nursery, design, and construction, and eventually to the employment of a workforce of 150. The partnership with Mattern and Hammerbacher ended in 1948, as there was no demand for designed gardens under post-war occupation, and this also temporarily ended Foerster's breeding programme. After a period of neglect in the 1970s the garden is now classed by Potsdam as an historic monument.

It is clear that Foerster had no truck with the thinking of the National Socialist Party. Whilst Lange supported the Nazi regime, Foerster did not, and his anti-nationalist book *Glücklich durchbrochenes Schweigen* (Happily Broken Silence) published in 1937, was quickly withdrawn.[65]

Where did Hammerbacher and Mattern stand in this troubled period? Mattern joined forces with Alwin Siefert in the autobahn project from 1936, and their motives for planting native species along roads may appear questionable.[66] Mattern went on to hold the chair of landscape architecture in West Berlin. Hammerbacher seems to have expressed views, common to those attempting to square their consciences, by linking the natural garden with the concepts of the eighteenth century, where 'natural' spoke of freedom and liberty. Hammerbacher's gardens have unseen boundaries, long grass, and unclipped trees. However, Van Groeningen highlights the strong social commitment of the partnership of Foerster, Mattern and Hammerbacher, who designed gardens cheaply for the 'small man' to 'create a paradise by using simple plants'.[67] And if one put together the efforts of many small men, 'one large garden landscape would develop'.[68]

In the eighteenth century the philosophy of the Enlightenment spilled over into its 'natural' gardens. By the end of the nineteenth and beginning of the twentieth century England and Germany recognized the value of wild species in gardens and the Dutch sought to protect their vanishing countryside; in the United States Sessions and Jensen valued indigenous wild plants for gardens, private and public parks. In the 1930s plant-breeding entered the warped political philosophy of the German Nazi Party. The resurrection of Foerster's garden has helped to lay this ghost to rest. Of the perceived roles of 'natural' planting – pioneer planting, politics and conservation up to the Second World War – conservation has become the most significant and continuous issue.

Modernism: art and architecture in the garden to the 1930s

'Modernism' meant different things to different branches of culture at the beginning of the twentieth century, but broadly it was concerned with breaking with old ways of thinking. In the visual arts, new ideas almost invariably arrived first in painting, spreading next to architecture; garden design, a most conservative and reactive art form, followed on, often decades later. This conservatism was confirmed by some of the landscape paintings exhibited at the 1900 Paris 'Exposition Universelle'.[1] These underlined established positions regarding plantsmen's and architects' gardens, and national attitudes towards nature and art. Of them, the placidity of the fruit and vegetable garden in the Dutch Ferdinand Hart Nibbrig's (1866–1915) *Abundance* (1895) points to the preoccupation with plants and the 'natural' landscape in the Netherlands, while the Catalan modernist Santiago Rusiñol's (1861–1931) sun-soaked garden terraces in *The Green Wall* (1901) shows the formal designs of Spain which are repeated in the 1990s by his Spanish compatriot, garden designer Fernando Caruncho. Pieter Cornelius Mondrian's (1872–1944) painting of *Pollard Willows on the Gein* (1902–4) only hints at his later concern with the stern geometry of the De Stijl movement which found its way into some town planning.

If Modernism meant the breaking from old patterns and ways of thinking, was there a body of 'rules', or a common language of ideas, which could be assimilated between different branches of culture, and which could then be adopted by the landscape makers? Those seeking to identify such rules for garden-makers included the Canadian-born Christopher Tunnard, whose dilemma and lack of success is explored here.

To some extent we have to agree with art historian H. H. Arnason's comment that 'in the study of art the only primary evidence is the work of art itself',[2] and therefore a body of rules becomes impossible to achieve. But some common thinking can be traced between art, architecture and landscape design, including the search for the essence of form, whether human or inanimate, uncluttered by cultural associations. Such thinking is seen in the sculpture of Constantin Brancusi (1876–1957) who influenced the later sculptural gardens of Isamu Noguchi (1904–88). From similar beginnings came abstraction and surrealism, explored by modern painters such as Englishman Ben Nicholson (1894–1981) and Belgian René Magritte (1898–1967) and which appeared later in the landscapes of Geoffrey Jellicoe.

Falling Water, Pennsylvania, by Frank Lloyd Wright
Built for Pittsburgh businessman Edgar Kaufmann in 1936, this stunning view of the house with its concrete terraces cantilevered over the waterfall of the Bear Run stream, seemingly fixed into the rocky hillside by its long vertical chimney, established Falling Water as a supreme example of the synthesis of a modern house with its landscape.

Jellicoe later identified the all-embracing subconscious influence of modern art in his designs.

Symbolism in art was not new, having its beginnings in the eighteenth century. But two centuries later its revival had a dynamic effect on the designs of American landscape architects. However, it was the pattern of the shapes in the paintings of the Russians Vasily Kandinsky (1866–1944) and Kasimir Malevich (1878–1935) which found their way into the gardens designed by American Garrett Eckbo, not their underlying symbolism.

Similarly, it was not the underlying philosophy of the De Stijl movement which captured the imagination of house and garden designers, but the colourful geometry of Piet Mondrian's (1872–1944) paintings. De Stijl took its name from a journal founded by Theo van Doesburg (1883–1931) in the Netherlands, published between 1917 and 1932. He had been much influenced by the paintings of Paul Cézanne and Vasily Kandinsky, and explored mathematical ways of expressing images in a strong revolt against 'Baroque' and Impressionism. The movement attracted a group of like-minded architects and painters including Gerrit Rietveld (1888–1964), Cornelis van Eesteren (1897–1988), J. J. P. Oud (1890–1963) and Piet Mondrian (1872–1944), sharing ideas in the years leading up to 1920. Van Eesteren moved into town planning, and designed social housing for the Amsterdam Department of City Development in the late 1940s, with communal gardens by Mien Ruys. He also proffered plans for Amsterdam's Bospark (1945).[3]

De Stijl's painters adopted geometry and primary colours in their search for clarity and order. Piet Mondrian progressed through Naturalism (as in his early *Pollard Willows on the Gein*) to abstraction, still using familiar objects such as trees or sand dunes, but taking them as references in an exploration of tensions between the vertical and the horizontal. His pictures became grids (perhaps reminiscent of the sixteenth-century pattern of drainage canals in the Netherlands) with a few primary colours, and without perspective.

J. J. P. Oud used a similar manner of restricting architectural features to the vertical and horizontal, in housing he designed for Scheveningen's seaside in 1917, and for factory housing at the Hook of Holland (1924–27), and his Rotterdam Café de Unie was an architectural expression of Mondrian's style of painting.

Later modernists also borrowed from De Stijl, and especially from Mondrian. Garrett Eckbo's wall screen for the pool at the Wohlstetter garden in Laurel Canyon, Los Angeles, in the 1950s uses primary-coloured rectangles in a Mondrian manner. Lotte Stam-Beese, a Dutch city planner, designed layouts for Penderecht in Rotterdam, whose ground plan is based entirely on long verticals and short horizontals.[4]

Opposite, top
Ferdinand Hart-Nibbrig,
***Abundance*, 1895**
The Dutch have long demonstrated skills in horticulture and agriculture, which have led to their now predominantly plant-centred approach to garden design. At the end of the nineteenth century, Hart-Nibbrig set the scene for the future in this flower and vegetable garden.

Opposite, bottom
Santiago Rusiñol,
***The Green Wall*, 1901**
Modernist Rusiñol, who lived in an artists' colony at Sitges near Barcelona, painted this view of a formally terraced landscape. It highlights the Spanish delight in the architectural garden, where the hard landscape form is given strong shaping by green hedges and trees.

The Parque del Calamot, on a hilltop in the Gavá district of Barcelona, was planned in the 1990s, based entirely on Mondrian's 1917 *Composition in Blue*. The picture was interpreted by its Spanish architects Carles Llinás and Fidel Vázquez Alarcón as a hierarchy formed by red, orange and blue rectangles, with small black rectangles punctuating the groups. The white background was taken to represent the park as a whole, and the areas for activity in the park were related to the coloured rectangles. The hilltop, squares, esplanades, and lookout points also acquired a hierarchy according to their placing in the park. *Pinus pinea* and carob trees remain from the estate which the park replaces, and are enclosed by the rectangular slabs of the path.[5]

Cubism emerged from a productive relationship between Pablo Picasso (1881–1973) and Georges Braque (1882–1963) which lasted until the Frenchman Braque went off to fight in the First World War in 1914. Cubism was to play an important part in the Modern Movement long after Picasso had moved on to other styles of painting. Cubists wanted to experience all sides of an object, to question its boundaries and even the concept of boundaries, and as a consequence artists experimented with different planes in their depictions of landscape, still life and portraits.

Cubism translated readily into architecture. Le Corbusier's (1887–1965) houses in France used variations of the hollowed-out cube and stacking cube. And at the same time as the evolution of painting away from the representational towards geometric and abstract forms, there was experimentation with new materials with which to build, particularly steel and concrete. The adoption of such materials and its development for the mass market in Germany under the auspices of the Bauhaus helped to create a new approach as to how the modern house could be used, with flat roofs for gardens and sunbathing and swimming pools accompanying the trend for healthy outdoor living.

The Bauhaus in Germany, a school of applied arts set up in Weimar in 1919 by Walter Gropius, remained active until the Nazis caused it to be shut down in 1933. Like the Arts and Crafts movement, Gropius and others believed in the value of excellent workmanship and the honesty of the quality of the materials used, and decried the rift between industry and crafts. Garden design was not taught at the Bauhaus (though Gropius made a design for Dartington Hall, in southwest England) but the Bauhaus concept of an all-embracing complete work – the *Gesamtkunstwerk* – later found its way into houses and gardens designed together. But where Morris resisted the influence of the machine, Gropius believed that there could be co-operation between art and industry, making products available to a wider public.

But at the beginning of the twentieth century, garden-makers were still loath to abandon styles of the past. Illustrations of Victor Bourgeois's 1932 garden at 10 rue Marianne in Brussels, with its narrow pool, line of standard roses, and zig-zag raised edging to its path, Otto Zollinger's Streiff House (1930–31) on Lake Zürich, with its swirling balconies above a bank of flowering plants, Sutemi Horiguti's Kitikawa House (1928–30) in Tokyo, with its pruned shrubs and simple green lawn forming sections cut from a circle on two levels, joined their flat-roofed English counterparts of Amyas Connell's High and Over (1929) at Amersham in Buckinghamshire, with its steep concrete steps leading down from a building whose two wings opened to the sun, and Orchard House in Bristol, whose dart-shaped flower bed full of dahlias was kept in check by a zig-zag path. But these were the exception rather than the rule, made by architects, not landscape designers. And much of this chapter describes the tensions between well-known modernist architects, who built houses based on geometric shapes with an eye to form following function, and garden-makers, who did not know how to apply Modernism to the garden.

Despite the example of lavish villa gardens on the Mediterranean coast, the early twentieth century saw a continuation of the decline in large-scale garden-making by the traditional British and European aristocratic landowner, whose wealth was based on agriculture. The economic recessions of the early 1920s and the early 1930s prompted the sale of a number of whole estates and the fragmentation of many others. The economic depression of the 1930s also affected large estate owners in the United States; garden designers had to seek work with public bodies, reduce the scale of their work, or go to the wall.

However, British and European landowners' misfortunes were opportunities for others, including the middle classes, who bought parts of fragmented estates. Industrialists, railway magnates, film makers, food manufacturers, and large agricultural estate owners in the Americas (and eventually Australia and New Zealand) became garden owners. As cities grew, technology enabled the building of the skyscraper, the value of land soared, and often the only space for greenery was at roof level, in atria as 'interior gardens', or around the base of the skyscraper as a display of corporate wealth. Demand by private individuals for gardens was joined by demand from public and private sources, from museums to business headquarters.

The Elements of Modernism – Art Nouveau

Modern landscape designers failed to explore Art Nouveau, despite its appeal being apparently so closely connected with the 'natural'; parterres in particular seem adapted to this art form. Described as 'the first self-conscious, internationally based attempt to transform visual culture through a commitment to the idea of the modern',[6] this form of decorative art took its name from a gallery, La Maison de l'Art Nouveau, which opened in Paris in

Projekt einer Kunsthalle mit Schmuckplatzanlage.

Kurt Hoppe – Art Gallery, Wiesbaden, Germany

Hoppe's 1909 design to landscape an art gallery shows how the decorative Art Nouveau form was applied to landscaping around buildings in Germany. Neatly trimmed trees rise from even neater containers, around which flowers stud their beds like jewels. Terraced steps descend to a sunk garden in front of the gallery.

1895 to sell modern objects. Nationally diverse, the movement was known as Jugendstil (youth style) in Germany, Stile Liberty (after the London store) or Stile Floreale in Italy, and Sezessionstil in Austria, where it was associated with Secession artists. Expressed in urban settings, nature was the most influential of its attractions. Sinuous leaf and flower shapes made in metal by Otto Wagner (1841–1918) for stations in and around Vienna at the turn of the century, by Hector Guimard (1867–1942) for the ironwork of the Paris Métropolitain's stations, by the Belgian architect Victor Horta (1861–1947) for the stairwell in the Tassel house in Brussels, and the elaborate cast-iron detail on the front of Louis Sullivan's Carson Pirie Scott and Company department store in Chicago, form some of the lasting images of Art Nouveau. To these must be added the Celtic forms evoked by the curved metalwork of the windows of Charles Rennie Mackintosh's (1868–1928) Glasgow School of Art, and the asymmetrical, looping curves, varying from breaking wave, weeping candle-wax, to whiplash in shape, appearing in jewelry, glass, metal and wood.

Austria and Germany's own versions of Art Nouveau, show close connections with the British Arts and Crafts Movement. Some designs for gardens in Germany in 1908 seem nearer to the decorative work for house interiors, with stylized trees forming a backdrop to neat hedges, and rows of standard roses emerging like jewelled hat-pins from a border.[7] Architect Kurt Hoppe's designs for gardens around an art gallery in Wiesbaden (1909) echo

the decorative theme, with pergolas, pavilions, pools with fountains, and an enclosing hedge from which rise trees trimmed like lollipops.[8] Others reflect the low-roofed cottage 'folk art' tradition, with the lawn and flower bed area of the front divided from the vegetables and flowers at the back by a pergola. Many such gardens were planned by garden architect Leberecht Migge (1881-1935) and appear in 1913 in his book on twentieth century garden design.[9]

Although it might have been expected that Charles Rennie Mackintosh, commissioned for two houses in Scotland, Windyhill at Kilmacolm for William Davidson in 1899, and the Hill House in Helensburgh for publisher W.W. Blackie in 1902, would have been asked to translate his Art Nouveau designs into garden plans, he was only required to design the garden furniture.[10]

However in Belgium, at his country house La Bastide at La Hulpe in 1912, architect Victor Horta (1861–1947) appears to have married the Art Nouveau of the interior to the landscape outside. Though the garden in front of the house was formal, the plan of the 7-acre (3-hectare) site on the steeply sloping

Above

Charles Rennie Mackintosh – design for Hill House and garden, southwest perspective
Charles Rennie Mackintosh's Art Nouveau style was not appreciated in Scotland quite as it was among the Austrian Secessionists. Although he successfully designed W.W. Blackie's house overlooking the Firth of Clyde in 1902, with stylized and symbolic plant forms decorating the interior (as Frank Lloyd Wright was doing at the same time in Chicago), he was not asked to create the garden.

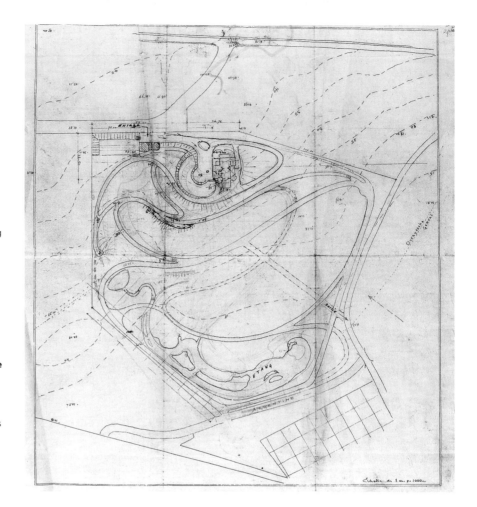

hill shows a deliberate series of whiplash paths made to the bottom of the
slope. To add to the composition, the stream which made its way down the hill
had been shaped into a sinuous lake with curling edges.[11]

Perhaps the richest expression of national diversity in Art Nouveau lies
in the landscape created by the architect Antoni Gaudí y Cornet (1852–1926)
in Barcelona. On the one hand Gaudí regarded the term *modernista* as
representative of all the social ills that had beset Spain at the turn of the
century, and held to the teachings of Catholicism which had denounced
Modernism as decadent and amoral. He designed the still unfinished Church
of the Sagrada Familia, with its sculptural shape and natural decoration.
On the other hand, the occult symbolism in Parque Güell suggests that
his Catholicism became remarkably elastic.

From 1891, Gaudí received the patronage of a wealthy Barcelona
businessman, Eusebio Güell y Bacigalupi (1846–1914). A supporter of the *Lliga
Regionalista de Cataluña,* the Catalan nationalist movement, Güell wanted
to improve living conditions amongst the working-classes. In 1891 Güell
employed Gaudí to design housing and a church to support an industrial

community at Sta Coloma de Cervelló some distance out of Barcelona. In 1900, Güell's ideas had moved on to building what was to be a garden city, with housing in green surroundings. What transpired was a curious mixture of the sacred and the occult, which adopted the decorative forms of Art Nouveau.

Parque Güell was sited on a hillside overlooking Barcelona, with a wall surrounding its twenty hectares, and plots for sixty houses. The main entrance, between two colourful pavilions for gatekeepers reminiscent of folklore gingerbread houses, is dominated by a staircase leading to a Doric colonnade which supports a large square for festivals, plays and dancing, with seating in the undulating mosaic bench which curves round the edge.

Above and below the square wind wide, palm-edged walkways, some on rough colonnades of local stone whose arches are shaped in asymmetric curves. Some of the arches themselves resemble palm trees. Near the top of the hill, the arches straighten to become columns bearing large pots of aloes. On the hilltop of the Turó de les Menes, originally

Parque Güell
Top left
Pots with agaves.
Bottom left
Whiplash balustrading.
Top right
Doric colonnade.
These pillars support the
square above, giving a
further, shaded place for
assembly. The roof also
shows masonic and
metaphysical symbols.

planned as the site of a chapel, is a Calvary with three crosses; the way to it is marked by giant stone beads representing the rosary.

Gaudí ensured that the indigenous trees and shrubs – pines, carobs, evergreen oaks, palms, rosemary, thyme, genista, sage, pittosporum and ligustrum – were maintained in the park.[12] Trees create shade along the paths; it becomes difficult to distinguish stone pillars from tree trunks.

No house plots were sold, apart from one for the lawyer Martín Trías Domènech; only Güell, Gaudí and Domènech lived in the park. The three appear to have shared interests in Masonry, the occult, and possibly Rosicrucianism, a cult concerned with alchemy and metaphysical ideas, all blended together in their Roman Catholicism. Symbols relating to these themes appear in the park, especially in the crypt under the square.[13] Gaudí's home, with its terraced garden and metal gates with sinuous leaf shapes, was once the show-house (1903–4), and seems very large in relation to the ethos of a garden city. In addition, the restrictive conditions for sale and the park's limited access led to the failure of the settlement. The park was bought by the city in 1924 as a public garden.

Art Deco

If Art Nouveau was the art form of the sinuous, Art Deco can be said to have re-established the straight line and angularity; Art Nouveau disappeared with the First World War. Art Deco evolved from 1908 and was into full stride in the 1920s. It took its name from the Exposition Internationale des Arts Décoratifs et Industriels Modernes in Paris in 1925. Eclectic in composition, it appeared where new building emerged to satisfy the demands of a new age – airports, brash cinemas, bright factories, petrol stations, newspaper offices, lavish department stores and corporate headquarters, even, in more muted form, in convalescent hospitals and schools.

Art Deco was distinguished by its use of chevrons, zig-zag lines, arrow shapes, overlapping arcs and squares, sunburst designs, large patterned plaques and friezes mounted over doorways, and tiers of rectangles diminishing in size. In gardens, the more adventurous hung wooden sunburst gates (now long rotted and replaced by garden-centre metal), built stepped-rectangle walls, their rhythms reminiscent of Scott Joplin's tunes, incorporated chevrons into brickwork and hinted at the connection with luxury liners with their porthole windows.

In Czechoslovakia, Modernism arrived from Vienna and Paris before the First World War, finding its way into architecture, interior and some garden design. In Prague, styles were moving between Art Deco and Cubism. Villas were built along the Vltava River, still with pitched roofs, and with strongly geometrical facades, such as architect Josef Chochol's (1880–1956) building in Libušina Street (1911–12). Its river front had an austere but appropriate small garden whose design was based on sloping triangles, seeming to anticipate the designs of the Noailles residences in France in the 1920s. Artist Josef Gocar's (1880–1945) Bohdaneč spa (1911–12), to the east of Prague, similarly matched the repeated chevron windows of his long ground floor facade with large, triangular beds. A poster of 1913 shows a softening of the facade by the use of flowery cascades from planters on the first floor terrace and bedding with the ubiquitous standard roses in the zig-zag beds below the windows.

However unlike Art Nouveau, Art Deco lent itself to the incorporation of decoration in the hard landscaping of gardens, and the eyes of the world were opened to the style at the Paris Expo in 1925. France had long claimed itself as a leader in the world of decorative arts – furniture, graphics, jewelry, sculpture, glass, metalware

Poster for Bohdaneč spa, Czechoslovakia
A 1913 poster by Antonín Brunner shows how Art Deco used chevrons and arrowheads on windows, and matched them with raised beds. Landscaping around this spa was severe, with large triangular beds set in the lawn, filled with single-colour blocks of plants.

Above

**Robert Mallet-Stevens,
Garden with
Concrete Trees**

This indeed was the shock
of the new at the Paris
Exposition in 1925.
Concrete was one of
the defining materials used
by modernists, and plants
were relegated to
second place.

and textiles. Garden design was not only to be part of the exhibition
(it appeared under Group IV exhibits, which were the Arts of the Theatre,
Street and Garden) it was even regarded as a fashion accessory to match
the house interior, which could be changed as rapidly as, say, changing the
pictures in the living room.[14] In this exhibition, horticulture was a low priority;
an Art Deco house had a garden – with or without plants.

The Exposition site extended between the Esplanade des Invalides on the
left bank, to the right bank of the Seine via the Pont Alexandre III; the bridge,
over a railway, posed limits to the weight of soil it could support. Like the
London Millennium Dome in Greenwich (2000), limits to planting led to
artificiality in display, though this may well have been exploited in Paris to
promote the use of new materials. Some of the most arresting representations
of gardens included those constructed by architects Robert Mallet-Stevens
(1886–1945) and Gabriel Guevrekian (1900–70).

Mallet-Stevens' 'Garden with Concrete Trees' (*Jardin de l'habitation
moderne*) puzzled, amused, shocked, and awoke the public to the realization
that Modernism had reached the garden. From each end of two large,
rectangular plant containers emerged trees made of cast concrete by Jan

Above left
**Gabriel Guevrekian,
Jardin d'eau et de
lumière**
This garden used materials
new to the garden – glass,
concrete and electric light
– providing the hard
landscaping with a lively
pattern of raised beds with
tilted planes giving colour
and excitement.

and Joël Martel. They stood like signals from the railway lines over which the garden was built, with many arms resembling planes from a cubist painting, their girder-like 'trunks' lost in grass slopes leading to the bottom of the planters in which some insignificant flowers made a gesture towards reality. The garden was intended to be a representation of nature, not a copy.

Guevrekian, a Persian of Armenian background who trained as an architect in Vienna and who worked in Paris and Manchuria, contributed the *Jardin d'eau et de lumière* (water and light garden) to the Paris Expo. In a small, triangular site surrounded by a chevron-patterned fence, Guevrekian used contemporary materials – glass, concrete, and electric light, and tilted planes of single-colour planting. In the centre of a concrete-framed pool, Louis Barillet's revolving, illuminated sphere of patterned glass sent images across the pool and interrupted fountains on each side with its rays. Beyond the pool, triangular beds of red begonias, blue ageratum, orange pyrethrum and green grass evoked Chevreul's guide to complementary colours. Each bed was set at an angle to give the picture more than one dimension. In this way, Guevrekian's garden, far from being recognized as presenting 'elements from Persian décor' as suggested by J. C. N. Forestier, the garden supervisor of the expo, became acclaimed as 'cubist'.[15] The garden attracted the attention of wealthy art patron Vicomte Charles de Noailles, who had commissioned Mallet-Stevens to design him a villa at Hyères, near Toulon. The villa, a flat-roofed building occupying a steep site overlooking the Mediterranean, spread its rooms in tiers down the hillside.

Below
Villa Noailles, Hyères
Guevrekian again used a
play of planes and colour
to create a rooftop garden
filled with tulips and citrus
trees for the Mediterranean
home of the Vicomte
Charles de Noailles near
Toulon, in 1927. The house,
designed by Mallet-
Stevens, occupied a
triangular site which lent
itself to Guevrekian's cubist
designs on the roof.

Noailles garden, Place des Etats-Unis, Paris. Photo by Man Ray
Attributed to Paul Vera, though possibly made with help from Jean-Charles Moreux, the garden design was created for Charles de Noailles in the Place des Etats-Unis, from 1924. A startling example of Art Deco, this was a theatrical display to be looked at from the first floor window; it had little to do with nature.

Accordingly, several different gardens occupied different levels about the house. But the garden for which Guevrekian became best known internationally occupied a triangular site, like the prow of a yacht, on the rooftop. The design was composed entirely of square and triangular beds separated by rectangular spaces, an exercize in geometry fitting neatly into the prow. André Lurçat's photographs of the villa in 1928 show the square, raised concrete planters filled with tulips, clipped plants forming pyramid shapes in side beds adjoining the walls, and orange trees emerging from planters on a surface covered with small tiles of black glass outside the lower salon. At the tip of the prow is a revolving, abstract statue, *La Joie de Vivre* by Jacques Lipchitz (1891–1973). The rectangular spaces were floored with brightly-coloured mosaics, a rectangular pool reflecting the statue. The Villa Hyères demonstrated that a garden could be small-scale, and made on a new space provided by a flat-roofed building, which was decorative, cubist in influence, and embraced abstraction in its choice of statuary.

Though the height of fashion, the garden was not conducive to plant health. Recent restoration showed that the sprinkler system had calcified the mosaic tiles and probably killed off the citrus trees. The heat of the roof and exposure to drying winds made it difficult to keep plants for any length of time, for 'the plants refused to obey the totalitarian symmetry the designer had wished to impose'.[16]

Equally progressive was the garden which Noailles had previously commissioned from the Vera brothers for his hôtel particulier in Paris, on the Place des Etats-Unis. Architect and writer André Vera (1881–1971) and his

engraver brother Paul (1882–1957) created an image to be seen from the
first-floor windows; asymmetrical, triangular, two-dimensional, its designs
anticipating the lightning bolts of the Art Deco decorations on electricity
companies' buildings in America, this was not a garden in which to stroll. Its
colours were provided in thin, sharp wedges by red brick, grey and yellow
stones, and black and white minerals divided by boxwood, with grasses and
perhaps a single, replaceable planting such as blue lobelia according to
season. The unreality was accentuated by mirrors in the surrounding walls
which reflected the broken pattern of the garden. However theatrical this
must have appeared, the Noailles gardens and others such as Pierre-Emile
Legrain's (1889–1929) Tachard garden in La Celle-Saint-Cloud, Paris (1925) and
André Lurçat's (1895–1970) villa garden for Edmond Bomsel in Versailles in the
same year, showed a remarkable adaptation of the parterre to accommodate
modern design and the small garden. The use of minerals as well as (and
sometimes instead of) plants was not new; a variety of brick, coal, gravel,
copper ore, shells, slate, glass and other mineral detritus as infill, or as fanciful
decoration had been used at Henry VIII's privy garden at Hampton Court, by
André Mollet in the seventeenth century at Versailles, and in the nineteenth
century by William Andrews Nesfield at Witley Court, Worcestershire. In France
in the 1920s they seem to be part of a conscious desire to replace plants with
a representation of nature. The 1925 Paris Expo and the gardens of Tachard
and Noailles had a far-reaching influence on the next generation of garden
designers in Europe and the United States of America.

There were other, less avant-garde modern and 'architectural' gardens
in Europe and the United States, which did not abandon the classical past
entirely, but which used strong colours, clear lines, concrete in hard
landscaping and modern art forms in their decoration.[17]

In Spain, such an example was provided by the painter José Maria
Rodriguez-Acosta, who built a house on a hillside in Granada between 1910
and 1920 to accommodate his collection of art, sculpture, and architectural
artefacts. A combination of castle and villa, with pillars, porticoes, arcades,
staircases, screened windows, arched entrances and ironwork balconies in a
grand mix of Moorish and Roman, the house's claim to modernity lies in its use
of concrete and its cubist appearance.[18] Several levels adapt the building to its
steep site on Monte Mauror; on the lower terraces between retaining walls,
formal gardens have been made. Tall green, clipped hedges enclose private
spaces centred by fountains and rectangular pools; pencil cypresses growing
from the first terrace outline the building, keep it cool, and allow some shelter
from outside eyes. About the garden are pieces of statuary including Venus
and Diana; a medieval tomb; sixteenth- and seventeenth-century columns,
some with figures; and a pillared walk with luxuriant climbing roses. A series of

flat roofs have tiled floors, benches to sit on to look out over the city of Granada and to the Sierra Nevada, and places to display sculpture. The roof spaces are too hot for plants, but geraniums in large containers give colour next to the stone of the lower terraces.

The large-scale provision of garden space on the flat roofs on the tops of London department stores were seen as customer attractions as early as 1909; large stores built in the first half of the century readily adopted Art Deco in construction and interior design, but not in their gardens. Even the cautious chairman of the Institute of Landscape Architects, Richard Sudell, had taken to the idea by the 1930s, helping Lady Allen of Hurtwood to design (at the time) the largest roof garden in the world at the top of Selfridges' Oxford Street premises. It replaced a tea garden, American soda fountain, miniature golf links, ragtime orchestra and ice rink. The design incorporated the usual elements of the English country house garden, with only a slight nod to the Art Deco modernism of the store, with herbaceous borders, rose and bulb gardens, a pergola, a rockery, water gardens and a winter garden, and paved vine, acacia and cherry walks.[19] A nursery was opened at the sports ground at Harrow to supply the store.[20]

However, new centres of urbanization in other parts of the world were inspired to create landscaping to match their domestic buildings. In February 1931, an earthquake destroyed the business centre of Napier, on the east coast of North Island, New Zealand. Despite the prevailing economic depression, the town was rebuilt by 1933, and the suburb of Marewa became an example of Art Deco for ordinary people, like the Arts and Crafts garden suburbs built by speculative builders in England at the same time.

The Napier Harbour Board and the city's Borough Council considered the type of construction which would be practicable, and even favoured a more severe form of Art Deco.[21] Inexpensive houses were to be made of concrete, and were designed to withstand another earthquake. Designs were be painted onto the concrete and low relief patterning to prevent injury that might be caused by pieces of falling decorative masonry. Because of the difficulty of raising resources, one-storeyed flat-roofed bungalows were built, decorated with a few chevron, triangle, arrow-head and grouped straight-line motifs. The buildings were painted white, with a spare application of colour – dusky pink, green, and blue outlining the top, window ledge, motif, or base of the house. They have remained intact as a group, escaping enlargement or alteration, although some flat roofs have been replaced by pitched ones.

Marewa's gardens link them firmly to the style of the houses. The hard landscaping of low walls, some stepped, and some banded with colour, were required by a Napier by-law to be no higher than a metre. This was mainly for safety, but low walls also allow the open-front ethos of the garden city, which

influenced the building of the suburb. The same height restrictions were required for fences and hedges. The wall piers form raised cubes at the junctions, some serving as post boxes. Gates, as elsewhere, have largely disappeared, but some were originally made in a half sunburst design.

The shape of the garden was defined by its concrete path, its steps with concrete planters by the front door, and trimmed evergreen shrubs placed symmetrically by entrances or in lines. Standard roses lined the front path in some gardens, lessening the severity; island beds were placed in some lawns. Tall, slim cypresses offset the flat roofs.

References abound in Art Deco design to the prevailing symbol of leisured vacations – the ocean liner – in the fabric of houses in the 1930s. These include

Above and left
Art Deco gardens at Marewa, Napier, New Zealand
These one-storey homes were built following the earthquake of 1931, which destroyed much of Napier. The bungalows of the new settlement of Marewa were made with concrete, painted white, and given spare touches of colour and Art Deco motifs. Marewa gardens are equally austere, their character given by pruned conifers, standard roses and island beds, contained by brick walls.

coloured glass sailing boats inset on bathroom windows and panelled wood interiors evocative of the ship's cabin.

Villa Marina (now Condover House) in north Wales manages to combine ship, house and garden. Built on the edge of the shore overlooking the Irish Sea, it was built as a private house for Harry Scribbans in Llandudno in 1936 by the designer of Odeon cinemas, Harry Weedon. Shapes echo one another in house and garden. The house, made of reinforced concrete with white rendering, has a flat roof. The chimneys look like funnels; the round concrete planters along the garden walls have a similar connotation. Changes of slope from terrace to terrace are accompanied by tubular railings, like those on a ship's deck; the same detailing surrounds projecting balconies. A garden pavilion overlooks the sea, with views similar to those from the ship's bridge. It, too, is made from white concrete, supported on six concrete pillars. A dolphin emerges from a blue sea in the terrazzo flooring in the pavilion; a path leads down to the shore. Planting, appropriate for drying salt winds, includes evergreen shrubs, sempervivums, senecio and griselinia, with hebes in raised beds. Set against all the ocean-liner detailing, the house and its garden evoke a desirable lifestyle open to the rich and famous.[22]

Le Corbusier and the Virgilian landscape

Charles-Edouard Jeanneret (1887–1965), who later adopted the pseudonym Le Corbusier, raised in Switzerland but resident in Paris from 1917, took upon himself the mantle of the architect of the Modern Movement. He was arguably the most influential in his profession during his lifetime, but, as Charles Jencks relates, his work is full of 'interpretative paradoxes'.[23] His plans for houses so dazzled his disciples that they, like Corbusier himself, were unable to see that his provision of gardens to go with the modern house had not been successfully resolved.

Le Corbusier's architecture derived from Cubism and advances in building methods which accompanied the use of new materials, in particular, pre-stressed concrete, and the ability to make large sheets of glass. He had been educated at the Ecole d'Art in La Chaux-de-Fonds, Neuchâtel, in art, architecture and sculpture, and took issue with the architectural curriculum of the Ecole des Beaux-Arts in Paris, which he saw as producing heavy, formal, over-decorated buildings with little attention to the landscape in which they were placed, which were slow to erect, and which (to Corbusier) related to élitism in the form of the titled and powerful classes. Over time he established a new set of rules for architecture which were every bit as dogmatic as those produced by the establishment he was criticizing. The brushstroke guidance he gave for the space around his buildings (as he did not employ landscape architects) was minimal and difficult to interpret. Corbusier became interested in Cubism with its concerns for sculptural shapes and geometry. Free of revivalist and classical associations, and less about subject matter than the way of presenting it, Cubism lent itself to Corbusier as a manner in which he could construct buildings. This invited the viewer to relate to the house from all angles.

Corbusier had absorbed the techniques of making reinforced concrete buildings from Auguste Perret (1874–1954), for whom he worked in Paris. Perret's office in the Rue Franklin was a nine-storey apartment building with pilotis (pillars), much glass in its external walls, and internal divisions which were made entirely from glass. There was a roof garden with evergreen poplars planted in boxes.[24]

Another significant influence was artist, designer and architect Peter Behrens (1868–1940), who designed the glass and steel Turbine Factory for the electrical company AEG in Berlin in 1908–9. Corbusier left Perret's office to study advanced arts and crafts in Berlin as a Behrens apprentice. Here he met Ludwig Mies van der Rohe (1886–1969) and Walter Gropius (1883–1969). They used a new utilitarian architectural language which concerned itself with geometry in cubes, spheres, cylinders and cones; they borrowed from engineering where efficiency of form was important. Thus the term functionalism entered the vocabulary of architecture; 'the house is a machine for living in' Corbusier repeated throughout *Vers une Architecture* (1923, published in English as *Towards a New Architecture*, 1927).[25]

The term 'functional' applied not only to the capability of the materials used to construct a building. Arriving at the same time as the movement for the healthy lifestyle, functionalism related to a new way of constructing houses. Nor did it end at the garden door, as house and garden were perceived by Corbusier to be mirror opposites of each other: 'the *exterior* is always an *interior*' he declared.[26] In Paris Corbusier joined forces with the cubist painter Amédée Ozenfant (1886–1966). Both were interested in a theoretical form of their art which they called Purism, rejecting the degeneration of Cubism into decorative art. They painted, produced books and started a journal called *L'Esprit Nouveau* .

Corbusier's *Vers une Architecture* was immensely influential. Throughout the 1920s he produced plans for buildings incorporating five rules which he set down in 1927. These amounted to the use of a simple load-bearing framework of slim concrete-encased metal pillars to support pre-stressed concrete floors, leaving the outside walls free to accept ribbon windows extending all round the building allowing uniform daylight to the interior. Since the outer walls carried no weight, pilotis could raise the base of the building, accentuating the concept of lightness and space. Living accommodation would then be on the first floor, and the inside spaces could

Above, right
**Le Corbusier, Villa
Savoye, Paris**
Le Corbusier's Villa for
the Savoye family at Poissy,
built from 1928, a 'box in
the air with light', was
designed to be seen from
all angles, as were all cubist
constructions. The Villa's
relationship with its garden
was problematic: Corbusier
described this as a Virgilian
landscape which should
not be disturbed by
his building.

be open-plan. The flat top made by the upper level would regain space lost
in the traditional pitched-roof building, and this could be used for healthy
sunbathing and a roof garden.

However, Le Corbusier had no rules to offer for the landscape around his
houses, other than it should be treated as natural, undisturbed, and 'Virgilian'.
Corbusier considered that a house should be placed in grass and trees, with no
design, which evoked the pastoral landscape of the Roman poet. The restored
Villa Savoye near Paris offers an impressive example of the Corbusian view of
the cubist house in the natural landscape. Corbusier called it 'a box in the air'[27]
created from 'an architectural play of solids and voids'. The theatrical setting of
white villa hovering against its green backdrop has become something of an
architectural landmark. It is also fertile ground in which to question
Corbusier's relationship with house and nature.

The Villa was made for a rich insurance company director, Pierre Savoye,
who gave him the commission in 1928 for a country weekend house to be
built on a parkland of trees and meadows. The living rooms reflect the
'exterior–interior' quality which Corbusier described. The first floor opens
onto a terrace with planters which are visible from the full-length windows
in the living-room. Corbusier described this as the roof garden.[28] The outer
windows look towards grass fringed with trees; long, rectangular window
openings on the terrace frame the view. The second level (as the first) can
be reached by means of ramps, which lead to the solarium – a round-ended
space for sunbathing with another of Corbusier's framed views in the outer
wall. Filled planters break up the whiteness of the roof space.

The ground floor has accommodation for domestic staff and a garage,
hidden behind green-painted exterior walls. The Villa is frequently described

as having been based on the turning circle of the automobile, and no doubt the client here dictated the conveniences of modern living which prevented Corbusier from running his pristine meadow under the house. Repeating the 'exterior–interior' theme is a very simple plan for the garden, which used the pattern of paths and grass to repeat the plan of the ground floor in reverse, flanked by two straight lines of roses which mark the approach to the house.

Villa Savoye, view across the first floor
Light floods in from the picture-frame ribbon windows, the outside greenery seemingly part of the interior. The roof garden, outside the lounge, has concrete planters with a lilac and some flowers.

Villa Savoye, view to the solarium
Looking up from the first floor, the references to a ship become evident. The curve of the solarium becomes the funnel, the ramps and railings leading to each floor (just visible in the reflections in the lounge windows) suggest movement between decks. Such references were common in modernist houses, as travel became part of the lifestyle of the rich at that time.

Le Corbusier's attitude to the natural background emerged most clearly from his frequently quoted comment that his houses would rise 'above the long grass of a meadow where cattle will continue to graze', where 'dwellers in these houses, drawn hence through love of the life of the countryside, will be able to see it maintained intact from their hanging gardens or from their ample windows. Their domestic lives will be set within a Virgilian dream'.[29] Corbusier's intention was to cherish the beautiful view and the beautiful grass, and leave the forest untouched. 'The house will be placed on grass, like an object, disturbing nothing', he claimed.[30]

Recent commentators have questioned his ambiguous definitions of 'nature' and whether or not man controlled it; how 'nature' could remain 'undisturbed' by the placing of a man-made object within it; and the minimal amounts of vegetation on the roof garden.[31]

However, the placing of the Villa Savoye in its surroundings gives interior visions of restful greenery flooding through continuous window space, justifying the perception of natural surroundings. From outside, the white villa against the green backdrop, the metaphor for the machine for living in, asserts its personality from all sides. The painted green base to the villa sufficiently anchors it to the earth; the simple garden, shaped like the floor plan, creates the minimum disturbance. The minimal vegetation on the roof gardens may reflect a token relationship with the greenery outside and the practical problems of maintenance in sun and wind. More justified would be criticism of the lack of 'efficiency' and 'functional' skills which the architect showed in constructing a building which was leaking along the ramp by 1931, in need of restoration two years after building began, and was uncomfortable enough for its inhabitants to desert it soon afterwards.

For the garden historian there remains an 'interpretative paradox' which is difficult to solve. The 1925 Paris Exposition successfully demonstrated, as in Guevrekian's *Jardin d'eau et de lumière*, how cubist ideas could be used in gardens. But the Purists disliked the Expo's 'debased' form of Cubism. Instead, Corbusier chose the pristine landscape as one which did not vie for attention with his villa as solo performer.

Corbusier's roof gardens were some of his most controversial features. In 1930, Comte Charles de Bestegui asked Corbusier and his cousin Pierre Jeanneret to design him a rooftop area for his apartment in the Champs Elysées in which to entertain his guests. There were two stepped levels as terraces overlooking the street. Planters containing hedges formed a secluded sitting area. This was reached by steps from a partially paved, partially grass-carpeted level below. The hedges obscured the view until, at the touch of an electric switch, they could be moved aside. Bestegui had furnished his apartment in rococo style, and continued this theme on the roof with furniture of the same period on his grass carpets. The whole gave a bizarre tone, especially as the Arc de Triomphe appeared partially, like the rising sun, above the parapet.

The English landscape architect Russell Page (1906–85) visited Corbusier in his roof-top apartment in Paris, and inspected the garden 'where Le Corbusier had been content to spread earth and, as he said, leave the birds and the wind to do the rest. So here were tufts of grass and weeds, dandelions and willow-herb and even young laburnum trees'.[32] Though it is unlikely that Page, a popular garden designer for the rich, with a conservative approach to his work, would have approved of any modern design, his description illustrates Corbusier's difficulties with gardens.

Corbusier has attracted sharp criticism for his promotion of high tower blocks as his answer to the garden city solution for the overcrowding of cities. He had experimented in the early 1920s with the concept of stacking mass-produced maisonettes with 'hanging gardens', which were terraces with plants, covered by a roof formed by the maisonette above and open at one end, and which were more like interior or atrium gardens. Two-storey blocks with additional small front gardens and central courtyards filled with trees were planned for Bordeaux- Pessac.[33]

A visit to the USA in 1935 introduced him to the skyscraper. Following the Second World War Corbusier built his seventeen-storey poured concrete apartment block, the Unité d'Habitation, at Marseilles between 1946 and 1952. There were gardens, play-areas, sports facilities and other communal facilities on the roof, and a proposed two-storey high shopping zone taking up the length of the building. Such tower blocks, grouped with space between, Corbusier defined as garden cities in the sky, claiming they released ground-level space, removed people from traffic, and formed high-rise communities. The reality – and countless bleak imitations – failed the inhabitants they were designed to serve, and their ideal gardens, above and below, never developed.

The legacy of Corbusier's uneasy – and unresolved – relationship with nature, and therefore its place in the 'garden' which surrounded the house, was perpetuated by his followers, and remained unresolved in Europe at the outbreak of the Second World War.

Ludwig Mies van der Rohe (1886–1969)

Ludwig Mies van der Rohe and Frank Lloyd Wright were architect-contemporaries of Corbusier whose interpretations of the relationship of buildings with nature were less intrusive.

Mies van der Rohe was born in Aachen, Germany, the son of a master mason. Trained in trade schools and then by apprenticeship to architects, he valued the quality of the materials with which he worked. Two of his buildings

The Barcelona Pavilion
Mies van der Rohe designed this pavilion as the German entry to the 1929 International Exhibition, and the elegance of the minimal thin planes making divisions within the rectangle which enclosed the living space had a lasting effect on architects and landscape makers alike. The view from the interior towards green marble walls, perhaps echoing the colour of the trees outside, looks to a figure in an interior pool.

remain as icons of lightness, minimalism, and exemplars of the best use of modern new (and old) materials – the Barcelona Pavilion and the Villa Tugendhat.

The Pavilion was made for the 1929 International Exhibition in Barcelona, dismantled at the end of the event, and re-erected in the mid-1980s. It is a single-storey rectangle divided by glass and marble walls, the flat roof supported by slim chromium-plated steel pillars, mounted on a travertine terrace beside which was a pool lined with black glass. Its asymmetry and overlapping planes had a lasting effect on the garden designs of the American landscape architect Garrett Eckbo (this theme is pursued in Chapter Five).

The Tugendhat house made in 1930 at Brno, Czechoslovakia, returns to the modernist ideal of the flow of landscape outside into the living space. Closely resembling the Barcelona Pavilion in construction, harmony with the landscape was achieved by the surrounding floor-to-ceiling glass wall, which brought trees and grass, shadows and reflections into the living space. Outside, the glass mirrored the passing clouds.

Modernism was outlawed by the Nazis, and Mies's influence in Europe disappeared as he closed the Bauhaus and emigrated to the United States a little later, where he continued to design houses which gave equal importance to their surrounding landscapes.

Frank Lloyd Wright (1867–1959)

The American architect Frank Lloyd Wright, on the cusp of Arts and Crafts and Modernism, had an organic approach to house and landscape, which he saw as indivisible. Influenced by the long, horizontal lines of the prairie landscapes in which his early houses were built, the Martin house at Buffalo, New York State (1902–3), and the Robie House, Chicago, Illinois (1908–10) show the low roofs, rectangular shapes and long groups of windows which characterize his 'Prairie' style.

Following the World Columbian Exposition in Chicago in 1893, with its adoption of the neoclassical or Beaux-Arts style of building, Frank Lloyd Wright and architects who were unhappy with what they saw as this natural intrusion into the landscape (including Hugh M. G. Garden, Dwight H. Perkins, George Elmslie, Walter Burley Griffin, Robert Spencer, William Purcell, George W. Maher, Robert E. Schmidt, and John S. Van Burgen) became a more recognizable Prairie school of architects.

Wright's love of his prairie surroundings emerged in the plant forms he used in decorating the interiors of his houses, whether in the ash leaves in the skylight of his children's playroom or the oak leaves of the back-lit ceiling grille of his dining room in Oak Park (1889). These echoed the wild plants he brought into the house, and reminded the family of sunlight slanting through the forest. Highly stylized plant forms filled windows, skylights and glass doors in his studio (1898), the Unity Temple (1905–9), the Robie House and elsewhere at Oak Park, Chicago, and further afield in the USA.

Wright worked with Jens Jensen on a number of commissions, including the Avery Coonley House at Riverside, Illinois (1908–17), and the Roberts House in Marquette, Michigan. Jensen's horizontal stonework in his park waterfalls and swimming pools was matched by Wright's horizontal lines of brickwork in his houses, where he painted out the vertical mortar joints to accentuate the long planes of the walls. All these features were in sympathy with the vernacular shapes of the prairie.

Writing of his country estate at Taliesin at Spring Green in Wisconsin (1912–59), where he moved in 1909, Wright said in his autobiography that 'no house should ever be on any hill or on anything. It should be *of* the hill. Belonging to it. Hill and house should live together each the happier for the other'. Here Wright planned gardens watered by cisterns, plantations, fruit trees, and fields of crops as 'a garden and farm behind a workshop and a home'.[34] Falling Water, the Kaufmann House, made at Bear Run, Pennsylvania, in 1936, built on a rocky ledge above a waterfall as a series of interlocking horizontal planes, has a stunning simplicity. It needs no garden, for garden, landscape and house are one.

Taliesin West was built as Wright's office and became an architectural school at Scottsdale, Arizona, in 1938. Described as a low complex of 'buildings, courtyards, and gardens aligned, notched, and knit into this landscape' it had gardens on slopes or elevated above the desert.

A pergola roofed a cut in the slope; a prow garden, built in 1942, had a pool and a massing of cactus, yuccas and prickly pear.[35] Wright achieved the unity of house and landscape which Le Corbusier neither achieved nor wanted.

Dartington Hall, William Lescaze and Beatrix Farrand

The difficult relationship between modern architect and conservative garden maker arose on the Dartington Estate in Devon, with its partly fourteenth-century Hall surrounded by agricultural land on the edge of Dartmoor. It was purchased by Leonard (1893–1974) and Dorothy (1887–1968) Elmhirst in 1925 to regenerate rural life which continued to suffer between the wars. Leonard Elmhirst sought rehabilitation of the agriculture and crafts of the countryside, involving everyone employed in the fullest sense. Elmhirst, a Yorkshireman from a landowning family, had graduated from a course in agriculture at Cornell University in the USA and there had met his wife, Dorothy Whitney Straight, the daughter of a rich businessman and the widow of an American diplomat. Sharing her husband's ideals, she contributed financially to their joint venture.

They were able to rescue the Hall from its ruins and the farming estate from dilapidation, and the rehabilitation process helped to strengthen the local community. In this process, education became a key element. A progressive school was opened. As with all of their enterprises, education was a broad and all-embracing concept, involving adults and young people working together, with encouragement for the influence of contemporary culture. The Elmhirsts had contacts in Europe and the United States with talented artists, musicians, architects and craftsmen. In this they were helped by the situation in Germany, where the Bauhaus was threatened by the influence of the Nazis. The Elmhirsts were in sympathy with the Bauhaus's promotion of the blending of skills of artists and craftsmen, and when it finally closed in 1933 many Bauhaus students came to Dartington. Walter Gropius was invited to join the staff; he never did, but visited several times between 1934 and 1935 before emigrating to the USA. He left Leonard Elmhirst a plan for an amphitheatre, a strongly sculptural, modern design to seat 604 people, to be modelled in grass at the end of the remaining tiltyard below the Hall. The plan was never executed.

Modernism appeared at Dartington in the buildings for the school, placed discreetly away from the Hall and its courtyard core. The rectangular office block and boarding houses supported by pilotis, and the cubes and

Walter Gropius design for an amphitheatre at Dartington, Devon, England
Walter Gropius designed this sculptural, grass amphitheatre for Dartington's tiltyard in the late 1930s, before leaving Europe for a post at Harvard's Graduate Design School. The design was never implemented.

rectangles of the staff houses provoked local criticism. The new headmaster for Dartington School, the American William Burnely Curry (1900–60), knew the Swiss/American architect William Edmond Lescaze (1896–1969), and persuaded the Elmhirsts to employ him to design his new house.

Lescaze, influenced by De Stijl, Le Corbusier and the Bauhaus ideals, was one of the earliest exponents of the International Style in the United States.[36] Lescaze was also to make plans for a modern holiday resort on land owned by the Dartington estate at Churston Ferrers near Brixham, Devon; but because of the war, this was never completed.[37]

Somewhat grudging approval for William Curry's new house – 'the residence that symbolizes the extreme contemporary side of the Dartington programme', the dazzling white concrete building with its Crittalls' metal window frames – came from Christopher Hussey.[38] Set amongst trees and the surrounding farmland, High Cross House is two storeys high with a third storey opening on to the flat roof; Curry was a naturist and liked to sunbathe in privacy. The second floor bedrooms had terrace balconies. The servants' block, with garage underneath, was painted sky blue, like some of the interior walls of the Villa Savoye (dispelling the belief that all modern houses were white). The garden was entered via a terrace through a sliding glass door from the living room. The outside made its presence felt in all the rooms as the large expanses of glass admitted garden, trees, and the countryside beyond.

Problems developed over the gardens. There had been no overall landscape plan for Dartington; its history points to traditionalist design with the Elmhirsts' first appointment of the *Country Life* writer and garden designer

Above, left

William Lescaze, High Cross House, Dartington, Devon, England

A house designed in the International Style for the headmaster of Dartington School in the grounds of the fourteenth-century Dartington Hall in the early 1930s evoked criticism from conservatives. The garden gave rise to equally heated argument: the conservative garden designer Beatrix Farrand clashed swords with the modernist architect Lescaze.

H. Avray Tipping (1855–1933) as gardener in 1928. In 1933 Beatrix Farrand was appointed as gardens adviser. Her work on the medieval courtyard at Dartington seemed entirely appropriate; she had worked on the campuses of Yale, Chicago, Princeton and Oberlin Universities, producing restrained, traditional designs. Farrand was a friend of Dorothy's, having made a garden on Long Island for Dorothy and her first husband. Dartington was Farrand's sole commission outside America; she visited only four times. The Dartington gardeners were sent to America to learn from Farrand; the rest was done by letter. Much of what she did around the Hall concerned hard landscaping, with walls to accommodate falling ground levels, giving shape by making paths and planting flowering trees in the woodlands, and opening up the Sunny Border of herbaceous plants by the bowling green.[39] The trouble began when she was appointed landscape adviser to the Churston estate, and there were clashes over the house for William Curry.

A plan and drawings attributed to Farrand for the modernist Churston estate, with its hotel, club, swimming pool and development of flat-roofed terrace and detached houses, show herbaceous borders alongside brick walls and steps, backed by clipped, tall hedges, with a rockery hiding the change in grade between the lawn and house base, and a sunken rose garden – all the accoutrements of the traditional 1930s garden, which took no account of concrete and Cubism.[40]

There was friction between Farrand and Lescaze, who met in their offices in New York. Lescaze wrote to Leonard Elmhirst in February 1933 saying he felt he could do everything himself with the help of the Dartington Nursery department, thus saving the fee of the landscape architect and ensuring that 'house, trees, shrubs and site will go together'. But Elmhirst wrote back to say that he had accepted Farrand's plans, essentially because she knew how plants reacted on English sea-fronts, and would leave in place what was already growing around the houses, thus effectively accepting a compromise solution.[41]

Lescaze had planned a garden for William Curry's house in 1932 which left intact large trees on the boundaries, with grass up to a paved terrace, and was partly enclosed on the south and east by a hedge. On the eastern side, the hedge formed a rectangular room, open to a path on its western side, with four long narrow beds filling the middle space.[42] This gave lawn space for the children to play on, beds for cultivation, and a terrace on which to sit. But as soon as Farrand had visited Dartington, Lescaze's plans were eclipsed by Farrand's, with their 'cottage garden flowers… such as lilacs, forsythia, delphiniums and hollyhocks'.[43]

The compromise garden, shown in its very early stages in *Country Life* in 1933, displays rectangular beds on both sides of the house edged with the bristles of young hedges, with paved paths and the token deckchair on the terrace in front of the grass; this was commended to the public in 1936 as a model of low maintenance and practicality[44] and one suspects that the modernist Curry did not keep the delphiniums and hollyhocks for long.

Christopher Tunnard (1910–79)

The concept of the 'functional' landscape was first promoted by Christopher Tunnard as a new approach to the making of modern gardens. A Canadian who had been brought up and educated in Victoria, British Columbia, before moving to Britain, he trained for a diploma in horticulture at the Royal Horticultural Society at Wisley, then for a qualification in building construction at Westminster Technical Institute. Between 1932 and 1935 he worked for the landscape designer Percy Cane (1881–1976), whose clients were mainly the owners of small country houses, before setting off on his own.

Tunnard became increasingly irritated by the inability of garden-makers to relate their work to the modern house and its connection with modern lifestyles. In a review of the 1936 Chelsea Flower Show, Tunnard refers to the institution as 'The Royal Academy of Garden Architecture [which] appears to be fast approaching the moribund state of its prototype, so little can be found of evolution, originality or evidence of a well-balanced sense of values among the exhibits', and asks, 'What relation do these horticultural creations of Chelsea bear to everyday practical gardening?'[45] He wrote a series of articles for the *Architectural Review*, which were published in 1938 as *Gardens in the Modern Landscape*, and an essay in the January 1942 edition of *Landscape Architecture* (by which time he had emigrated to the United States). In these, Tunnard took on the gardening world.

Garden books, he argued (he wrote for the conservative *Landscape and Garden*, the journal of the Institute of Landscape Architects), were full of vistas, axes, oval lawns and picture-making, producing 'second-hand designs' full of remakes of the traditional formal garden. Alternatively they came up with the informal or naturalistic, the 'dying breath of the romantic age'.[46] He had in mind the inability of the English garden-maker to emerge from his nineteenth-century massed herbaceous border, his colourful bedding, and his revivalist myth of Merry England. Tunnard condemned contemporary garden-making in England as suffering from the burden of past history and an excess of horticulture. There was, in America and England, an 'almost complete lack of [landscape] designers skilled in the technique of planning for modern architecture, or even aware of the implications of this new movement',[47] so architects did not take on landscape designers who they reckoned would be hostile to their views.

The modern house, said Tunnard, was planned for multiple uses and easy expansion, which should be reflected in the garden. Modern houses had been criticized for their hard outlines and lack of decoration by those who were not aware of the satisfaction of clean lines, or alive to the beauty of the new materials. Glass could be used for walls, pools, and fountains, reinforced concrete for ramps and bridges, weatherproof plywood for shelters – even asbestos had been used for screening and plant containers on a roof garden.[48] In language which evoked the simplicity of the De Stijl movement, and quoting Corbusier's 'the styles are a lie',[49] he claimed that 'the right style for the twentieth century is no style at all, but a new conception of planning the human environment'.[50]

Three guiding principles emerged from his analysis of the concept of the modern garden. The first was that it should be functional, reflecting the needs for rest and recreation, with perhaps some provision for the growing of food; though this was questionable considering modern mass production. A garden should have an aesthetic appeal, that is, there was to be room for flower cultivation, though the aesthetic had to be non-ornamental and free from sentimentalism and romantic nature-worship.[51] Tunnard's second principle was empathy, which he related to the placing of the garden in the landscape. There should be freedom from the 'tyranny' of symmetry, with axes and vistas leading into the landscape. Instead the garden-maker should hope to achieve an 'occult balance', between the designed landscape and nature around it – a quality which he admired in Japanese gardens. Finally, he urged the use of art in the garden, especially non-representational sculpture, where the honesty of the modern materials would not be obscured by design.[52] Work by Alexander Calder and Willy Soukoup appears in his illustrations. Perhaps the principle of function is the most interesting in view of what was to come in the post-modern period, as for the first time in England, people were seen as a participating part of the garden, rather than mere spectators.

Tunnard urged designers to make models of their proposed gardens, so that they could see how uses could be linked from space to space. In a television broadcast in 1938, he showed a model of a suburban garden with fruit trees underplanted by spring bulbs in rough grass, mown paths, and a flower garden near the house designed with simplicity 'in order to throw into relief the pattern and texture of the plant arrangements'.[53] With an eye on exotics, he reflected on plants 'out of context' with their surroundings. Shrubs and flowers should be selected for their separate values, not massed for pictorial effect or used as collections. The effects of light in a garden should not be submerged in the desire for startling colour combinations.[54]

Tunnard's philosophy on the relationship of the house to the wider landscape came from a desire to be part of it, and not to shut it out. Nature

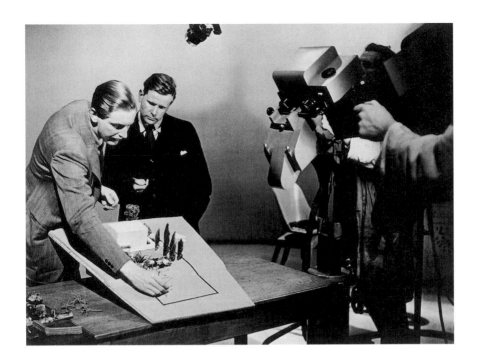

should be controlled, but not imposed upon with wasteful designs.
In agricultural landscapes 'that which is productive, balanced, and orderly',
should be left alone. Taking his lead from Corbusier, Tunnard recommended
abandoning the formal drive with its avenue of trees for a winding route
through the meadows.[55] After his return to North America in 1939, he
witnessed the search for wild nature in a landscape damaged by
industrialization and made too accessible by the railroad. With his ideas
mulling around the openness of the English landscape movement, and at the
same time looking for an acceptance of the new prospects of urbanism,
Tunnard was searching for an amalgam of the two. Why screen out silos and
smokestacks and not 'accept them for what they are'? Why should New York's
skyscraper landscape 'be considered ugly' because 'it is all man-made'?[56]

Tunnard's best-documented house and garden is at St Ann's Hill (now St
Ann's Court) at Chertsey in Surrey, where he lived with Gerald Schlesinger. The
architect was an Australian, Raymond McGrath; the house was built between
1935 and 1936 on the crest of a rise in the triangle formed by three cedar
trees, replacing the demolished mansion at the heart of an eighteenth-
century estate. The house used pre-stressed concrete with a central cylinder
containing the staircase and storage cupboards on each floor, with the rooms
forming semi-circles about it. Roof terraces adjoining bedrooms sat above a
south-facing colonnaded ground floor living room, its pink front relieved by a
wisteria. The bedroom and living room levels appeared as circular cut-outs
springing from the middle of an opening section in the centre of the circular
building. From the western end extended a garden wing – an open paved

**Christopher Tunnard
with J. M. Richards
demonstrating a model
of a garden for television
transmission at the
BBC, 1938**
Tunnard demonstrated
how different functions
may be placed within a
garden, and how one space
should be linked with
another. A model helped to
bring the design stage to
life, and many modern
young garden makers
moved away from
two-dimensional
representations on
drawing boards.

Above

St Ann's Hill – a recent view of the garden wing
The sheltered garden wing has retained the concrete terrace and pools from 1935–36, with its winter garden and glass doors accentuating the flow of space from the garden to the house.

Above right

St Ann's Hill – the swimming pool from the balcony
Raymond McGrath's house was built to capture the sun, and the balcony at the top of the house with its ribbon of picture-frame windows looks down on a pool which was curved round a clump of rhododendrons, presumably for the foliage and the reflections.

terrace with Corbusian framed views, flower beds and sculpture, linking via a winter garden to the house.

From the first, the relationship of the house and garden to the wider landscape posed all manner of historical tensions, which remain unresolved. Looking northwards to the back of the house, the garden wing seems so close to the eighteenth-century stable block that it appears to be elbowing it out of the way, and one wonders whether it was built in the expectation that the block was to be demolished. There are the remains of a temple which seem disconnected from both house and landscape. Down a slope from the back of the house, and not visible from the house, seventeenth-century geometrical beds line a central grass path, remaining in cultivation until recently, with no change from their original design.[57] Where was the pioneering zeal of the reformer who wanted to sweep away the baggage of the past?

Looking south and east, however, the whole becomes more coherent. The garden wing forms a sheltered sun-trap, its pool, concrete planters and simple arrangement of flowers and dwarf junipers visible from the house, reflecting the inside-outside connection urged by Corbusier. Within sight of the house, set asymmetrically and a little below it, a bathing pool curves around a bank of rhododendrons and reflects the building; widely-set shallow steps link the pool to the fall of slope and then to the informality beyond. Looking south from the house during the late 1930s, the landscape of the middle distance was being shaped into tree-clump and tree-belt, with grassland between; the break of slope and the trees served to hide the discordant features created by the formal garden and the kitchen garden to the west.[58]

Here was the functional garden with pool, sunbathing area, terrace for entertaining, flower garden, vegetable and cut-flower areas. One area flowed into the next. The architectural design linking house to garden was asymmetrical, taking the historic features of terrace, pool, and steps and shaping them to match the modern house. The historic landscape accepted its twentieth-century mansion. Looking southwards, Tunnard achieved his empathetic garden.

Looking north, to the house, the garden becomes discordant and difficult to comprehend as the well drawn plan (which contradicted Tunnard's preference for a model)[59] is distorted by the break of slope and the vastness of the lawn. Had Tunnard stayed beyond three years, these difficulties might have been resolved.

At Bentley Wood, Halland, in Sussex, Tunnard was able to develop his landscaping concepts further for Russian émigré Serge Chermayeff (1900–96). Chermayeff, a designer who was educated in England from the age of ten, bought land at Bentley Farm to build a house for his family. In 1936 his planned timber house was rejected by the local authority, Uckfield Rural District Council, on the grounds that its design and elevation contrasted with that of the locality and would prejudice its amenity value. At a public enquiry in 1937, Chermayeff won his case.

The rectangular two-storey house was made in modular timber units.[60] Its frame of Australian jarrah provided a grid-pattern of large squares within which were placed ceiling-height windows on the ground floor, and balconies before large windows above. The cladding was western red cedar, which weathered to grey. The house was set on a low terrace, which extended beside

Bentley Wood, Halland, Sussex, England
Although Serge Chermayeff employed Tunnard to design the garden for his house at Halland (begun 1937), he had already done much of the garden landscaping himself. Tunnard was responsible for the terrace borders and probably augmented Chermayeff's natural planting in the thinned woodland beyond.

the house to give a sheltered area bounded on two sides by a tall brick wall with its flower border. On the garden end, the terrace opened to the horizontal view of the South Downs, seen through a rectangular timber frame. The frame has been likened to the work of Paul Nash whom Tunnard also admired.[61] This large, but unintrusive unit was glazed at the bottom and left open above. On the house side of the frame, a paved terrace and lily-pool gave on to a lawn divided by a paved path; in the junction of the wall and the frame stood a tall tree; on the other side of the path was Henry Moore's *Recumbent Figure*.

Chermayeff felt himself in tune with landscape gardening, seeing it as a part of architecture in its widest sense,[62] thus agreeing with the philosophy expressed by Tunnard, who was called in before the house was built. However, Chermayeff had already made a start on thinning the trees and underplanting them with daffodils, and he had planned the route of the drive.[63] Scrub was cleared, and oaks and birches left intact as a light woodland cover, with an irregular lawn in the middle. Water from the house supply and ditches drained into a woodland dell which was planted with grasses, astilbe, primula and iris. The woodland's natural flora of bluebells, primroses and foxgloves graded into planted drifts of scilla and crocus. All of this, said Tunnard, gave a frame, which 'needed the extra stability that new planting alone could bring'.[64]

Chermayeff decided on an informal approach, dubbed 'atmospheric' by Tunnard, as a foil to the formally shaped building. A chain of rounded evergreens was planted along the edge of the woodland, interspersed with varied groups of red, purple and grey flowering and fruiting shrubs. A more traditional planting plan was adopted for the terrace, where the wall allowed camellia, choisya, and *Azara microphylla* to survive with summer bedding of red and white nicotiana at their feet. But even more surprising for Tunnard was his despised Victorian 'mingled flower bed' along the end of the screen wall and terrace border in front of the living room. Here penstemon, salvia, helianthemum, dianthus, phlox and cistus were planted amongst ceratostigma, cytisus, and yucca, with sedum and equisetum in cracks in the paving, and with wisteria forming a frame; Alan Powers argues that the colours matched the materials.

Here again was Tunnard's functional garden, with sunbathing and entertaining areas, kitchen garden and orchard screened by gorse, plans for tennis courts and a pavilion, and attempts at a low-maintenance design for modern living overall. Sculpture answered the need for art in the garden, but also, the creation of space by the thinning of trees became as important as the trees themselves.[65] Empathy, the third principle, Tunnard saw achieved at Bentley Wood in 'the recognition and use of natural features on the site in any building scheme which make architecture a part of the countryside'.[66] But like St Ann's Hill, Bentley Wood was occupied for only a short time by its architect.

In 1939 Chermayeff was declared bankrupt, and the house was sold in 1940 to Dorothy Elmhirst's son, Whitney Straight. Chermayeff was eventually made Director of the Department of Design at Brooklyn College, New York, after his emigration to the United States in 1940.

Christopher Tunnard had little time to mature his views before the war overtook him. He planned other gardens at Cobham, Surrey, and Galby, Leicestershire which are known mainly as drawings by Gordon Cullen in Tunnard's book. Nevertheless his angry batterings at the complacency of English design aroused response, if not imitation. Finding himself a lone voice in his endeavours to evolve a garden which matched the modern house and to encourage other landscape designers to do the same, he gladly accepted an invitation from Gropius to lecture at the Harvard Graduate School of Design, which was just emerging from the constraints of the Beaux-Arts tradition. Two years after conscription in 1943, he became assistant professor of city planning at Yale University, moving away from garden design. In England he had become interested in social housing in common with many left-leaning architects of the 1930s, and was connected with the Modern Architectural Research (MARS) Group. He wrote about communal gardens for housing schemes, and his admiration for the community gardens of Römerstadt, near Frankfurt in Germany[67] (discussed in the next chapter) and approved of the Dutch Bos Park. Later, in America, he began to question the teaching of his earlier idol, Corbusier. He mocked young architects for 'swallowing [the] dogma' of the 'no-style' debate in his examination of urban planning in the *City of Man* (1953), and Corbusier's assertion that beauty emerges from form and function.[68]

Tunnard was a brave promoter of the modern garden, attempting to engage both mind and eye in a *Gesamtkunstwerk* for the modern lifestyle. His ideas fell on deaf ears in very conservative England and on the equally conservative Anglophile-American east side of the USA, though he must have influenced the avant-garde at Harvard – Dan Kiley, Garrett Eckbo, and James Rose – and the students whom he taught, including Lawrence Halprin. In many ways he had arrived too soon. The essence of his approach – that the style for the twentieth century was no style at all – now sounds very post-modern. The 'no style', abstract concept was too difficult to communicate, and it is debatable whether Tunnard had fully explored its implications. But his work before the war established people as participators, not observers, in gardens, encouraged the use of sculpture, and searched for a simple, beautiful, framework shaped by use or 'function'. In the words of one contemporary writer, Tunnard 'detonated the accepted canons of the arts and crafts garden and the residual gardenesque in England, and the blast reverberated across the Atlantic'.[69]

Garden Spaces for the People: the Garden City

Although gardens have been portrayed up to this point as the provinces of the upper and middle classes, where they walked, talked, directed their gardeners to shape and plant, admired scenes, and entertained their guests, there was another group – the labouring class – for whom gardens and allotments were more a way of supplementing income through growing food. During the nineteenth century, green spaces were vanishing as towns expanded in Europe and America. But the problems of the town and countryside were related, prompting initiatives for better housing, garden ground, and parks for the people.

In Britain Ebenezer Howard (1850–1928) believed that the answer lay in an attempt to provide the best qualities of town and country in the Garden City, an ideal which embraced all classes and occupations, but which evolved into the middle-class garden suburb and village. The Garden City was copied elsewhere, with national variations.

One factor common to large towns in Europe and America in the nineteenth century was the expansion of populations. In America, this was the result of large-scale emigration from Europe, by people seeking a better life, or to escape persecution. In Europe, agriculture offered a poor return in prices, rent and land values, as virgin territories were opened up for farming in the Americas, Australia, and New Zealand. Over time, agricultural labourers whose housing was poor and wages even poorer, were attracted to large towns in the false hope that there would be better paid employment in towns. The problems were worst in London, for this had the largest population in Europe at the end of the nineteenth century, though overcrowding was equally a feature in Paris, Berlin, New York, and Chicago.

Workers were housed in tall tenement blocks or houses often built round unpaved courts where light and air seemed never to penetrate, often back to back, entered by tunnels, and without sanitation. Some lived in cellars above sewers. Life expectancy was low; cholera and typhoid rife. The problem lay in the density of occupation as much as in total numbers. Henry Mayhew's study of poverty in overcrowded London in 1861 gives many glimpses of attempts by the poor to brighten their lives with small backyard gardens, or even plants in pots. But in 'Lisson-grove, Islington, Hoxton, Hackney or Stepney – where the inhabitants formerly cultivated flowers in their little gardens [cottages] are now let out in single apartments, and the gardens – or yards, as

William Stephen Coleman (1829–1904), *A Cottage Garden in Summer*
Coleman's watercolour of a cottage garden, with its vegetable patch occupying the centre ground, beehives behind, and with flowers around the fence, reminds the viewer that it was a necessity for the labouring classes of the nineteenth and early twentieth centuries to grow their own food.

Gustave Doré,
Over London – By Rail,
1872, engraving

Doré vividly depicts the
overcrowding of labourers'
housing, created by people
flocking into London in
search of work; he shows
the loss of space caused by
new industry and railways.
These terrace houses were
sub-let to so many tenants
that the back yard quickly
became an extra room –
not a garden.

they mostly are now, were [sic] used merely to hang clothes in.'[1] Gustav Doré's
1872 engraving *Over London – By Rail* presents the same picture of cramped
backyards full of washing and the spill of people from over-occupied terraced
housing, with no room for greenery.[2]

In the countryside, housing suffered most from the late 1870s onwards,
when landowners claimed they could not build new cottages or mend old
ones because of the fall in agricultural returns; this, together with low wages,
accentuated the stream of labourers towards the town.

Little advance in the improvement of housing could be made without
influencing public opinion, and much middle-class opinion remained in the
grips of the picturesque and images of rural arcadia, well into the beginning of
the twentieth century. The reporter from the *Illustrated London News*, visiting

LABOURER'S COTTAGE, NEAR BLANDFORD.

Dorset in 1846 to report on the plight of the labourers there, put the case succinctly in his description of a cottage at East Morden as 'a charmingly picturesque *bit* for the painter; though its propped-up walls and decaying thatched roof but too closely indicate the privation and suffering of the inmates'.[3] Even the 'model' village of Milton Abbas, in the same county, with its grassy fronts to pretty rose-clad thatched dwellings, had privies – and water supplies – placed close together on the slope of the garden-ground at the back of the cottages, with the inevitable outbreaks of cholera.

Painters such as George Elgood (1851–1944), E. A. Rowe (1860–1922), Alfred Parsons (1847–1920), and Beatrice Parsons (1870–1955) portrayed the gardens of country houses, in which cottage garden plants were featured, but not cottage gardens. The arcadian image was promoted by the paintings of Helen Allingham (1848–1926), one of the few who portrayed the planting layout in cottage gardens. She was taught by the Birmingham and Royal Academy Schools of Art, and she lived much of her life in Chelsea and Hampstead, mixing with an artistic and literary circle. She painted cottages in many southern counties, with straight-backed, slim young women with clean aprons standing contentedly in doorways or by gates, angelic (and very clean) children playing nearby to illustrate *Happy England* in 1903 and *The Cottage Homes of England* in 1909. *The Clothes Basket* shows a true cottage garden, with delphiniums, peonies, and lupins massed around the cabbages grown in the middle, pansies edging the path, and roses climbing round the cottage windows.[4] Allingham painted what she wanted to see, never the corrugated iron which covered a hole or the broken window. By contrast Gertrude Jekyll's

George Elgood,
Cottage garden plants
at Cleve Prior, c. 1904
Edwardian painters such as
George Elgood delighted
in portraying what they
considered to be cottage
gardens. What they
showed was cottage
garden plants – without
the vegetables.

Above right
Helen Allingham.
The Clothes Basket, 1909
Allingham helped to
promote the arcadian
image of idealized country
life by prettifying some
of her scenes, and
sentimentalizing the
cottagers. In this painting
she shows a little of the
cabbage plot, which is well
concealed by delphiniums,
lupins, peonies, lilies
and pansies.

Old West Surrey, published in 1904, contains her photographs of real, plain-faced cottagers bent by toil, admiring their gardens in which 'the smaller the space the more is crammed into it'.[5] Again, roses clamber round windows, pot plants fill the porch, and everlasting sweet peas flank the door; but the text is full of villagers' accounts of long hours of backbreaking work, and long walks to reach it.

Were artists, however unwittingly, who tried to portray 'Merrie England' and a 'contented countryside' in their images of cottages and gardens during this period, turning their backs on the realities of rural hardship? The Cotswold gatherings of the followers of Arts and Crafts attracted 'intellectuals and middle classes' – many Americans amongst them – 'escaping the misery of the towns'. It seems that the English garden so identified in paintings at this time may have reflected the predominant and preferred middle-class view.[6]

The philanthropists were finally stirred into action in 1883 by the clergyman Andrew Mearns' book, *The Bitter Cry of Outcast London*.[7] His description of filth and degradation in which much of the labouring poor of London lived shocked and alarmed the middle class. A Royal Commission followed which began the slow process of introducing the state as provider of housing.[8]

Some industrial and agricultural paternalists sought to ameliorate the situation by providing good housing, parks, allotments and communal space for cultivation. In the countryside, men such as William Henry Berkeley, second Viscount Portman (1829–1919), typified the enlightened landowner. With 24,000 agricultural acres in Somerset, 8,000 in Dorset, just under 2,000 acres in Devon, and 270 acres of lucrative Marylebone and Baker Street London,[9] Portman was able to juggle the falling fortunes of agricultural rents with the rising ones of London. His Dorset seat was at Bryanston, rebuilt by Norman

Shaw in the 1890s. The heir in waiting (who died before his father), Edward, lived at Hestercombe in Somerset.

About four hundred people were employed on the 3,000 odd acres around Blandford, virtually the entire population of the two parishes of Bryanston and Durweston.[10] They were housed in three-bedroomed cottages which had been praised by a Royal Commission in 1885.[11] These were a far cry from the one-up, one-down variety with ladder staircase and earthen floor found in the worst cases elsewhere. The Portmans gave their workers long leases for security and let their cottages directly to the labourers. It was usual for cottages to be let by the tenant farmers, but the Portmans felt that they could better keep an eye on conditions in this way, and prevent the farmers from bullying their workers. However, this was 'tied' accommodation, which meant that the cottage came with the job, and wages were accordingly depressed; workers were expected to make up that shortfall by 'perquisites' such as free gleaning and garden ground on which to grow food.

H. Rider Haggard expressed his admiration for the estate in his accounts of his rural journeys in 1902. 'Here, as might be expected, everything is managed without thought of cost. Never before have I seen such buildings of cottages: the very cows are provided with softer sorts of wood on which to kneel, and the electric light machinery reminds the visitor of the engines of some great ship'.[12] The cottages had large gardens, and allotments were provided in the villages. Accounts show that rents were often in arrears, but it appears that Portman realized that nothing could be done in the prevailing economic climate. For thirty years the family shouldered the falling returns, but finally death duties caught up with them as two viscounts and the heir to the estate died between 1911 and 1923. Gradually parts of the estate were sold off, including the mansion, which became a school, and the family ran the rump of the estate from London until after the Second World War.[13] There was little demand for paternalists to provide public parks in country villages, though in north Dorset, F. J. B. Wingfield Digby (1885–1952), owner of the Sherborne Castle Estates, gave the Pageant Gardens site in the town in the 1920s for use as a public park.

William Lever and Port Sunlight

Following the example of northern model housing such as Saltaire, Bradford (1850–63) and Ackroydon, Halifax (1861–63) with their allotments and parks, the soap magnate William Hesketh Lever (1851–1925) established an industrial village settlement at Port Sunlight (1888–1934) in which he combined good housing and green space for recreation and cultivation with a desire to construct a memorable designed settlement. He was sufficiently concerned about town planning to use money he won in a libel

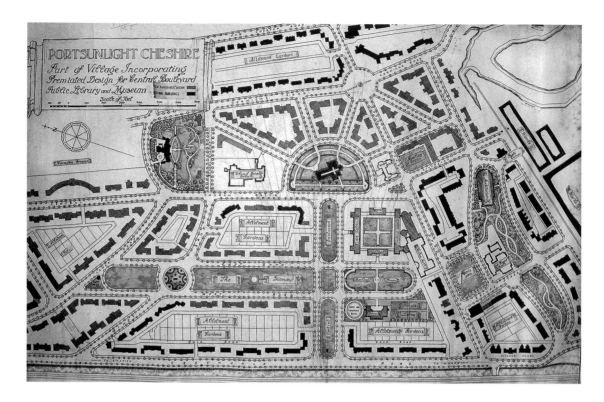

Thomas Mawson, plan for Port Sunlight, England, 1910

Mawson's plan shows his provision for parks, at the far right and top left, and the formal green in the middle, as well as gardens and allotments for the housing which he designed for Lever's soap workers at Port Sunlight.

suit to set up the Department of Civic Design at the University of Liverpool in 1909. Lever employed architects such as the American Charles Reilly (who was Director of the School of Architecture at the University of Liverpool), Ernest Prestwich and later, Thomas Mawson, to plan his settlement. There was a rather formal Beaux-Arts civic centre to the village although Lever also encouraged building in the traditional black and white Cheshire vernacular.

Mawson's revised plan of Port Sunlight for 1910, incorporating earlier ideas by Prestwich, shows the central stroke of a cross formed by the long green – 'the diamond' – linking a museum and library; the eastern arm of the cross leads to a church. All round the diamond are blocks of houses, enclosing allotment gardens; there are informal parks around the edge, and formal public gardens in the diamond.

The houses, eventually built in groups of up to seven, would have been occupied solely by workers in the soap factory which was set beyond public gardens by the side of the river. Lever wanted low density housing and wide roads, no more than twelve houses to the acre in order to maintain health and avoid the overcrowding. Lever had strict rules for the maintenance of the open front gardens, to promote harmony and prevent the dumping of rubbish. Eventually the dreary absence of flowers led the company to relent, and offer reduced rents for the best-kept gardens.[14] Port Sunlight was one of the last paternalist industrial settlements; further south, a different type of provision was being made.

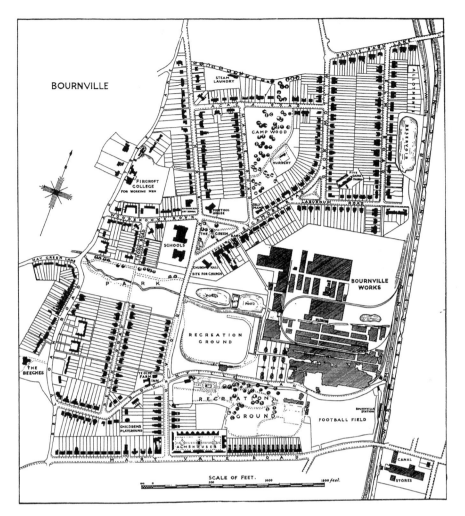

Map of Bournville, 1914
Despite the rapid growth since 1879 of this planned settlement for workers in George Cadbury's cocoa factory, about a third of the acreage remained in recreation grounds and parks. As well, each house had a substantial garden, and there were allotments.

George Cadbury at Bournville

At Bournville, on the outskirts of Birmingham, Quaker cocoa manufacturer George Cadbury bought 330 acres of land in 1879 for 'a practical experiment in social reform'.[15] Cadbury placed the administration of the village of 2,000 people in the hands of a trust, which maintained the houses, built new ones, could buy land, and which was independent of the Cadbury works. In that way profit would go straight to the village, and would help to keep rents down. The houses were intended for working men who wanted them, not exclusively the cocoa workers. The original intention to sell to those who wanted to buy was abandoned in favour of renting, after those who bought sold them on at a profit. The architect, W. Alexander Harvey, designed vernacular houses in brick, half-timbering, and an eclectic Arts and Crafts style, semi-detached or in blocks of four. They were built mainly from 1895. Each house had a generous garden of about six hundred square yards, planted with fruit trees, and its occupier could call on advice from the trust's gardeners. Gardening had a high profile, with lectures and classes for the young men (surprisingly, also the

Above
**Bournville, near
Birmingham, England**
W. Alexander Harvey
designed comfortable
half-timbered houses in an
Arts and Crafts idiom for
Bournville. Set in tree-lined
streets (that were also
named after trees), the
settlement was intended
to establish decent
housing in a garden
village for working
men and women.

Right
**Bournville,
recreation grounds**
Set next to the cocoa
factory, a large and
pleasant recreation ground
and half-timbered pavilion
provided good facilities
for workers and helped
to preserve the green
surroundings which
Cadbury saw as important
for the welfare of
his workers.

young women). There were, in addition, allotments available. The reason for encouraging such spade-work, apart from promoting good health, was that the value of the produce helped to offset the rent, thus carrying on the policy which had been followed by agricultural landlords. There were debates about the greater productivity and therefore greater value of the garden ground in garden villages. However it was also suggested that gardens would keep men out of the public house – the inn at Bournville was a 'dry' one – and Cadbury felt that men would eat more vegetables and less meat, which, as a vegetarian, he felt 'would improve the general health of the country'.[17]

Garden villages were not only to be utilitarian. Flowers appeared at annual shows. Hedges protected front garden displays. In addition, the landscape was to make a contribution to the settlement. Bournville's site, on a gentle decline and rise northwards, was laid out fairly informally with wide roads named after the trees planted along them. The works, with its railway station, abuts the line to Birmingham and Bristol, but by 1914 it was surrounded by green, tree-fringed sports grounds. In addition, a small park followed a stream leading into the grounds at the bottom of the valley, and a woodland formed the heart of a horseshoe of housing in the north. The Girls' Recreation Ground in the south utilized the landscaping of the eighteenth-century Bournville Hall. An account in 1936 described the ornamental nature of the grounds adjoining the factory, with lawns, flower beds, and tree-lined grass verges 'thickly planted with crocus, narcissus, snowdrop, scilla and meadow saffron'. Forty-three gardeners maintained the grounds and greenhouses so that the factory and offices could have indoor plants, hanging baskets, and seasonal bedding outside.[18] The emphasis on recreation surrounded by beauty reflected Cadbury's concern – shared by William Morris – that factory work could diminish humanity. And like Lord Leverhulme, Cadbury was prepared to promote the education of those landscaping the environment by endowing a lectureship in civic design at Birmingham University, to which Raymond Unwin was appointed in 1911.

Parker and Unwin and Joseph Rowntree's New Earswick

Another Quaker cocoa manufacturer, Joseph Rowntree, had already availed himself of Unwin's services at a settlement he was making at New Earswick, some three miles northeast of York. Purchased in 1901, the village on the flat site west of the river Foss was to retain all original trees and water features, and have roads named after the trees which lined them, as at Bournville. In addition, workers could vary their routes home according to the street trees which were in flower at that time. The overall plan resembled Port Sunlight, in that houses were grouped around a hollow centre, in which were planned a village green, a folk hall, and facilities for sports – football, tennis, bowls, and hockey. Footpaths were made so that children had no need to cross roads on their walk to school. Rowntree shared his ideas with Cadbury, and as at Bournville, the settlement was administered by a trust, with profits being ploughed back to the advantage of the village.

New Earswick displays the thinking of two influential planners – Raymond Unwin (1863–1940) and his business partner Barry Parker (1867–1947). Unwin had married Parker's sister, both had been brought up in the environs of Sheffield, and shared a common social outlook. Parker and Unwin went into partnership in 1896. Neither was a trained architect; Unwin served an engineering apprenticeship, and Parker trained as a craftsman.

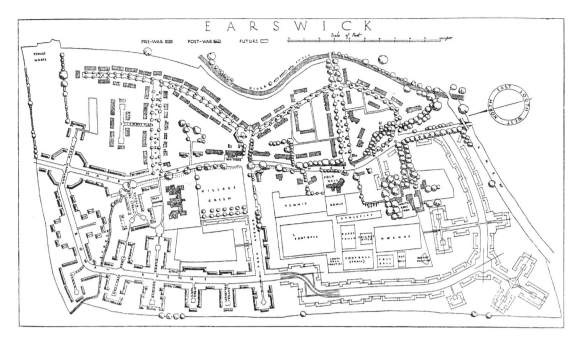

**Barry Parker's plan for
New Earswick, York,
England, 1901**

Joseph Rowntree
employed Raymond Unwin
and Barry Parker to design
a settlement for his cocoa
factory workers. Parker's
plan shows his design
pulling away from the
straight lines of the by-law
housing of the time.
By grouping houses
in a semi-circle, he had
invented the quiet cul-de-
sac, and the spaces at
the centre of blocks of
grouped houses could
be turned into greens.

New Earswick was planned at the same time as Unwin was considering the layout of settlements to give the maximum environmental benefit possible to their inhabitants. In *Cottage Homes and Common Sense* (1902), Unwin argues for the replacement of rows of street houses with back yards and alleys, common to industrial towns and mining communities with which he was familiar, in favour of the grouping of the open space thus released into a common garden or square. By turning a group of cottages to face the sun, and linking them together, it would be possible to evoke university quadrangles like those of Oxford and Cambridge.[19] In a plan made for the Northern Art Workers' Guild in 1903, Parker and Unwin had shown how staggering the layout of separated cottages would open them up to air and sun, and surround them with garden space.

In another influential publication in 1912, *Nothing Gained by Overcrowding!* Unwin promoted the cul-de-sac.[20] Local by-laws, introduced to bring clean air into towns by widening streets, had resulted in dreary, grid-pattern layouts. Unwin was able to demonstrate that costs could be cut by reducing the width of the road, and this would leave more space available for gardens and open spaces. Cul-de-sacs appeared in the later stages of New Earswick, with houses slightly offset in a wide curve round a peaceful green centre. Grass verges between road and house aided the tranquil setting. Thus, in Port Sunlight, Bournville, and New Earswick, landscaping and the abolition of narrow-fronted housing with dismal back yards had begun to create an environment fit for working people. Unfortunately apart from men such as Cadbury and Rowntree, there were few entrepreneurs who were willing to forgo profit, and the cost of such housing became too high for the working classes.

Ebenezer Howard (1850–1928) – the Garden City

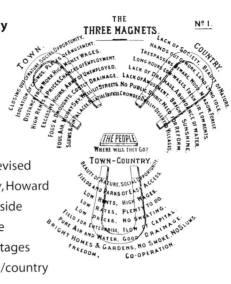

Howard's solution to the overcrowding of cities was based on an entirely new concept – that of corporate ownership. It came to fruition at about the same time that Cadbury was building Bournville, Lord Leverhulme, Port Sunlight, and Parker and Unwin, New Earswick. In *To-morrow: A Peaceful Path to Real Reform*, published in 1898, revised and re-issued in 1902 as *Garden Cities of To-morrow*, Howard analyzed the results of migration from the countryside and overcrowding in the cities in his diagram of the three magnets. Each magnet represents the advantages and disadvantages of town, and country, and town/country offers the best of each lifestyle.

Howard had learned about country life the hard way. Born in Sudbury, London, he emigrated to the United States in 1871 to farm in Nebraska, without success. Howard had witnessed the rebuilding of Chicago after the 1871 fire; due to its parks it was known as the garden city. In America he absorbed the utopian ideas of Edward Bellamy, author of *Looking Backward* (1888) and Henry George, author of *Progress and Poverty* (1879).

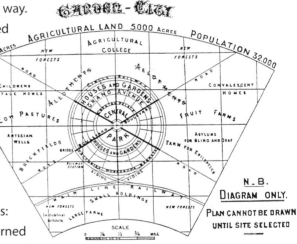

Howard's thinking was inspired by many sources: the rejection of capitalist landlords pocketing unearned increments from the land, from Henry George; the belief in co-operative society without interference from government, church, army or any other body, in parts from Morris, Bellamy and Russian anarchist geographer Peter Kropotkin; and the belief that the working classes could be moved out of cities. Added to this were the convictions of many thinkers that the country was a better place in which to live, and that getting back to nature was best for society. From these influences, and many others, including the non-conformists and socialists already involved in housing experiments, Howard devised a model which would solve harmoniously the problem of people leaving the countryside to overcrowd the towns: the Garden City.

It was to be built on cheap agricultural land some distance from a town with money put up by a group of investors who would wish to plough back profit for the benefit of society. It would grow to a certain size, when it would spawn another, similar, town beyond a green belt. The green belt would provide space for agriculture. The settlements generated in this way would

Top

Ebenezer Howard's 'Three Magnets' diagram, 1902

Howard's diagram illustrates the best of the attributes of town and country which combine to form the garden city.

Bottom

Ebenezer Howard, diagram of a Garden City, 1910

The garden city was to be set in the centre of green space which could contain colleges, institutions, and agriculture.

form a region of towns, or a 'social city', which would be linked by rapid transit railways. Each town would recycle its waste for use on the agricultural land. It would provide infrastructure such as water supply, work in agriculture and industry, craft and small businesses, education including agricultural colleges and colleges for the blind, institutions such as hospitals and asylums – in short, the garden city was to be self-contained and all embracing. Because city dwellers would see the benefits of living in the countryside, the cities would empty and their rents would fall, and it would be possible to clear the slums and rebuild in the towns. There could be parks, recreation grounds and allotments on the sites of the cleared slums.[23]

Because Howard did not specify exactly how the garden city was to be laid out, it has proved to be an adaptable model. Howard urged that people 'should forthwith gird themselves to the task of building up clusters of beautiful home-towns, each zoned by gardens, for those who now dwell in crowded, slum-infested cities'.[24] But the underlying assumption was that the garden city should instil the overwhelming benefits of country life, which was demonstrated in his second diagram in *Garden Cities of To-morrow* by the encircling acres of green farms and forests. Agricultural land should take up five-sixths of the space, and the city buildings, the rest. The ideal population would be 32,000. There should be large gardens with the houses, and allotments. Again, the produce of both would offset the rent. The country, said Howard, 'is the symbol of God's love and care for man… Its beauty is the inspiration of art, of music, of poetry… It is the source of all health, all wealth, all knowledge… Town and country *must be married* , and out of this joyous union will spring a new hope, a new life, a new civilization'.[25]

Letchworth

The realization of the model was a slow process. Howard had led the way in setting up a Garden City Association in 1899. The First Garden City Company was formed in 1903, after a complicated buy-out from fifteen owners of 3,818 acres (1545 hectares) of cheap agricultural land at Letchworth. But from the beginning there were differences between the ideal and the reality. The site was bisected by the railway, which was needed to locate industry. Thus it would be difficult to separate areas for industry away from housing.

Directed by Parker and Unwin's 1903 Master Plan, the planned density of housing was low – some twelve houses to the acre – comprising short terraces and cul-de-sacs. The town centre was to have civic buildings, and be framed by

The Spirella Corset Factory, Letchworth, Hertfordshire, England, c. 1910
Letchworth, the first built garden city, provided work opportunities such as printing and the making of corsetry. Howard's zoning of areas of the city for industry and housing within its green surroundings was not easily achieved here, because a railway cut the site.

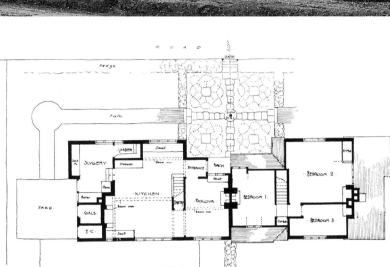

Half Ground Floor   Half First Floor

Left and below

Elmwood Cottages, Letchworth

M. H. Baillie Scott's paired Elmwood Cottages, built following the 1907 Cheap Cottages Exhibition in Letchworth, with ground plan and garden (below). The simple plan for a low maintenance paved rose garden with its sun dial, and path through a lawn with a boundary hedge, suggests that this was intended for the office worker rather than the labourer.

radial avenues, which were not completed. By 1910 Letchworth was home to the printers and bookbinders J. M. Dent and W. H. Smith and Son, the factory of Lacre Motor Car Company Ltd, the Garden City Embroidery Works, and the Spirella Corset factory, whose 'Viennese *Jugendstil*' building,[26] designed by Cecil Hignett, a former assistant of Parker and Unwin, has been recently restored. Other factories followed, including war-time ventures for making parachutes and munitions, uncomfortably accepted by pacifists, mixing with the farms, dairies and market gardens.

The building of housing for the low-waged was given an impetus when the Cheap Cottages Exhibition was held in Letchworth in 1905, showing semi-detached and single houses. A second, Letchworth Cottages Exhibition, was held in 1907, this time concentrating on groups of houses.[27] House design was mostly conservative and inspired by the Arts and Crafts movement. Architect

Mackay Hugh Baillie Scott (1865–1945), perhaps more used to country house size, designed the semi-detached Elmwood Cottages later built in Norton Way North. Parker and Unwin designed vernacular cottages around large greens, and larger detached houses, some with balconies for sleeping on in the summer. Their public buildings included the non-alcoholic Skittles Inn, supplied by Cadbury with cocoa, and the Mrs Howard Memorial Hall beyond which is the Howard Park. Parker designed an office for the partnership as a thatched cottage, although by 1906 Unwin was busy with Hampstead Garden Suburb and never worked there.

Letchworth's reputation for attracting eccentrics and cranks, left-wingers, vegetarians and strange religious groups, was shown in a mocking cartoon of the time depicting the town as a zoo. The leading lights of the town are dressed in smocks and sandals, wielding spade and offers of plots.[30] In reality the reputation may have been deserved by the inhabitants of The Cloisters, a slightly sinister-looking building of 1906–7 with its tall bell-tower and chimneys, isolated across the fields until fairly late in the town's growth. It was built by architect W. H. Cowlishaw for Miss Annie Jane Lawrence, a wealthy but perhaps gullible lady, in which she was to encourage followers of 'the New Life'. She appears to have been persuaded by J. Bruce Wallace, a founder member of the Garden City Association, to make The Cloisters a residential centre for a group he had founded, called the Alpha Union. This was a movement similar to theosophy, concerning itself with 'wholesome thought and labour'. The residents slept in hammocks outside, and unsuccessfully attempted to cultivate wheat according to the rules of Kropotkin by giving loving care to each grain.

Garden design in the first Garden City depended on the buyer. Baillie Scott, writing in 1906, questioned the modern trend towards the functional garden, which was seen as a place to grow fruit and vegetables for the average household, with another part for 'outdoor apartments for the use of the family in fine weather'. The occupier of the 'smaller type of suburban or country house' would have 'neither the time, knowledge, nor inclination to grow [his] own vegetables or flowers'.[31] Baillie Scott realized that agricultural labourers, or people who would have cultivated their own gardens, were difficult to find in Letchworth. He foresaw that those buying houses would probably employ gardeners who knew about bedding out, clipping hedges and managing lawns and gravel paths – which would be labour-intensive and expensive. Trying to balance the wild and the formal, Baillie Scott recommended the William Robinson type of wild garden and orchard as the best solution for the larger middle class house such as Tanglewood, at 17 Sollershott West, with perennial borders, unmown grass (apart from lawns for tennis, croquet or bowls) bulbs under the fruit trees, and few paths. But for the confines of the smaller working-class plot, such as Elmwood Cottages, a formal garden with paving and a square rose garden centred by a sundial, with some regularly placed fruit trees, seemed more suitable.

Letchworth did not begin to pay dividends – and low ones at that – to its investors until a decade had passed, underlining the difficulty of attracting capital to a corporate, low profit-making venture. By 1960 it almost lost its identity as First Garden City Ltd was taken over by a property company intent on asset-stripping[32] and only a parliamentary private member's bill saved it as a public authority – the Letchworth Garden City Corporation. This was replaced by charitable status in 1995, as Letchworth Garden City Heritage Foundation.

Hampstead Garden Suburb

The garden suburb concept grew from the needs of the poor in Whitechapel, the drive to save open land from the developers at Hampstead Heath, and the work of Henrietta Barnett, the wife of Canon Samuel Barnett, who linked them both together. Henrietta Barnett had worked with her husband at Toynbee Hall in Whitechapel, a settlement where Oxford graduates could live and help to educate the underprivileged, a group made up amongst others from immigrants who worked in the warren of garment sweatshops. Barnett was also a follower of Octavia Hill, who had relentlessly pursued the rescuing of open spaces at the end of the nineteenth century, believed in gardens in the heart of the slums,[33] and with Canon Rawnsley, lawyer Sir Robert Hunter and the Duke of Westminster, had founded the National Trust.

The Barnetts had a weekend retreat from their good works at Heath End House at the edge of Hampstead Heath. Land owned by Eton College next to the Heath, the 323-acre (130-hectare) Wyldes Farm estate, looked as if it might fall into the hands of developers as the underground railway moved towards Golders Green and Edgware, with a proposed station on Wyldes Farm. Barnett organized a Heath Extension Council to acquire the estate in the name of public amenity (and to protect her own outlook from Heath End House). At the same time her conscience persuaded her that land to the north of the proposed Extension could be used to construct a garden suburb, which, if planned with housing for rich as well as poor, would be socially and financially successful. Although Eton College delayed negotiations until 1906, the schemes were finally agreed.

Barnett set out her aims in December 1903. She hoped that 'the rich may live in kindly neighbourliness with the poor; the dwellings of both attractive with their own distinctive attractions, as are the cottage and the manor house of the English village. The larger gardens of the rich helping to keep the air pure, and the sky view more liberal; the cottage gardens adding that cosy generous element which ever follows the spade when lovingly and cunningly

**'Oxford Quadrangles',
Hampstead Garden
Suburb, from 1907**
Raymond Unwin's early
experiences of mining
communities convinced
him that by grouping
cottages together he could
create shared green spaces
that would be like Oxford
college quadrangles.
The Orchard, with the
spire of St Jude's in the
background, evokes the
artisans' cottages intended
for the northern part of the
Suburb, where doors open
on to the green.

Right

**Edwin Lutyens's
'Queen Anne' houses**
Approaching North
Square, Lutyens (and other
architects influenced by
him) built large houses
in his Queen Anne style.
Here, the quadrangles are
more formal, with a road
marking a dignified
separation of the house
from the green square.

wielded as a man's recreation'.[34] The original plan made by Parker and Unwin in 1905 showed large houses next to the Heath Extension and working-class housing, with allotments behind, in the far north. Barnett's comments reveal the paternalistic influence of nineteenth-century Christian Socialists who wanted to improve the lot, but not the status, of the working man. She also appears to suggest that the garden would not be required to provide food, and that by implication, the agricultural poor were less likely to live in Hampstead. Barnett's Garden Suburb had drawn away from Howard's Garden City in its acceptance of class divisions and its orientation towards the town worker. As no industry was provided in the Suburb, the inhabitants were expected to take advantage of the twopenny fare to London. This did not

quite square with the earnings of those who would be hiring 'barns for tools and coster barrows', shown on the 1905 plan, and in the end demand for housing pushed up prices beyond the pocket of the working classes.

The Barnetts hoped to raise the horizons of the working classes through visual education. As at Port Sunlight, an art gallery was provided in both Whitechapel and Hampstead Garden Suburb, and it could be said that it is the planning of the street picture which provides the lasting image of the Suburb, not its social message. Raymond Unwin, Letchworth's architect, had hitherto concentrated on cottage and road layout and orientation to bring decency to housing, and like others, he had been much influenced by what he saw in visits to European towns. John Nettlefold, Chairman of Birmingham Corporation Housing Committee, was an admirer of Cadbury's low density layouts and private provision of housing at Bournville, though his book *Practical Housing* of 1908[35] is full of advice from German sources. However, T. G. Horsfall, Chairman of the Manchester Citizens' Association, also a great admirer of German housing, preferred the power which German town councils had to plan their own schemes, which was similar to the 'owner of a large estate' in England.[36] Horsfall was one of many pressing for more state intervention in housing at this time.

Above and below
Hampstead Garden Suburb
The Great Wall (above), dividing the Heath Extension from the Suburb, evokes a German medieval castellated city boundary. Allotments (below) were more for hobby gardening than for supplementing the wage of the inhabitants.

Unwin was more interested in the appearance of the buildings of old German towns, especially Nuremberg and Rothenberg, and the informality and picturesqueness of medieval Italian cities shown by Viennese town planner Camillo Sitte (1843–1903).[37] Rothenberg's city wall, dividing the town from the country,[38] appears along the edge of the Heath Extension, as do the arches and gables of Rothenberg's town gateways[39] at the Temple Fortune entrance to the Suburb.

The Artizans' Quarter on Asmuns Hill was built early on, with allotments reached by footpaths at the back, the houses steep-roofed, and the whole following the bend of the Mutton Brook. The cul-de-sac made by Asmuns Place required an Act of Parliament to avoid the restrictive by-laws on road width. But the cultivation plots, gardens and rural greenness created by the Mutton Brook Valley and new road design also gave the less wealthy more pleasant surroundings in which to live. The grouping of buildings at road junctions, the setting back of houses in rows to allow better vision, the small tower-like features on houses on the sight-line, all speak of Sitte's influence combined with the Germanic style. Many well-known architects as well as Parker and Unwin were involved in cottage plans, such as Baillie Scott, Courtenay Crickmer (1879–1971) and Geoffrey Lucas (1872–1947), and with garden designs to match the cottages, thus helping to give diversity in design but posing difficulties for Unwin's overall vision of the Suburb. Unwin gave preference for quiet roads, with road traffic kept to a minimum by the provision of closes, cul-de-sacs, 'Oxford quadrangles', and a meandering layout. All of these designs gave space for gardens, communal grassy spaces in front of houses, and trees, realizing Henrietta Barnett's original wish for trees along the streets, where they married with Unwin's grass verges and green-centred courts.

The central square is dominated by the spire of Edwin Lutyens's St Jude's Church and Byzantine dome of the Free Church across the square, and the Queen Anne-style Institute between them, separated by green grass and formal flower beds. There is a change of tone as houses round the central square, designed by Parker and Unwin and others including the Michael Bunney (1873–1926) and Clifford Makins partnership, display a more sedate Queen Anne Revival manner. The change of emphasis from encircling village style with gardens and informality to authoritarian ecclesiastical at the Suburb's heart is all the more emphatic as the buildings of the central square are set on a hill. It is difficult to imagine any light-hearted games on the public green between the two churches.

Apart from a post office, the Suburb has no shops. Would the central square have been better served by a smaller church in the centre of a marketplace, similar to the ones Unwin had been sketching on his travels in England and abroad?

Inevitably Hampstead Garden Suburb has undergone metamorphosis from social experiment to much-copied commuter suburb. Its desired social mix was perhaps unattainable from the outset, and its influence has been on the promotion of the separation of through traffic from the village layout and an appreciation of artistry in town planning both in Britain and abroad.

Petts Wood – Garden Village Suburb

One of many Garden Village Suburbs, Petts Wood in Kent followed just this model in the 1920s. It was largely created by a developer from Essex called Basil Scruby (1876–1946) as a 'quality' settlement.[40] He raised capital to buy 400 acres (160 hectares) of woodland and common near the South Eastern and Chatham Railway line, between Chislehurst and Orpington, on which to make a garden suburb, and persuaded the railway company to build a station in 1928. The suburb was called Petts Wood, after the sixteenth-century Deptford shipbuilder, William Pett, who leased the woodlands now owned by the National Trust and which form part of the amenity of the settlement. The journey to London took twenty-two minutes, which, together with the countryside setting, helped to sell the settlement to the middle-class commuter.

Scruby then divided the site which lay to the east of the station into plots to sell to builders, such as the Welshman Walter Noel Rees, who created housing in the Arts and Crafts tradition, with low roofs, prominent chimneys, brickwork with occasional patterning, half-timbering, and diamond-paned leaded windows. This style was soon named Tudorbethan by those who mocked the cottage pastiche, but it sold well. The houses had large gardens, and were set back from the tree-lined, gently curving roads with grass verges. Typically the front gardens had low, dry-stone walls, and the back a large lawn, perhaps a rockery, crazy paving, and herbaceous borders. Standard roses joined the hybrid tea roses. Wherever possible, trees were retained, and buyers often found themselves the possessors of a small woodland in their back gardens.

The visual connection with Unwin's work at Hampstead cannot be ignored. On the site of a demolished nineteenth century mansion and its grounds, Rees built a select cul-de-sac called The Chenies, now a Conservation Area. The cul-de-sac enabled large gardens at the back of the buildings. Its half-timbered detached houses were protected along Willett Way by a wall resembling a lesser version of that along the Hampstead Heath Extension. The Chenies was approached on one side through an arched gateway like the one at Asmuns Place. Other builders such as Cecil Pamphilon, son of architect Walter Pamphilon, continued the theme of comfortably sized cottage-style houses with large gardens in the 1930s, whose trademark was a wooden diamond and

**'The Chenies',
Petts Wood, Kent**

Part of the lingering Arts and Crafts movement, Petts Wood was built from 1928 by Basil Scruby, a developer who saw the selling power of the garden village within commuting distance of London. This quiet cul-de-sac, with its trees, grassy verges and half-timbered houses, is typical of many private developments of the time whose aims were commercial rather than egalitarian.

a slot in the gable. They were intended for the better-off, with prices up to £1,450. The exclusive end of the settlement was Birchwood Avenue, whose Tudor House on an acre of ground had a lychgate entry from the road into a large garden in no particular style, a short drive, topical ship designs in stained glass in the bathroom, front and back stairs inside for staff, and a cottage for the gardener-chauffeur.

The brick and timber cottage-shops around the station square enclosed the Daylight Inn, named after daylight saving pioneer, William Willett, and a garden was made in the estate office grounds which adjoined the Inn. There was York stone paving around the Inn, which was built as a larger version of the cottage shops. Even the garage in the square had petrol pumps hidden under tiled roofs. The high Anglican Church of St Francis of Assisi was consecrated in 1935, again following the Arts and Crafts theme. Its Roman Catholic architect, Geoffrey Mullins, designed it to be built in hand-made Sussex brick to resemble a medieval tithe barn with a wooden hammer beam roof. Spread below the building was a green sloping apron of grass, with woodland trees.

However the modern house also made an appearance in the 1930s in Petts Wood, as it had in Hampstead, though not as part of the Scruby development. Davis Estate housing was built along closes named after the trees planted along their verges. These were less expensive, being mass-produced and built on smaller plots with smaller gardens. They had metal window frames, and black tiling beside the front door, and a handful had flat roofs.

Intended by Scruby as a picturesque middle class garden village suburb, Petts Wood managed to keep its character with its surrounding green belt of woodlands and recreation grounds, and the high cost of its housing. This greenness – the interspersing of houses with gardens, grass verges, tennis courts and a cricket ground, the woods to walk in – was typical of the loosening of urban texture so well loved by house owners in garden city, suburb, and village. But Petts Wood had no allotments. It was part of a trend followed by the private developers who sensed the selling value of the term 'garden', but had none of the democratizing social aims of the Garden City.

There were difficulties posed by the shortages of building supplies after the World Wars, political debates about whether state or private money should be used to house the masses, the changing nature and place of employment, the unstoppable expansion of towns and the rising cost of land. Almost inevitably, the Garden City became an impractical ideal for widescale use, though its blueprint was admired by many, as this chapter will show.

Instead, parts of its ethos became the estate-agent's bestseller: the suburban cottage with good garden in a respectable area, the tree-lined road, the grass verge. No longer were allotments required for working men. There were parks for the masses to walk dogs and for children's games. English people were more interested in gardens than schemes for egalitarian ownership.

Allotments and land colonies

Small, detached cultivation patches can be spotted on early Ordnance Survey maps, usually outside towns.[41] Mostly they were to produce food, but some, like the 'guinea gardens' or 'hobby gardens' of the eighteenth century outside Birmingham, were ornamental, giving flowers, vegetables, 'healthful exercise and rational enjoyment among families of the artisans'.[42]

In the nineteenth century, allotments were closely associated with the need to defuse mounting discontent amongst both rural and urban poor. As already described, produce from the rural allotment served to augment the low wages of the agricultural and industrial labourer so he could pay his rent, and it was also a way of giving him 'self-respect, independence and thrift'.[43] The rural volume of *The Land Enquiry* reported in 1913 that 'so highly are gardens valued that we often find a man will live in a bad and insanitary cottage which has a large garden, in preference to a good cottage the rent of which is the same, but which has no garden'. But the same Enquiry noted that the majority of allotments were in the hands of 'village tradesmen, artisans, pensioners and others, and that the labourer seldom has time to cultivate them'.[44]

The convention of allotment letting was adopted by the providers of housing for industrial workers, and Ebenezer Howard allowed considerable space for allotments in his model of the Garden City. The Liberal Party's Jesse Collings was a supporter of allotments for the poor, and in the 1880s used the slogan 'three acres and a cow!' as part of a drive for publicity. Fear of compulsory purchase led landowners to form the Landowners' Voluntary Allotment Association in 1886, ahead of legislation in 1887 which gave local sanitary authorities the power to organize allotments for letting, and again in 1892 for smallholdings. Two years later the Parish Councils Act gave powers of compulsory purchase, without compensation, for one acre plots for a penny rate. Because the business of rural allotment provision had become so entangled with politics, some landowners had become wary of letting plots on their land to the labourers, and the Duchy of Cornwall found itself the centre of local newspaper attention for letting to the better off – including superintendents of police and army personnel with pensions – in Dorchester at the end of the nineteenth century.[45] Others were only too glad to let their agricultural land as allotments during the worst of the depression between the two world wars, getting more return from the rent than from farm produce.

Urban fringe allotments, such as those of the Nottingham's hosiery workers, could be rented for £1 per annum at Hunger Hills in the early nineteenth century. Here they grew flowers and roses for sale at the Manchester and Liverpool markets, as well as fruit and vegetables. By 1920 this area comprised 60 acres (24 hectares) with a main avenue and a maze of side paths, with neatly trimmed hedges including soft fruit bushes around the plots. They probably exhibited their produce at the local floricultural and horticultural societies which had flourished from the eighteenth century; Nottingham's hand-loom weavers produced prize-winning carnations.[46] But in the 1920s some of their sheds for storing tools and potting up plants actually housed families, with children taking water from the standpipes, and light from lamps.[47] These allotments have been listed and are in the process of restoration by English Heritage.

Allotments played their part during both world wars. Before the start of the First World War, the Board of Agriculture and Fisheries asked private landowners to keep their surplus vegetable seeds for distribution by the Royal Horticultural Society to allotment holders. Land was requisitioned for allotments. Urged to garden for patriotic reasons, the holders were anxious to continue after the end of hostilities. There was then the problem of providing cultivation ground and housing for returning soldiers and unemployed munition workers. Once again, housing and food provision were intertwined.

The alternative to providing patches of ground to top up the wages of the poor was to move them out of the city altogether. The concept of land colonies had been talked about in the nineteenth century, and was tried, with no great impact, after both world wars. Ebenezer Howard's Garden City employed people in agricultural surroundings by moving them from the town. But moving the unemployed from South Wales or Durham to farm in the south, as the government tried to do in the late 1930s, cannot be seen as part of Howard's pattern. Land settlement was promoted again in 1945, extolling the nineteenth century values of self-help, character-building, and stabilizing the countryside. Co-operation had been the glue of society in Howard's model. But country life for the unemployed and demobilized soldiers was hardly likely to succeed unless they were part of co-operative farming units as in Denmark, Holland or Belgium, and farming co-operatives were never developed in England.[48]

Workers on allotments, England, 1939
With the outbreak of the Second World War, there were concerns that Britain's supplies of food from abroad would be interrupted. The Ministry of Agriculture began a scheme to encourage the growing of vegetables. Parks and gardens were converted from amenity use to food production – at the same time some historic sites were destroyed.

County authorities provided training, tools, seed and land to cultivate, and unemployment pay, 'the dole', was to be saved to help set the man up once he had finished his training. Some authorities renovated cottages which had been deserted for the trainees to live in. But there was a considerable wastage as men who were unused to the land had no heart for the life; and moreover, land and cottages given to the settlement movement had been originally rejected as unsuitable for farming. Land Settlement never really got further than good intentions.

America – settlement and suburb

Americans studied the English experiments closely, because their experience of overcrowding in the city was similar. Chicago, due to its industrial growth and its position as a gateway to the agricultural interior, found itself an uneasy host to a multitude of immigrant Irish, German, Russians, Italians and Poles, who settled between the Chicago River and the stockyards. The reaction of the City was to stuff these impoverished people into wretched tenement blocks which had few basic amenities. Jacob Riis, who, like Jens Jensen, had emigrated from Denmark, wrote a polemic in 1890 called *How the Other Half Lives*, which stated the facts about overcrowding and played on middle-class fears about the disintegration of society. Others took a more compassionate line. Canon Barnett's Toynbee Hall Settlement became a source of inspiration for American philanthropists such as Jane Addams (1860–1935), who had visited the Barnetts in London and read Mearns's *Bitter Cry*.

She took over a house in Halsted Street, in the centre of the worst of the slums, and turned it into a community centre for immigrants in 1889, called Hull-House, after the merchant who had built it. Hull-House became a force for integration. Addams quickly found out 'that private beneficence is totally inadequate to deal with the vast numbers of the city's disinherited', and her campaign for better education and environmental conditions for working people won her the Nobel Peace Prize in 1931. She sought, as she said, to 'build a bridge between European and American experiences'.[49]

Hull-House demanded attention. It began summer schools attached to Rockford College, eventually helping to create University Extension courses in Chicago. It attracted visitors such as Frank Lloyd Wright and Peter Kropotkin,[50] whose decentralizing ideas would have agreed with Howard's at the movement of a group of Italian agricultural workers to form a farming colony in Alabama.[51] Hull-House was one of many settlements in American towns before the First World War which were to influence the provision of parks and better town planning.

It was photographer and journalist Jacob Riis whose talk in Hull-House in 1898 led to the creation of Chicago's Special Parks Commission in 1899, which involved Jensen in the provision of children's playgrounds and swimming pools in parks, and field-houses – the equivalent of settlement houses – to provide social services.

In 1923 the Regional Planning Association of America was formed, a body which saw the relevance of garden city ideals. Most of its drive came from New York left-wing intellectuals including architects Clarence Stein (1882–1975) and Henry Wright (1878–1936), and from writer Lewis Mumford (1895–1990) in particular.[52]

Mumford's main concern was to find an alternative to urban sprawl and congestion which followed the dominance of the automobile. As these were remote from the concerns which had driven the original Garden City, the examples which followed were likely to be very different, especially as their sites, within reach of New York by train, were affected by the cost of land.

Radburn, a settlement built at Fairlawn, New Jersey, incorporated ideas tried at Sunnyside Gardens near Manhattan between 1924 and 1928, where housing was built in a 'superblock' which enclosed green space for gardens and recreation, and the concept of the neighbourhood unit, recognized by planner Clarence Perry (1872–1944) in his Forest Hills home. The 'neighbourhood' was identified as a small social unit with a school, which could act as a building focus for part of a larger whole. Radburn was begun in 1929 and remained unfinished in 1933 as the recession began to bite, but created sufficient interest to be influential. The safe environment created by the separation of traffic from pedestrians by means of the superblock has been the feature most noted. The central enclosure thus created was accessed by footpaths, with a 'core of parkland or open space for recreation, circulation and general amenity'.[53] But Radburn was not able to build the full complement of schools, shops and play spaces which should have accompanied the central green space. Early photographs show detached housing around a green which looked as if it would be at home in Letchworth, with children riding bicycles along grass-edged paths. Radburn was copied successfully in Greenbelt, Maryland (1937–43) and Baldwin Hills Village, California (1941) amongst others in the USA, and the Radburn principle of town planning was to appear in Britain after the Second World War.

The Greenbelt Towns

Perhaps the thinking behind the construction of three towns during the period of the Wall Street Crash and agricultural depression during the 1930s owes more to the Howard Garden City ideal than its apparent paradoxes would allow. At this time the United States faced the possibility of social unrest due to agricultural workers leaving the land, and finding no work in the overcrowded towns with their high rates of unemployment. This was due to two main causes – farm machinery, and the Dust Bowl. The introduction of technology to farms resulted in the need for a smaller workforce. The Dust Bowl followed the ruin of the farmland in the southern mid-west due to the indiscriminate ploughing up of land which should have remained under pasture, and the subsequent blowing away of the topsoil.

Franklin Delano Roosevelt, President from 1933, favoured the traditional image of the good life on the land with its message of the benevolent forces of nature civilizing mankind. His preferred remedy was land colonization, with the return of men to the land. However, his economic adviser and then Under-Secretary of Agriculture, Rexford Guy Tugwell (1891–1979), thought differently. Tugwell, an agricultural economist at Columbia University, had no illusions about the harsh life farming could bring, with 'vicious, ill-tempered soil… makeshift machinery… happenstance stock, tired, overworked men and women… and all the pests and bucolic plagues that nature has evolved'.[54] Brought in to serve Roosevelt's New Deal, Tugwell's advice was to accept rural decline, and the need for new housing that would be required in Greenbelt Towns. This went along with some current thinking which saw the sense of supporting the 'growth poles', or places to which people migrated in search of work.

Plan of Greenbelt, Maryland, USA

One of only three planned towns built to alleviate the movement of people from the land during the time of the economic depression of the 1930s. Greenbelt, Maryland was built outside Washington, D.C. on the 'neighbourhood' principle developed in Radburn, New Jersey, ten years before, with blocks of houses enclosing green centres.

The Greenbelt Towns were satellite towns, placed on the outskirts of large towns similar to the Howard concept of the Social City. But Tugwell was not particularly influenced by Howard, and the significant factor in planning towns at this time was the need to accommodate the automobile. Tugwell was initially tempted by Le Corbusier's solution to urban pressure of an extensive green belt surrounded by high rise blocks. However this was dependent upon the availability of cheap land. Thus planners looked to Radburn and Clarence Perry's neighbourhood units.[55] There were twenty-five hopeful candidates for Greenbelt status, but the difficulties posed by attempting to achieve a similar concept with different state governments, were legion.

Finally only three Greenbelt towns were built, and a fourth, Greenbrook, planned. Greenbelt, Maryland, is outside Washington, D.C.; Greenhills, Ohio, is on the edge of Cincinnati; and Greendale, Wisconsin, is outside Milwaukee. All three were built on relinquished agricultural land with low housing densities; the first two adopted the superblock, the third, the grid pattern. Greenbelt was protected from private development from outside its edges by an encircling wide band of woodland; it had no industry. Housing design was in the modern style and with communal green provision in the centre of the two superblock layouts;[56] for Greendale, town planner Elbert Peets used the house style of colonial Williamsburg.

Distrusting Tugwell's perceived socialist ideals, and objecting to planning as a threat to private enterprise, Congress turned on the Greenbelt concept as interventionist, repealing legislation which gave power to appropriate land for building and funding. But Tugwell had achieved the near-impossible by the construction of his three Greenbelt towns in eighteen months, and his ideas re-emerged in the British New Towns programme after the Second World War. The Greenbelt plan lay less store by the value of contact with the soil than Howard's Garden City, but its origins were similar. Tugwell also wanted a more equal society to live in his new settlements, akin to the American small town in which 'no-one was very rich there, but no-one was very poor either', seeing that the advances of science could still go along with 'simplicity of life',[57] by managing one to meet the needs of the other.

Planning and the German garden cities

While Americans refused to have state control over their house building, Germans used planning to re-order both settlements and the people who lived in them. Before the First World War there was an exchange of planners between Germany and England, with each side discovering from the other ways to deal with the common problems of migration from the countryside and overcrowding in towns. Industrialization led to the development of allotment gardens to help feed the industrial poor, and *Schrebergärten* for the

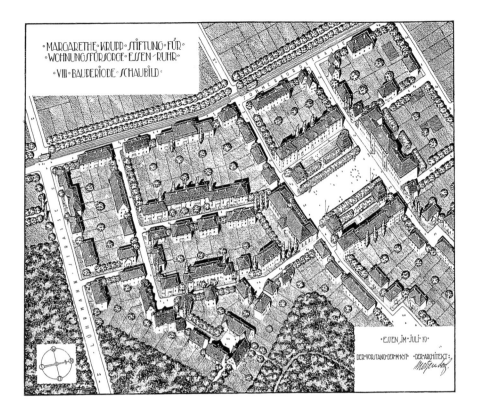

·MARGARETHE·KRUPP·STIFTUNG·FÜR·
·WOHNUNGSFÜRSORGE·ESSEN/RUHR·
·VIII·BAUPERIODE·SCHAUBILD·

·ESSEN·IM·JULI·19·
DER·VORSTAND·DER·M·K·ST· ·DER·ARCHITEKT·

improvement of health and education by exercize, founded by orthopaedic specialist Dr Schreber in Leipzig. Eventually these allotments became educational gardens on the edges of playgrounds.[58]

In 1902 a salesman, Heinrich Krebs, took Howard's ideas back to Germany and began the *Gartenstadtbewegung* (Garden City Movement). There were similar industrialist-paternalist settlements in Germany to the English ones, including Margarethenhöhe, built by the industrialist Krupp family in 1912 outside Essen. The plan for the settlement with cottage homes and terrace housing, with each family's garden forming part of an enclosed centre, was reminiscent of Unwin.[59] Hellerau, outside Dresden, was another such example, reflecting the Arts and Crafts ideas adopted by furniture-maker Karl Schmidt. Schmidt had founded the Dresden Craft Workshops in 1898, and decided to move his workers and build a garden city. Like Cadbury, he gave the control of the city to an independent company. The garden city was designed by architect Richard Riemerschmid according to Camillo Sitte's principles, and was intended to be a social experiment. Hellerau 'gave a massive stimulus to the general debate within the German Garden City movement'.

In Frankfurt a public housing plan was drawn up by Ernst May (1886–1970) who had been part of Unwin's team at Letchworth and Hampstead. His design approached the idea of the satellite city network, with a narrow green belt, each town made up of long terraces of modern houses. These had flat roofs

Above, left

Plan of Margarethen-höhe garden village, Metzendorf, Germany
This German village was similar to the earlier paternalist settlements in England. Built by the industrialist Krupp in 1912, the block of allotments in the west, the alignment of the cottage gardens towards the sun and the communal layout of the centres are reminiscent of Thomas Mawson at Port Sunlight and Parker and Unwin at New Earswick.

with gardens, and were single-family homes with gardens aligned to gather
the best of the sunshine. The green space along the river Nidda at Römerstadt,
Frankfurt-am-Main (admired by Christopher Tunnard), was used for
allotments, gardening schools for the young, market gardens, and sports
grounds, and originally housed blue-collar workers. Martin Wagner
(1885–1957) also designed modern garden cities during the Weimar period,
on the west and south sides of Berlin. Typical of his enterprise is Siemensstadt,
built round a Siemens factory, with four- and five-storey blocks placed in a
garden context, but with an accessible underground station. Architects such
as Gropius, Bartning and Scharoun contributed to Wagner's cities.[59]

But during the Nazi period, planning became a part of the sinister policy of
reshaping settlements with approved groups of people. Hitler's 'ethnographic
reorganization in the east' announced to the Reichstag in 1939, together with
Himmler's expression of his policy of Germanization as 'we have to take care
that only men of German – that is Germanic – blood will be living in the
eastern provinces'[61] explains the parallel indigenous planting policy explored
in Chapter Two. The physical expression of Nazi planned settlement was a
return to the traditional German village, with its roots in agricultural society,
based in the eastern provinces as towns were required also elsewhere to build
the industry needed for world domination. Allotments became part of the
process, as they were seen to bring about 'direct attachment to the soil'.[62] The
model for resettlement was provided by the geographer Walter Christaller
(1893–1969), who had studied population patterns in southern Germany and
discovered a hierarchy of settlements based on the distances people could
travel to market. This presented itself in a series of hexagons, each fitting into a
larger shape, as certain specialist functions provided by places on the hexagon
called forth longer journeys. Christaller's Central Place theory was extended
by the Nazis, to determine where country towns, railway stations and villages
would be built on land cleared of undesirables, and 'Germanized' by the
inward movement of more suitable populations.

Ebenezer Howard's Garden City concept attracted attention worldwide;
the 'Three Magnets' diagram was translated into Russian, Japanese, French
and German. An International Garden Cities and Town Planning Association
was formed in the 1920s. At a conference held by the Association in 1922 to
promote garden city ideals, it was recognized that there would be adaptation
of these ideals to suit different countries. The later American and German
examples in this chapter show how far it was possible to become removed,
both physically and philosophically, from the original.

Eventually most countries were to adopt the high-density, high-rise
solution to overcrowded cities. In France, Georges Benoît-Lévy, a paternalistic
industrialist, author of *La cité jardin* (the Garden City) in 1904, and one of its

chief promoters, saw the value of allotments (jardins ouvriers) for apartment dwellers around Paris. The high-rise superblock *cité-jardin*, with space in the centre for allotments, continued to be built in the 1930s. Plessis Robinson, on the southwest edge of Paris, has recently employed landscape architect and artist Jacques Simon to renovate the gardens.

Remarkably, the USSR (which emerged after the Revolution of 1917 and the civil war which followed) paid great attention to the bourgeois Howard's ideas, which could be assimilated into its drive for collective (though not 'democratic') ownership of property. There was much pre-Revolution interest in 'garden villages' and 'garden suburbs', the garden settlement having some connection with Russian village life.[63] But in the end high-rise buildings in large cities housed more people. Green belts and wedges of green spaces around towns appeared in the First Five Year Plan in 1928–32, giving some semblance of the urban/rural connection; Moscow's general plan of 1971, projected to 2000, encompassed a green belt and better protection for the forest it contained.

The Australians took principles of housing, town planning and regional development from the Garden City (Howard had included a plan of Adelaide surrounded by parks in his books), and the garden suburb is still considered an ideal environment in a spacious country.[64] In Japan, neither government, academics, nor architects fully engaged with the meaning of the garden city in Howard's terms, and it was variously translated as the 'flower garden city' or the 'vegetable growing city', ignoring the social considerations and interconnections of both town and village. Den-en Toshi, the first garden settlement in early Japanese terms, was developed in 1911 by the Mino Electric Railway Company as a place where commuters could escape from the city. Later, the pressure of population growth underlined the inevitability of large cities, and planners abandoned the garden city in favour of the garden suburb.[65]

How successful, then, was the Garden City? Common ownership of property by a small community presents difficulties for profit-driven societies. The flight from countryside to town still continues; to this must be added the global pressure of international migration from war-torn, disadvantaged countries, where the very scale of the problem defies any Howardian solution. The garden suburb with its low-rise housing only remains an attainable goal in developed countries. Howard's awareness of the value of the countryside, of ground for cultivation, of green belts round towns with their spaces for recreation and the lifting of the spirit, should also remain goals, however difficult to achieve.

The Americas and the Search for Identity: Landscapes from the 1930s to the 1960s

A remarkable spell of self-discovery in garden design was beginning in North and South America at the end of the 1930s, as both continents looked to their cultures and questioned the imported Beaux-Arts tradition. The results of this questioning were best seen in Brazil, Mexico and western USA, where a new generation of landscape architects began to design for indigenous lifestyles which owed less to Europe than before. That said, the two continents welcomed the modernist émigrés from Europe. In North America this included Ludwig Mies van der Rohe, who went to the Illinois Institute of Technology, László Moholy-Nagy, who founded the Institute of Design in Chicago, constructivist sculptor Naum Gabo, painter Piet Mondrian, and Walter Gropius, appointed Head of Harvard's Graduate School of Design. Through these men, interest was awakened in the work of other Europeans such as Vasily Kandinsky and Constantin Brancusi in Paris, inspiring landscape architects such as Garrett Eckbo in North America and sculptural garden-makers such as Isamu Noguchi.

Wartime reduced much private demand but created a need for social housing and landscaping; in the postwar economic expansion landscape architects found themselves busy with schemes for corporate headquarters, interior and rooftop gardens for skyscrapers, parks, factories, industry, and housing estates, as well as the private garden. In each case, the garden-makers of this chapter absorbed European modernism, but used it creatively in combination with their own national styles and the climatic requirements of the countries in which they lived. In this way they helped to evolve national styles of their own.

'Brasilidade' – Roberto Burle Marx (1909–94)

Born in Rio de Janeiro, of a Brazilian Roman Catholic mother and a German Jewish father, Roberto Burle Marx was to be hailed as the 'real creator of the modern garden' by the American Institute of Architects, a title he displayed proudly on his studio wall. Burle Marx fulfils all the qualifications required for this title: he used new materials such as concrete in hard landscaping as well as natural stone, his designs were abstract, and he worked with modern architects Lúcio Costa (1902–98) and Oscar Niemeyer so that his landscaping perfectly complemented the buildings it surrounded and was an extension of them. But his position in history is due to his originality in his use of plants in

Mosaics and planting by Roberto Burle Marx at Copacobana Beach, Rio de Janeiro
Grey, white and brown mosaics in abstract patterns were much used by Roberto Burle Marx; this example in Rio is the largest, broken by alternate planting of groups of street trees.

The Kronsforth garden, Teresópolis, Rio de Janeiro, Brazil

Made in 1955 for Albert Kronsforth, the garden displays a biomorphically shaped lake with a promontory, set on a hillside where it repeats the shapes of the highlands beyond. The garden was renovated by Ralph Carmargo in 1987, with flowering shrubs and spring bulbs set around the lake.

the handling of shape, texture and colour, the replacement of European plants by species better suited to the climate, and the passion with which he designed his gardens. Burle Marx was a multi-talented artist, skilled at jewelry-making, lithography, sculpture and textile-making. But it was painting which guided his plantsmanship. As a self-taught botanist, he used plants in his schemes as if they represented colour on a canvas, building two- or three-dimensional patterns on large landscapes.

The Rio de Janeiro of Burle Marx's youth was the capital of Portuguese-speaking Brazil, and similar to Chicago in its attraction for European immigrants. One of the largest countries in the world, Brazil's climatic and vegetational zones extend from the lush equatorial rain-forest around the Amazon basin, to the dry cactus-growing tropical grasslands of the north-east. The Portuguese came in the sixteenth century with slaves from west Africa; eventually they were followed by many nationalities from Europe, some fleeing from the Napoleonic wars or, later, persecution of the Jews. The abundant tree-cover encouraged by the high temperatures and high rainfall encouraged settlers to exploit the timber – including *hevea brasiliensis*, the rubber tree. Later came the development of plantation agriculture, including coffee and sugar. The settlers stripped away the trees and grassland flora, and exposed the forest floor to soil erosion. Rio, with its harbour, became a trading centre with large, colonial-style homes, built on the wealth from agriculture and timber, diamonds and other minerals. Gardens were made in the formal Portuguese, English, French and German styles of the nineteenth century, matching the colonial architecture of the houses. Burle Marx grew up in this polyglot community, for which his landscaping helped to provide a Brazilian consciousness, and an awareness of the need for the conservation of its landscape and flora.

Burle Marx was awakened to the significance of indigenous Brazilian flora in the botanical gardens of Berlin-Dahlem at the age of eighteen, having come to Germany partly to see an eye specialist, but mainly to study painting.[1] The discovery underlined the restricted colonial outlook of his boyhood background, and also his growing interest in plants – he had grown vegetables to sell for pocket-money in his parents' garden. On his return to Brazil he enrolled at the National School of Fine Arts in Rio, to study art. Here architecture was beginning to be taught, but prior to 1930, there was virtually no architectural profession in Brazil. Rio was dominated by the Beaux-Arts tradition, in the belief that 'Europeanization' was 'civilization'.[2] Architect and city planner Lúcio Costa lived near Burle Marx and knew him from childhood. He was also Burle Marx's professor at the School of Fine Arts, recognized his interest in plants, and his talent in combining them in his garden at home. Burle Marx's career began with Costa's recommendation to friends that Burle Marx should design gardens for them; and through Costa, Burle Marx met Oscar Niemeyer (b. 1907), the cariocan who was instrumental in introducing free-form architecture to Brazil.

Burle Marx's career developed rapidly; by 1934 he had become Director of Parks and Gardens in Recife, and four years later, he worked with the Costa and Niemeyer adaptation of Le Corbusier's brief for the Ministry of Education and Culture in Rio. Marx designed two roof gardens for the tall building, and, round its base, the first public gardens in Rio. In the 1940s he worked on public parks, the most notable being the garden of the Pampulha Museum of Art at Belo Horizonte, and at Araxá, in Minas Gerais.

One of his best-known private gardens was created from 1946, for Odette Monteiro in Corrêias near Petropolis. He was to design many more into the 1950s and beyond. In 1949 he bought a property in the country within reach of Rio – the sítio Santo Antonio da Bica – with his brother Siegfried. It was to be their home, garden and nursery, and is now owned by the government of Brazil. Major projects for Rio followed in the 1950s, including the development of the Bay of Rio de Janeiro from the airport of Santos Dumont to the Copacobana beach, where Marx designed the long brown, black and white mosaic pavements. Here he landscaped the gardens of the Museum of Modern Art, and the Park of Flamengo, which was made on land reclaimed from the sea. The monotony of the long freeway system here was broken with different groups of street trees. He landscaped hospitals, embassies, banks, university campuses, civic centres and city squares. In 1954 Burle Marx was appointed Professor of Landscape Design in the School of Architecture, University of Brazil. By 1960 Rio ceased to be the capital, and there was more work, with Niemeyer, in the new capital at Brasilia for the Ministries of Foreign Affairs, Justice, and the Army, and the garden of the Vice-President of the Republic.

Burle Marx did not confine his work to Brazil. There were commissions in Argentina, Venezuela, Chile, California, South Africa, Washington D.C. and Paris. He visited Asia and toured Europe and North America, lecturing and visiting museums and landscapes. This brief history indicates the immense influence and energy of the man, and it is sad that so much of his work has vanished or been badly maintained. This is partly through the lack of public money to maintain the gardens. But in Brazil there has been resentment of what was considered a politically high-spending regime with which Burle Marx was associated.

All commentators stress the importance Burle Marx attached to the use of Brazilian species in his planting schemes. By 1940 he had banned the use of all European plant species.[3] There was, in the cultural discussion of the time, especially in the writing of Oswaldo de Andrade, a need to discover the 'national essence' of Brazil or *brasilidade*,[4] which could be done by absorbing imported material and turning it into something Brazilian. However in Burle Marx's work there was as much about ecology, the conservation of disappearing species, and the use of tropical plants for tropical climates, as there was about *brasilidade*. He also used plants from South Africa, India, Malaya, Hong Kong, Mexico, Australia, Central America and many other tropical sources in his gardens.

The artist in Burle Marx at first experimented with placing his plants in asymmetrical, non-axial shapes deriving from modernist Europe. From the 1950s he moved more towards the free-form designs of California, using the swinging, biomorphic rhythms which resonated so well with the swelling mountains and sinuous curves of the harbour at Rio and its hinterland.[5] Free form matched the natural world, the flow of the river, the shapes of leaves and trunks in the forest. Free form also suited the large spaces in which Burle Marx's designs were placed. In its simplest expression, a flowing tapestry was made by two swinging lines of different coloured grass – *Stenotaphrum secundatum* and its variety *variegatum* – at the Museum of Modern Art, Rio.

Burle Marx used water in his landscapes, with smooth-edged winding lakes interrupted by promontories, reflecting the sky or the shadows of tall trees, as at the Olivo Gomes residence at São José dos Campos. Here, tower trees, *Schizolobium parahybum*, helped to bring interest to a flat landscape beyond the lake. Some lakes had narrow stone insets, forming compartments for lilies and other water plants. At the Teresópolis garden of Ralph Camargo, golden hemerocallis formed a wide border to the water and palm trees gave a vertical dimension to the picture. In some gardens, such as that of Raul de Souza Martins, also at Teresópolis, there were formal water walls and cascades on different levels, using concrete and local stone. Planter boxes were set into the pools by the cascades, with a massing of the deep-cut leaves of *Philodendron*.

Local stone also appeared as boulder displays in Burle Marx's *sítio* and in other dry gardens contrasted with cactus, *Sansevieria*, and spiky, red-flowered Christ's Thorn. In the garden of the Museum of Modern Art, Rio, tall blocks of granite contrast with water-rounded stones. Sometimes boulders were arranged around the bole of a tree, or partly enclosed a small bed placed in paving.

Burle Marx used tiles in walls, as in Portugal. Here they metamorphosed into Brazilian mode with biomorphically shaped decoration; sometimes

Olivo Gomes garden, São José dos Campos
A flat site was transformed by Burle Marx for Olivo Gomes in 1950 by the wide spacing of *Schizolobium parahybum* trees (the Tower tree), which are mirrored in the lake; while below them, *Thyphonodorum lindleyanum* take on the appearance of water birds poised for a catch.

Opposite, above and below
**Odette Monteiro Garden,
Petrópolis, Rio de Janeiro**
The Fazenda Marambaia
was bought by the
Monteiros in 1946, and
Burle Marx fashioned a
sinuous lake, planting the
edges with arum lilies,
philodendron and
bamboo. He chose forest
trees to landscape the
wider site. A new owner,
Luis Cesar Fernandez,
asked Burle Marx back
to restore the landscape
in the 1980s, and he
defined the paths around
the lake and planted the
slopes with succulents,
grasses, flowering
shrubs and brilliant
mesembryanthemums.

tiles were placed in combination with mosaic as for Olivo Gomes at São José dos Campos. Murals were made of a mixture of mosaic and concrete panels, as for Francisco Pignatari at São Paulo. His characteristic brown, black and white mosaics evolved from the local use of natural stone for pavements.

Burle Marx sought out plants on expeditions into the rainforest and elsewhere. He must have been aware of the unique, animal shapes of individual plants: the raw and wild framework of the *Pithecolobium tortum* Mart tree; the strange winged outlines of giant arums, *Typhodorum lindleyanum,* and *Montrichardia arborescens* stalking through the pools. Mopheaded ponytail trees, *Beaucarnis recurvata,* seemed to wait for the take-off of *Vriesia imperialis* beneath them. Alien spikes of xerophytes crouched in rocks by paths. All manner of palms preened in the sun.

As there were few nurseries in the early stages of his work, only small trees or seedlings were available in large quantities at first. Burle Marx's own nursery therefore had a valuable role to play in the placing of appropriate species in the landscape. Two examples illustrate some of Burle Marx's characteristic landscapes: the private garden of Odette Monteiro from his early work in the 1940s, and the garden of the State University of Santa Catarina at Florianopólis, made in the 1970s.

Julio and Odette Monteiro purchased land in the rainforest region to the north of Rio, near Petrópolis, in 1946. The Fazenda Marambaia had been part of the sugar and coffee plantation economy at the foot of the Serra do Orgãos, dark, granitic mountains which rise like domes behind the valley in which the farm was located. Lúcio Costa and Burle Marx were asked to design a house and landscape the grounds; later modernist Costa was replaced by Wladimir Alves de Souza who built a neo-colonial house.

Plantation farming had stripped away the natural forest here, but Burle Marx sought to use the indigenous trees from the fringes of the estate. A lake was made at the bottom of the valley by damming a pre-existing stream. From the lake, a gentle slope led to the house. The lake edge was kept clear apart from boldly planted clumps of *Philodendron bipinnatifidum,* and the streamside was planted with bamboo and *Zantedeschia aetheopica,* the white arum lily.

The Fazenda Marambaia was neglected after the death of the Monteiros, and the new owner, Luis Cesar Fernandez, asked Burle Marx to restore it in the 1980s. The garden was visited by plantswoman Sima Eliovson for her book on Burle Marx's gardens, and by Rossana Vaccarino in the late 1990s. Their descriptions and photographs give some idea of the planting and the changes which took place in the thirty years from the sculptured and unrefined picture displayed in P. M. Bardi's *The Tropical Gardens of Burle Marx.*[6]

In the 1980s and late 1990s the estate was encircled by sandy paths which wound round behind the lake, joining at the front of the house where the colours of pink rhododendrons, azaleas and bougainvillea resonated together. There is a dramatic view of the peaks of the Serra do Orgâos rising above the trees from the path which winds away from the house, borrowed scenery whose black tops are accentuated and contrasted by the vibrancy of the colour in the valley – nature assimilated, controlled, and enriched. From the path, neatly contained by stone edging, short grass contains a vivid carpet of mauve mesembryanthemums. These lead the eye towards a startling juxtaposition of scarlet rhododendron set above the lake. Between the lake and the path are masses of golden-yellow, formed in part by hemerocallis. On the slope rising above the lake spiky bromeliads

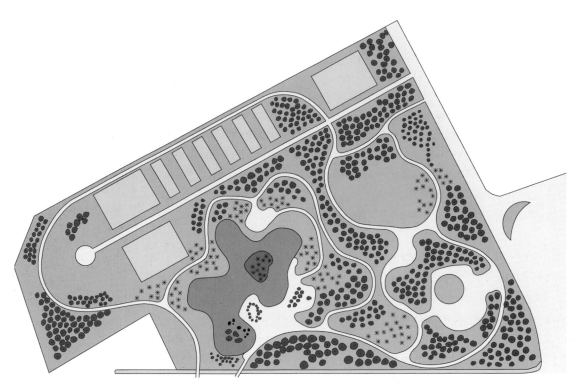

Ground and planting plan for Santa Catarina State University garden
In 1970, Burle Marx designed the mosaic pavement and planting layout for the university garden of Santa Catarina at Florianopólis, south of Rio. The swinging curves of the paths, the essential freeform design, was matched by abstract blocks of planting ranging from tall palms to smaller datura (*brugmansia*) in the centres of the beds.
See also planting list (opposite).

and tall flowering pampas grass add texture below the tree-line. As the path descends into the valley, sharp, sword-shaped succulents are planted beneath shrubs on the slopes, and the flowering shrubs interspersed with sinuous outlines of ground-cover. On the house side of the walk, different coloured bands of coleus – purple, red, and yellow-green – wind in and out of each other. The pattern is joined by white and yellow chlorophytum from South Africa.

Plans for the second garden, at the State University of Santa Caterina at Florianopólis, south of Rio on the Atlantic coast, show Burle Marx contrasting biomorphic garden shapes with the abstract geometry of the layout for the university. Made in October 1970, two years after the beginning of Burle Marx's partnership with architects Haruyoshi Ono and Jose Tabacow, the university's buildings are placed in spaces around an irregular rectangle. Each building is contained by a wide mosaic pavement, which is joined to an equally irregular grid-pattern ground plan. Seen from above, brown, white, and black mosaics establish an abstract shape on the pavement, suggesting a short-tailed fish with open mouth. A half-circle of trees at the entrance to the university is cut by a T-shaped asphalt path which bisects the ground plan and leads towards the faculty buildings, adding another dark element to the design on the ground. Everywhere the pavement mosaics are punctuated by round and square beds for trees and shrubs.

The gardens lie behind a flat terrace of white mosaics with bars and rectangles of coffee-brown breaking the expanse. The free-form shapes making up the garden are controlled within a triangle. Paths wind and snake around amoeboid spaces with their nuclei made from beds in their centres. Planting spills across boundaries and on to the terrace. Burle Marx uses groups of the same species which echo each other but never become repetitive. The centre of the space may contain scented, trumpet-shaped *Brugmansia suaveolens* with the evergreen shrubs philodendron and *Brunfelsia pauciflora* forming blocks around the palm *Euterpe edulis* as a centrepiece. Elsewhere the Queen Palm, *Arecastrum romanzoffianum*, with its yellow dates, joins the euterpe as block planting beside sinuous paths or a link between other green masses.

Ranches and gardens in Mexico: Luis Barragán (1902–88)

Luis Barragán shared a consciousness of nationality with his contemporary, Roberto Burle Marx. Both looked to their colonial homelands and sought to create something new; but where Burle Marx used plantsmanship in his native Brazil, Barragán's minimalist Mexican landscapes emerged from architecture, with plants giving structure to the whole. He was concerned to make gardens which were sensitive to the natural landscape, to its Spanish history, and to the modern Mexican culture. This led him to create contrasting landscapes – closed, Mediterranean courtyards in his early work, gardens related to the volcanic El Pedregal, and minimalist aristocratic ranches in his later years. Barragán's place in the history of landscape design is as important for his legacy of Mexican modernism, as it is for the legacy of colour, simplicity, and tranquillity which flow from his landscapes.

Luis Barragán was born in 1902, the third of nine children, eight years before the Mexican revolution. His parents had a farm – the Hacienda des Corrales – in the countryside in Guadalajara. Luis was educated at Roman Catholic schools, and remained strongly but quietly Catholic thereafter. Mexico had been colonized by the Spanish until 1821, which was reflected in the architecture of churches and large houses, and with which Barragán was familiar. After more than a decade of unrest, peace was only regained from 1924, when General Plutarco Calles (1877–1945) took control and began the reform of agriculture; he also set out to curb the influence of the Roman Catholic church. Calles's successor, General Lázaro Cárdenas (1895–1970), began the land redistribution scheme which led to the loss of much of the Barragán family estate in 1935. Barragán had become an outsider – rich, and a Catholic, and perhaps for these reasons, underestimated in his homeland.

Before the land reforms (which preceded their deaths) Barragán's parents had been comfortably off, and horses and the peace of rural surroundings were powerful images in his later work. He studied for a diploma at the Free School of Engineering in Guadalajara from 1919, presumably to work in the

Planting list (partial) for Santa Catarina State University garden
(opposite)
*Arecastrum romanzoffianum (Cham.) Becc.
Bactris lindmaniana Drude
Brunfelsia pauciflora (C & S) Bent.
Carinia estrellensis (Raddi) Ktze.
Chorinia speciosa St. Hil.
Cordia sylvestris Fresen.
Cordia trichotoma (Vell.) Arrab.
Coutorea hexandra (Jacq.)
Cybistax antisyphilitica (Mart.) Mart. ex D.C.
Datura suaveolens Humb. et Bonpl.
Erythrina crista-galli L.
Erythrina falcata Benth.
Erythrina reticulata Presl.
*Euterpe edulis Mart.
Lantana camara L.
Lushea divaricata Mart.
Matayba guianensis Aubi.
Peltophorum dubium Taub.
Philodendron bipinnatifidium Schott.
Plumbago capensis Thunb.
Pouteria lasiocarpa (Mart.) Radik
Randia armata (Sw) D.C.
Zebrina purpusii Brueckner

*palms

construction of houses for men of private means. But he found himself more attracted to architecture which he pursued at the School after his degree, leaving his studies unfinished to visit France and Mediterranean Europe between 1925 and 1927. Whilst in Paris, he went to the International Exposition des Arts Décoratifs of 1925, there coming into contact with European Modernism. This was, for him, a period of exploration of the Mediterranean roots of Mexican culture. In 1930 and 1931 Barragán briefly visited Chicago, then New York, where he wrote an essay on gardens[7] and later, returned to Europe, meeting Le Corbusier and French painter and garden-maker Ferdinand Bac. The early phase of Barragán's work therefore reflects a mixture of influences – Spanish/Moorish, Mexican, Mediterranean, combined with modern functionalism. Throughout, he designed houses and gardens together.

From 1935, following Barragán's move from Guadalajara to Mexico City, came a productive period in which he built modern houses and gardens and became involved in speculative development. Mexico City was expanding fast and he was able to buy land; in 1944 he acquired the lava field of El Pedregal, using this apparently harsh wilderness as a setting for houses with gardens closely linked to the landscape. At this time the Mexican artist Jesús 'Chucho' Reyes Fereira worked with him, enriching Barragán's choice of colour and his interest in traditional Mexican architecture. The 1940s saw collaboration with the modernist architect Mathias Goeritz in the remodelling of a chapel and the convent for Capuchin nuns: the *Capuchinas Sacramentarias del Purisimo Corazón de María*, with its serene courtyard garden and simple, glowing interior (1953–60).

Landscapes for larger residential development, such as Las Arboledas and Los Clubes, made between 1958 and 1964, stand out for their equestrian associations. Barragán's commission, with architect Sordo Madeleno, for a satellite city for Mexico was never realized, though the designs for Lomas Verdes illustrate an austere approach to town planning. Illness curtailed his output in the last twenty years of his life.

Barragán's attraction to the work of Ferdinand Bac (1859–1952) arose from the gardens which Bac drew in his book, *Jardins Enchantés*, and his landscape for Les Colombières, a house near Menton. Bac, like J. C. N. Forestier, rejected much of what he saw in the eclectic styles and undistinguished villa and garden building of the French Riviera.[8] Born in Stuttgart to illegitimate parents, his father from the French royal family and his mother from a French countess, Bac took up residence in France, learned to paint, and became a writer. He had come to garden creation late in life, wanting to create a new synthesis of Mediterranean culture in the landscape which would use the old forms but in a new assemblage of ideas, 'stripping them of every ornamental element specific to eras, religions, individual societies, to discover the ancestral sign that could unify them in a single culture, in a common climate from the same sea'.[9]

He made three gardens, one of which has been destroyed. The work for a rich banker's widow, Marie-Thérèse de Croisset, the mother of the notable patron Marie-Laure de Noailles, involved remodelling her villa near Grasse. Between 1913 and 1919 the house was extended, and the hill slope upon which it stood was terraced both above and below the villa. The finished picture, with its house painted deep Venetian 'Carpaccian' red, tiers of arcaded buttressing walls, pergolas and cloisters with clipped evergreen arches to match, and with contrasting pencil cypresses, created a very dramatic 'Franciscan simplicity' on the hillside. It also combined the styles of the Italian villa with formal pools and fountains, and replaced exotics with Mediterranean plants.[10]

But the work which captured the imagination of Luis Barragán was Bac's third garden of Les Colombières, begun in 1920 for his friends Emile and Caroline Octavie Ladan-Bokairy at Garavan near Menton. The house and garden were to be seen as one, with a common theme – the voyage of Ulysses; Bac, having found satisfaction in garden-making for friends with whom he would spend the rest of his days, felt himself at one with the returning hero.[11] Not understanding the modernist message, Bac had found the gardens he had seen at the 1925 Exposition to be constructs devoid of meaning. In Les Colombières he was able to pursue his aim of making meaningful gardens of enchantment, magic and tranquillity, weaving the themes into his *Jardins Enchantés*.

Whilst not imposing metaphor and meaning on his early gardens in Guadalajara, Barragán adapted the mystery and colour of Bac's courtyard gardens, which he saw in *Jardins Enchantés* and Bac's book about Les Colombierès. Later he wrote 'One must be suspicious of open gardens that allow the possibility of discovery at first sight. I love the beautiful gardens of the east, divided by arcades and hedges that form enchanting enclosures, that value spaces and transform nature into a true home'.[12] His houses are separated from the street by enclosed courtyards in which gardens link house with outside. In the courtyards are broad steps leading down to rectangular pools with simple fountains, as at the González Luna House (1929), and perhaps a tree or scented plant. Some houses had pergolas and pavilions; others had enclosed roof terraces with agaves and other plants in pots. Rounded archways, flat roofs and white surfaces decorated with triangles speak of a mix of Moorish-led Mexican influences.

In the 1940s, following Barragán's move to Mexico City, his houses took on more of the nature of the International Style. El Pedregal, the speculative

Painting from Ferdinand Bac's *Jardins Enchantés*, 1925
Colourful, mysterious depictions of Moorish buildings painted by Ferdinand Bac, find echoes in the courtyards of architect Luis Barragán's early buildings.

development made on the lava field, secured Barragán's reputation for house and garden-making in Europe and the United States,[13] largely as the result of the evocative black and white photography of Armando Salas Portugal. Show houses were built on the 800-acre (323-hectare) site , with courtyards full of strong sunshine and deep shadows. The geometry of the houses contrasted with the wildness around them, made all the more startling by the planes of colour of the house walls – introduced by 'Chucho' Reyes. Here Barragán's demonstration of the landscape cradling the house recalls the work of Frank Lloyd Wright. The contorted viscous shapes of the brown and black lava field were left intact, 'taking advantage of their texture and forms as the most decorative and impressive elements'.[14] In the gardens, little construction was needed apart from steps in the rock, some enclosing walls, and the necessary swimming pool. At Avenida de las Fuentes a pool was cut into the rock, with its formal rectangle at the house end transformed into irregularity as it sought to link to the landscape. A lawn and native rock, steps, and a way up to a balustrade were all reflected in the glass wall of the living room. Simple groupings of trees including pine, pepper and oak, some drought tolerant cacti, *Senecio praecox*, perhaps jacaranda and mimosa might be used in related gardens, and where topsoil had been added there were wider possibilities. The gardens of El Pedregal were enclosed, and the walls to the streets, with their trees and cascades of climbing plants, were to invoke a vertical walled garden. The simplicity of the theme resonated with Barragán's growing awareness of Japanese gardens; he had a large collection of Japanese books and prints, and considered making a Zen garden.

Mexico City was growing too fast for the comfort of its inhabitants in the 1950s, and where possible, those with sufficient resources moved out to its fringes. From 1958 Barragán became involved in developments for men who kept horses; firstly, at Las Arboledas, sited fourteen miles from the city, and later at Los Clubes nearby (1961–72). Here Barragán could please himself, ignoring the neo-colonial styles still preferred by some of the middle classes, and pulling away from Corbusian modernism. Together with other investors, Barragán bought the land, and divided it into single-family plots. Here he planned houses and stables, with leisurely, spacious, horizontal planes, water, and trees. Bridle-paths were established, and distances between features were spaced in relation to horse and rider. At the end of an avenue of eucalyptus trees was set the long, gently spilling water trough for the horses – El Bebedero. The success of this development led him to Los Clubes nearby.

Opposite
El Pedregal
Part of a development made from 1945 on a lava field, Barragán used the contorted shape of the volcanic outpouring as a surrounding mantle in which he placed his simple garden. Added topsoil enabled the making of a lawn, and indigenous trees were used, so that the houses and gardens appeared to have grown from their sites.

Below
El Bebedero, Las Arboledas, Mexico City
Las Arboledas (1959–62), like Los Clubes, was a development made for wealthy men who loved riding. Distances were measured in terms of travel on horseback. El Bebedero, the drinking trough, was a long shining rectangle of water like glass, set under eucalyptus trees – a park for horses and riders.

Folke Egeström House, Los Clubes, Mexico City, 1966

Los Clubes was built between 1961 and 1972. The white Folke Egestrom House contrasts with the strong colours of the horse enclosures, where the shallow pool for exercize was fed by a chute, and minimal container planting contrasted with the trees outside.

As at Las Arboledas, the horse was central to the design. A recurring feature was the water chute created from a girder placed high above a shallow rectangular pool, the plashing sound breaking the stillness of the courtyard and reminiscent of similar fountains from Barragán's boyhood village, where hollowed wooden logs had conveyed water to stone troughs. 'Chucho' Reyes had encouraged the use of colour, which from the 1950s became part of the dynamic rather than a decoration of a building, changing dramatically in the strong Mexican sunshine. At first Barragán's palette was made up of pink, chocolate, blue and white; at Los Clubes he used strong purple, magenta-pink and orange-red on the plain horizontal walls of the stables of San Cristóbal. Enclosed by these walls and reflected in them, were the expanses of water where the horses could exercize. A low planter with trees related the woodland outside to the horse-space within. The Folke Egerström house in Los Clubes echoed these features, perhaps presenting the best-known images of Barragán's landscaping for horses, with its space, water and colour in the rectangular planes of the walls. Here, in an inner courtyard around the one-storey house, the landscaping for man took on a similar pattern to that for the horse – at a smaller scale. A swimming pool echoed the exercize pool for the horses. Around it, a roofed terrace provided a cool retreat. Paving next to the pool gave onto a lawn which was greener than the grass for the horses, and beyond the lawn a rose-covered pergola softened the angularity of the courtyard. The landscape of Las Arboledas and Los Clubes created another dimension to Barragán's work, fusing the traditional Mexican solidity of structure with the geometry of the International Style. Colour is the decoration, minimalism the aim.

Barragán's work has attracted more influence beyond his own country, where he is still regarded as an outsider – one who supported the old institutions of church and society when both were unpopular. Elsewhere Barragán's colourful planes and sparing plant range have entered the vocabularies of other designers, such as Tadao Ando in Japan, Christian de Groote in Chile, Edouardo Souta de Moura in Portugal[15] and Fernando Caruncho in Spain.

The Room Outside: Thomas Church (1902–78)

If any landscape designer deserves the credit for launching the garden for outdoor living, it should be Thomas Church. In so doing he reflected, as did plantswoman Kate Sessions , the emerging Californian self-confident personality. But where Sessions was close to the pioneer fringe shaping settlements out of virgin territories, Church was part of the next wave, catering for a more sophisticated society. With some two thousand or so commissions to his name by the end of his life, Church helped to establish the garden for an 'outside' lifestyle for the consumer society which was part of a new Californian regional consciousness. In so doing he involved people with landscapes, as Christopher Tunnard had in England. His book, *Gardens Are For People* (1955), also made people the participants, not the onlookers, in the garden.

In 1848 Mexico ceded California to the United States, and it became the thirty-first state in 1850. From some two thousand settlers at that time, beginning with the gold rush of 1849, the population was set to double every twenty years. Incomers came from Spain, and other Europeans came after a generation's settlement on the east coast; there were also Chinese and Japanese. With an influx of that speed and complexity, young California became rapidly independent of its colonial parents. It was mature enough to celebrate its Spanish roots in San Diego in the first thirty-five years of the twentieth century; garden designer Florence Yoch incorporated Spanish themes in the gardens she designed for film tycoons in southern California.[16] Santa Barbara required buildings in its centre to be made in Spanish style in 1925.

California's large zones of predictable Mediterranean climate had launched a thriving agricultural industry, and had created a new one – the movies. Defence and high-tech industries were to join agribusiness at the time of the Second World War. It was a state which had survived the recession of 1929 – the year in which Church began to practise – and the Second World War, the involvement of the USA creating a temporary cessation of garden design due to the shortage of materials.

A Bostonian by birth, Thomas Church's formative years were spent partly in the dry Ojai Valley in southern California, and partly in Berkeley, San Francisco.

Rejecting the law as a profession, he took a degree course in garden design in the College of Agriculture, following it by an MA in landscape architecture at Harvard's Graduate School of Design. Having travelled on a scholarship to Italy and Spain, he presented a thesis comparing landscape in California and the Mediterranean. Church was interested in the similarities between the scale of the early Italian villa, the outdoor lifestyle, the resources making such lifestyles possible, and the need for irrigation,[17] themes which influenced his garden making for most of his career.

The recession reduced the availability of work, but Church did not seek out the flamboyantly rich who patronized the likes of Florence Yoch in the south. He was always concerned to provide what the client wanted; and his clients in the San Francisco Bay Area did not require large estate gardens or lavish houses. The owners needed 'a two-car garage and a place for guests to park'. The house should have its screened service area, privacy from the neighbours, a play area for the children, shade, a swimming pool and a barbecue area. There should be a lawn, and a paved terrace for sitting on and 'to entertain lots of people'.[18]

The garden was designed with the considerations of site, water supply, and the needs and capabilities of its owner. Required sites in the San Francisco region were often small or on steeply sloping ground, restricted or angular plots. Church's designs had to play with perspective, and attempt to contrive additional flat space. This he did by the use of wooden decking built out over the hillside – perhaps for the first time in gardens. To answer the demand for low maintenance, a narrow range of trouble-free plants was provided; it was no use placing fussy tender specimens if the owner did not know how – or have the time – to care for them. In a 'country garden' he suggested a mix of sedum, senecio, artemisia, and lavender, the shades of grey contrasting with colour provided by agapanthus, aster and pink canna.[19]

Readers of the popular gardening magazines of the west – *House Beautiful*, and *House and Garden* – saw and could identify with his designs. Church contributed to *Sunset*, 'The Magazine for Western Living', for whose ranch-style headquarters he designed a landscape. *Sunset* had been founded by the Southern Pacific Railroad, owners of large tracts of the west which they wanted to promote for settlement, attracting returning soldiers after the Second World War with their images of the outdoor lifestyle.[20] Church was one of the first to see the value of publicity to bolster the image of the landscape designer, and his regular contributions to *House Beautiful* from 1946 were to form the backbone of his book *Gardens Are For People* in 1955. Similarly, pieces written for the *San Francisco Chronicle* became part of *Your Private World: A Study of Intimate Gardens* in 1969. *Gardens Are for People* has been credited

with 'shaping a generation of informed clients and creating a demand for a specific brand of marketable skills'.[21]

Thomas Church set up an office in San Francisco in 1932, working frequently with architect William Wurster (1895–1973), whose office was in the same building. They joined forces in 1935 to design for a golfing community at Pasatiempo, near Santa Cruz in the Bay Area, when private contracts were difficult to find.[22] Coming from Harvard University, whose teaching of design was strictly Beaux-Arts classicism, it is not surprising that some of his early gardens showed classical-formal lines, with axes, avenues, and symmetry. He could, however, see how to incorporate classical ideas with modern lifestyles. In *Gardens are for People* he recalls the geometry of French parterres, recommending a modest version using boxwood or euonymus, santolina and teucrium, as 'suitable to our half-day-a-week gardening help' and 'biannual pruning'.[23] What he had seen at the 1925 Paris Exposition made its way into his gardens in the mid to late 1930s – in particular, Art Deco *motifs* such as the zig-zag, the right angle, and the arrow-head. The small Sullivan garden (1935), had a rectangular plot whose size was disguised by an L-shaped bed set at an angle into the lawn, neatly outlined by a low, clipped box hedge. The widest

Thomas Church, Sullivan Garden, San Francisco, 1935
This small town garden's design plays with right angles, especially the Art Deco zig-zag, which Thomas Church employed in his early gardens.

part of the bed sheltered a patio in the right angle formed by the two garden walls. Climbers were trained – again at right angles – up the wall backing the flower bed. Featured on the cover of the February 1937 edition of *Sunset*, the San Francisco Griffin garden displays a busy design using the zig-zag, cube and circle.

In the late 1930s, Church and his wife set off for Europe again. In 1937 they visited Scandinavia with Wurster, meeting the Finnish architect, painter and designer Alvar Aalto (1898–1976) in Helsinki before travelling on to Paris. After this, Church's designs underwent a change. Gradually, symmetry disappeared, and the shapes in his landscapes became rounded and abstract. However, Church never abandoned the zig-zag and the right angle – they were used in a different manner.

The explanation for this metamorphosis no doubt lay with Church's contact with European architects, painters and designers. Alvar Aalto's Villa Mairea, Noormarkku, Finland, made in 1939 for Maire and Harry Gullischen, encompassed much of Aalto's philosophy for the relationship of man with nature. There are many references to the forest in the Villa Mairea in the predominance of wood as a material, and the way it was used. The L-shaped, flat-roofed house enclosed an irregularly shaped swimming-pool, and its landscaping evoked a 'forest space' in the woodlands.[24]

Below

Plan for Martin Garden, Aptos, California, 1947
Possibly influenced by Burle Marx, Thomas Church later explored biometric forms in his gardens, though still finding a place for the zig-zag. In this simple beach-house garden, the design takes on the form of sand-dunes and waves, contained by angular decking.

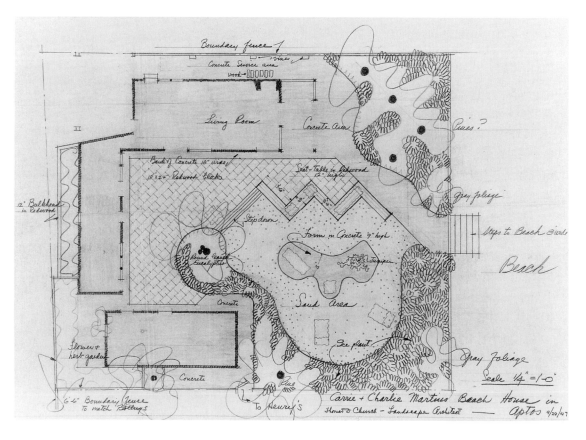

The Second World War increased the flow of talented Europeans to California. Thomas Church briefly put up architect Serge Chermayeff in his home in San Francisco in 1940, while Chermayeff searched for a job in the USA. Chermayeff saw a common purpose in the work of William Wurster, whose timber houses and view of nature accorded with his own.

Abstract art had little influence in the United States in the 1930s, but later the free-form paintings of Vasily Kandinsky (1866–1944), surrealist shapes of Catalan painter Joan Miró (1893–1983) and Los Angeles-born sculptor Isamu Noguchi (1904–88) began to attract landscape designers. Lawrence Halprin (b. 1916), who studied plant sciences and landscape architecture at Cornell and Harvard, joined Thomas Church's practice after the end of the Second World War, reinforcing Church's evolving modernism.

Ever since garden designer Peter Shepheard (1913–2002) identified them in 1953[26] the Martin Garden in Aptos and the Donnell Garden in Sonoma have remained as perfect illustrations of Church's move to abstract form and his strong connection of site with nature. Near neighbours in the northern California Bay Area, these surviving 1940s gardens link house, garden and coastal scenery. The Clark Beach House, a Wurster construction of timber from 1938, was landscaped by Church ten years later for the Martin family. A central sand area, occupying a position usually held by a lawn or pool, flows down to the beach via a serpentine path. The boundary between house and sand is a deck of redwood blocks, set in chequerboard fashion with a zig-zag edge. The sand 'lawn' (doubling as a play area for the children) has a rounded edge confined by a raised bed for mesembryanthemums, grading seawards into dune vegetation. Next to the house was a circular bed originally planned for eucalyptus.

Lawrence Halprin assisted Church in the making of the iconic garden at Sonoma. The cattle-raising Donnell family needed a new house on their ranch, and the site they preferred was the one on which they used to picnic, on a rise overlooking the bay with its sand and salt estuaries. The house had to wait, as in 1947 wartime restrictions prevented construction; but a pool could be made under regulations governing reservoirs for dealing with grass fires. The family wanted a swimming pool, changing facilities and a pavilion in which to lounge.

The Donnell Garden, Sonoma, California, 1947
Estuarine creeks appear in the distant haze over California Bay, framed by a live oak. Thomas Church wanted to preserve both. The creeks evoked the shape of the pool, which was designed by Church's colleague, Lawrence Halprin; the live oaks, some now gone, gave shade. Adaline Kent designed the sculpture in the pool (bottom) to be swum through or on which to sit or lie in the sun.

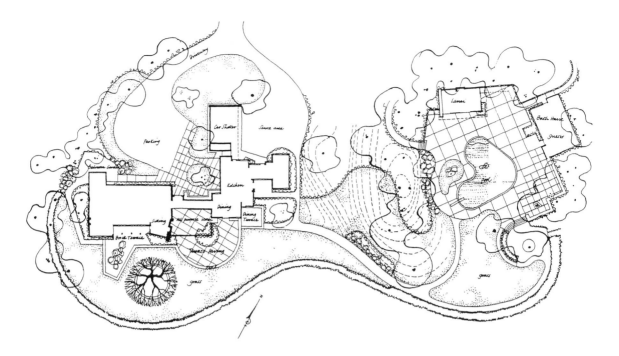

Plan for the Donnell Garden, Sonoma, California

Perhaps the best example of Church's freeform style of the 1940s, a juniper hedge encircles and combines the two elements of the Donnell garden – the house on the left and the pool and its 'lanai' changing room beyond the hillock to the right. Church's planting was spare but colourful, the green of the grass and live oaks reducing the glare of the sun.

The layout was discussed on site by Church and Halprin with Dewey Donnell; the bay was framed by a group of live oaks, which were to be incorporated into the design to give shade and wind-shelter. The shape of the swimming pool was Halprin's, but the overall landscape was Church's. The pool is a swinging curve beneath the trees, 'its shape inspired by the winding creeks of the salt marshes below'. At its centre is a concrete sculpture by Adaline Kent – one of the Bay Area's circle of artists – which can be swum through or sat upon. Granite boulders were placed as sculptural features. The concrete terrace round the pool was 'coloured tan to reduce glare'.[27] Redwood decking extended the area for activity, carefully cut to allow space for the live oaks. Later, when regulations allowed, changing rooms were made of concrete, and architect George Rockrise built the glazed *lanai* (Hawaiian for a sort of veranda, cabana or pavilion), again using local rock with a concrete roof.

Austin Pierpoint's house for the Donnells was built over the hillock, behind the pool, to which it was joined by a winding juniper hedge which encircled both pool area and house space in one biomorphic whole. To the indigenous live oaks Church added Monterey cypresses, with trees forming a screen on the northern boundary. The space between the boundary and the buildings was left under grass. Planting was spare, with rare splashes of colour from bougainvillea or wisteria. Paths were largely the result of 'desire lines' – the routes naturally followed by those using them. The Donnell house and pool garden forms the peak of Thomas Church's period of modernist design, an exercize in balance between nature and intervention.

Though he did design large projects – and he is likely to have been one of the first to use an aeroplane to make a preliminary survey – he is less known for the work he did with Wurster. This included the Valencia Public Housing Project for San Francisco (1939–43), planting for the Defence Workers' Housing project at Vallejo, California in 1941 (with Wurster as architect)[28] and the Park Merced middle-class housing project for Metropolitan Life in San Francisco (1941–50).[29] He also acted as consultant in 1957 for the landscaping of the General Motors Technical Center at Detroit for which the architects were Eero Saarinen and Associates, and he landscaped parts of Stanford University. Although he adopted European Modernism in design, it was his modernist friend and colleague Garrett Eckbo who is better known for its social application in California. Thomas Church stands as the first landscape architect to catch the imagination – through the press – of the new consumer society on the west coast of the United States, and to give it the stylish modern garden it desired.

The Harvard Rebels: Eckbo, Rose and Kiley

'Our grave is on axis in a Beaux-Arts cemetery.'[30]

Three young men arrived at Harvard's Graduate School of Design shortly after Church, at a point where a new dean, Joseph Hudnut, appointed in 1935, had begun to loosen its Beaux-Arts preoccupations. They were Garrett Eckbo, James Rose and Dan Kiley, who were destined to become, with the pioneering Thomas Church already a decade ahead, leading proponents of modern landscape design in the United States. There was a remarkable unity in their beliefs about the meaning of Modernism as a different way of comprehending landscape design. They wanted to shape this new discipline in a new university department, designing for house and garden together for outdoor living as 'a whole terrain of three-dimensional space made up of smaller units of design, some under roofs and some not, but all related.'[31] This philosophy had been expressed by Church, as had his belief that the client's needs were central to the garden. All were influenced by modern art, with shared admiration for designs coming from the Paris Exhibition of 1925 and Mies van der Rohe's Barcelona Pavilion of 1929. Each considered the Japanese approach to the spirit of the place – what Tunnard had called 'empathy'. But at Harvard they found their zeal for Modernism difficult to apply. A tale of the time has the chair of the landscape department announcing that any student attempting a modernist solution to the new assignment would 'automatically receive an X'.[32] Walter Gropius had been appointed to Hudnut's newly amalgamated faculty of architecture, landscape architecture and city planning in 1937. Marcel Breuer (1902–81), the Hungarian-born architect and director of the furniture workshop at the

Bauhaus, joined them in the same year, and Christopher Tunnard in 1938. Though landscape design was not taught at the Bauhaus, there were substantial links between the plastic arts and landscape; and Gropius and Breuer introduced the social awareness of European modernism. But Kiley found Gropius unsympathetic, and unwilling to 'accept the currency of fluid spatial dialogue between building and land'.[33] The result, according to their accounts, was much conspiratorial activity in the basement of Robinson Hall, where discussion led to articles which were later published in the architectural press. These set out approaches to modern landscape design[34] and damned the rigid historicism of the Beaux-Arts regime which Harvard seemed unable to replace.

Garrett Eckbo (1910–2001)

Eckbo, born in New York of an American mother and a Norwegian father, with 'limited social opportunities' and partly dependent upon his uncle in Norway to fund his university education, took up the landscape design course in the University of California's College of Agriculture in 1932 almost by accident.[35] The course was intended to lead to practical, professional competence, especially since the recession had led to more public work in parks, water management and land reclamation than private estates. After a short spell designing gardens for Armstrong Nurseries near Los Angeles, he won a scholarship to Harvard in 1936. He found the department under the rigid control of Henry Vincent Hubbard, and his 'Bible', *An Introduction to the Study of Landscape Design*. But, as Eckbo argued in the architectural magazine *Pencil Points* in 1938, 'Design shall be areal, not axial'.[36] 'By the eighteenth century the Beaux-Arts tradition was frozen in axial systems, yet the real world is only occasionally axial, and then by accident… Axial design tends to be static, its obvious purpose being to express and freeze the status quo'.[37]

Nevertheless Eckbo managed to use his years at Harvard to build connections with planners and architects and to establish himself by his writing and design work as a modernist following the lead of painting and the plastic arts. The first was a wise move in view of the growing demand for housing and the continuing effects of the depression on private work, but was also closely bound to Eckbo's social idealism. The second emerged very soon in his design for the Freeform Park for Washington, D.C. in 1937. Eckbo's master's thesis, which presented plans for the ideal American suburb,[38] respected the needs of the individual in a series of different designs for single-family households, each expressing the connection of house with garden. A central park provided coherence, featuring sports and community facilities and a social centre copied from Mies van der Rohe's Barcelona Pavilion of 1929, its reflecting pool remodelled for swimming.[39] The design, as with others

Eckbo presented as a student, took ideas from the American view of the garden city promoted by Clarence Stein (1882–1975) and Henry Wright (1878–1936), mentioned in Chapter Four.

The ideals were tested against reality in work done by Eckbo for the Farm Security Administration (FSA) for four years from 1938. California was perceived as the land of opportunity by victims of the 1929 Wall Street crash. The ploughing-up of land best suited to pasture, for grain cultivation in Kansas, Oklahoma and northern Texas in the early 1930s, was followed by a disastrous drought in 1934 and the blowing away of topsoil whose binding humus content had been destroyed by continuous cropping. The human fall-out from The Dust Bowl was the subject of John Steinbeck's *The Grapes of Wrath*. Thousands made their way into California.

Franklin Delano Roosevelt Memorial, Washington, D.C. (opened 1997)
Designed by landscape architect Lawrence Halprin as 'an experiential history lesson' to celebrate the life of President Roosevelt, the memorial incorporates a sculpture by George Segal called *The Bread Line*, recalling the queues at soup kitchens in the depression of the 1930s. Roosevelt's New Deal policy encompassed the Farm Security Administration which sought to alleviate homelessness and unemployment, and for which Garrett Eckbo worked.

President Roosevelt sought to relieve the hardship through the social and economic reforms of his New Deal during the 1930s. The work of the Farm Security Administration in California was only part of a wider initiative which, in its provision of work, encompassed reforestation and soil conservation, and included regional hydro-electric schemes such as that of the Tennessee Valley Authority. In the Central Valley of California temporary accommodation for large numbers had to be created quickly.[40] These planned, seasonal settlements somewhat resembled austere new towns in their prescribed configuration of hexagons and linear blocks. The sites, often on old ranch or farm space, were made more human by the division of lots by trees such as palms, eucalyptus, poplar, cottonwood, mulberry, and sycamore, with black locust and Siberian elm in dry hot areas of the southern Central Valley, and the provision of community facilities such as drying-yards for clothes, co-operative shops, parks and playgrounds. Residents were allowed small gardens. Tree-planting and trellises, magnolias, olives and oaks, provided

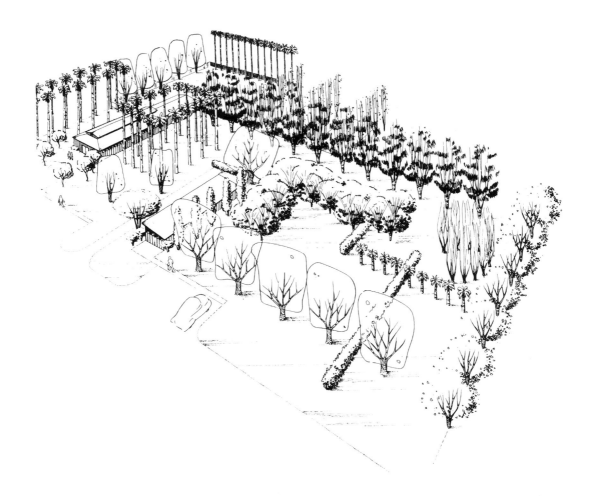

Weslaco Unit, Texas, 1939
Working for the Farm
Security Administration
gave Garrett Eckbo the
opportunity to design
camps for seasonal
agricultural workers that
used trees set in
asymmetric patterns,
shaping the spaces for
community needs.

shade and screening. Trees were excellent agents for stabilizing the soil in
large-scale enterprises. They also provided colour and inspiration. Eckbo, as
landscape architect for the FSA in San Francisco, tried to make the landscape
more human. He planned Winters, west of Sacramento, in apricot and walnut
orchards, disguising the formality with 'hedges, groves and lines of hackberry,
Chinese pistachio, and Chinese elm'.[41] Plans he made for Weslaco in Texas show
the influence of modern painting, with asymmetrical arrangements in grassy
spaces of right-angled, offset linear and part-circle hedges. The design for a
park for the settlement at Tulare seemed to garden historian Dorothée Imbert
'to draw more from patterns of paintings by László Moholy-Nagy [1895–1946]
or Kasimir Malevich [1878–1935] than from any rural precedent', which may
have given little comfort to the rural workers.[42] The FSA later embarked on
housing defence workers and internment camps for Japanese-Americans.

At the same time, Eckbo was involved in the setting up of Telesis, founded
at his house on Telegraph Hill in 1939. Telesis, described by Powers as 'a West
Coast equivalent of MARS [Modern Architecture Research Group] in England
but less riven by faction',[44] concerned itself with the environmental problems

of the Bay Area, seeking an holistic approach from all aspects of planning, whether cultural or physical.

The postwar period saw the further advancement of Eckbo as a leading landscape maker, through the firm he had created in 1945 with his brother-in-law Edward Williams, and architect and previous member of Church's practice Robert Royston. The economic climate was ripe for California's expansion, with new industries, new agricultural techniques, and a ready supply of incoming workers. As housing began to boom with the relaxation of building restrictions, Eckbo saw increasing opportunities in the south of the state. 'The south was larger, brighter, more powerful and impressive than the quiet, genteel north' he claimed,[45] and it was more dynamic and avant-garde with its collection of talented artistic émigrés around Los Angeles, to which Eckbo moved in 1946. The three men produced an impressive range of quality, modern work from then on, including parks, community housing, and private gardens.

It is perhaps easier to follow the influence of modern art in Eckbo's private gardens, than in his larger projects. In his student days he had been exercized by what he saw as false divisions in the gardening world between formal work, which 'forces architecture upon the landscape', and the informal garden, which 'forces the landscape upon architecture', arguing 'why not biology plus geometry?'[46] Eckbo's modern solution was a blend of skills within the firm, plantsmen who had been trained in design, and the placing of climatically appropriate plants in a setting sympathetic to landscape and its clients' needs.

There were no rules for design; like Christopher Tunnard, Eckbo disliked the concept of 'style'. He explored the modern artists' abandonment of perspective and their arrangement of objects within space to give meaning within an overall effect. Nevertheless there are features which he repeats in his gardens, but in compositions which are unique to him. His gardens invariably look inwards. Perhaps following Mies van der Rohe, he used overlapping planes in the garden form of offset hedges, to remove formal boundaries and invite further investigation of the spaces around. Like Church, he was intrigued by the zig-zag which he saw in Pierre-Emile Legrain's garden design for the Tachards near Paris in 1925, and which he used along edges of beds. Straight lines appeared in rows of trees, hedges, trellises, shadows cast by slim pergolas, and edges of pools. Sometimes these lines were grouped in swarms, as in his unrealized plan for the Burden garden in Westchester County, New York, in 1945, which has been likened to Vasily Kandinsky's *Composition VIII* of 1923.[47] Circular elements also appeared, as pools, half-circle hedges, beds, or paved areas joining one space to another, their origins perhaps again in Kandinsky or Moholy-Nagy. Most closely associated with abstract pattern is the Goldstone garden in Beverly Hills, made in 1948. Here, a biomorphic pool

Above
Vasily Kandinsky,
Composition VIII, **1923**
Eckbo's designs borrowed
Kandinsky's circles, half-
circles, triangles, grids and
darting lines, which
appeared in his 1948
Goldstone garden, Beverly
Hills (below left and right).

Opposite
ALCOA Forecast garden,
Laurel Canyon,
Los Angeles, 1959
Eckbo's own garden
was sponsored by the
Aluminium Company of
America to advertise the
versatility of the metal
used in making aircraft.
Screens and supports, even
a fountain, were made from
aluminium, with stone
and mosaic paving
acting in support.

lies across an elliptical space, its sunbathing patio sheltered by a triangular roof trellis, an irregular lawn joining pool to house area and planting restricted to tubs, a tree, and low evergreen shrubs. Eckbo's own garden at Laurel Canyon, Los Angeles (the ALCOA Forecast garden), was sponsored by the aluminium company ALCOA to demonstrate the versatility of the metal. Made in 1959, not only did the shape reflect Eckbo's use of geometry, but it demonstrated how a new material developed by the aircraft industry could be used to its best advantage in a garden. Aluminium fine mesh screens were used to make enclosures and to filter sunlight through pergola roofs. Triangular pyramids broke the shape of the trellis roof, and a triangular aluminium fountain splashed into a small pool. The patterns formed by light played through the screens on to the patterned paving below. But plants needed to be grown up the wooden supports for the structures above, as the metal grew too hot for the plants.

Four years after the ALCOA Forecast garden, Eckbo returned to his alma mater as chair of the Department of Landscape Architecture at the University of California at Berkeley, where he taught, wrote, and continued to practise, becoming involved in more public and large-scale enterprises. Working almost until his death in 2001, this part of his career was important in consolidating the academic basis for modern landscape design, though *Landscape for Living*, written in 1950, remains the best collection of his ideas. It was the first book on modern practice to follow Tunnard's *Gardens in the Modern Landscape*. Concerned at the lack of research and written record, Marc Treib urged Berkeley to hold a symposium in 1989, whose published papers helped to present a coherent picture of modern landscape design in Europe and the United States.

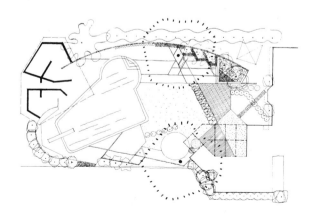

A garden in Pasadena, California, James C. Rose
Made in the early 1950s, the garden of this modern Spanish-style house reflects Rose's desire to link the interior and exterior living spaces with an informal design and simple planting. The garden features the aluminium-framed nylon-webbed chair which was a new postwar development for outdoor living.

James C. Rose (1913–91)

In many ways James Rose, the second of the Harvard rebels, was most closely in tune with Christopher Tunnard. He is also the most elusive of the trio, as there are few surviving examples of his completed work. He was expelled from Harvard's landscape course in 1937 (although he returned the following year) as a result of his intense dislike of Beaux-Arts teaching, which he expressed in a series of articles which he put together during his spell at Harvard and published later in *Pencil Points* in 1938 and 1939. These attacks form his lasting contribution to the 'war' on Beaux-Arts.

Though berating the criticisms of modernism, the body of these articles attempted to articulate a new approach to gardens, common to the three rebels, which drew on two lines of thought. One is the definition of landscape design as 'outdoor sculpture',[48] and therefore its links with the arts. The other is the establishment of design which emerges from the site, not plans, and with plants which are sympathetic to their site. He, like Tunnard, used models to demonstrate his designs, eventually abandoning models to create the garden entirely on site.

It was Rose's rejection of the two-dimensional pictures emerging from Beaux-Arts gardens which led to his perception of landscape design as sculpture; possibly he associated these demonstrations of man in control of nature with the authoritarianism of the Harvard course. He sought to find the spirit engendered by the site – Pope's 'genius of the place' springs to mind, though this is not a phrase which Rose would have used, given his dismissal of romanticism. He conceived a landscape which would evolve from its site. 'earth is a plastic medium which holds an infinity of sculptural combinations', he claimed.[49] Rose admired the rounded forms of the sculptor Constantin Brancusi (1876–1957), whose search for the essence of objects struck a chord with his own. The third dimension given by sculpture was enhanced by the spatial arrangements suggested by the work of Picasso, Theo van Doesburg, Mies van der Rohe, and Naum Gabo. Rose used the drawing of Picasso's *Figure* of 1910 in his student project for the Bibby Estate, Kingston, New York, in 1938.[50]

In 1941 Rose worked with a firm of architects and engineers in New York, before becoming briefly drawn in to the large-scale construction of military installations in New Jersey. After the war, his preferred small gardens appeared in the *Ladies' Home Journal,* and later in his *Creative Gardens* of 1958.

Rose saw no value in paper plans for designing gardens, with set paths, vistas and 'ornamentation with plants to create pictures.'[51] Plans were to be drawn afterwards, to record what had happened. Instead he sought to allow the site to suggest its own limits and the way which people would move in it, the materials used to reflect their own qualities, and planting to relate to the way each specimen developed over time. If these ideas were followed through, 'an organic style' would emerge.[52]

This 'organic style' was difficult to communicate to client and contractor, added to the fact that Rose was not always inclined to give the client what he wanted. In *Gardens Make Me Laugh*, written in 1965, Rose suggested that Americans regarded gardens as a mark of their position in life, and where possible he avoided putting in the lawns, massed flower-beds, the lifestyle barbecues and imposing entrances to which they aspired.

Dan Kiley (born 1912)

It is perhaps ironic that the third rebel felt sufficiently disassociated with Harvard's 'conservative, historicist tone'[53] to leave without his master's degree in 1938, yet was eventually to develop a modern style more akin to the grand manner of classicism.

Kiley qualified for entry to Harvard by virtue of hard work. Brought up in Massachusetts, he left school with an aspiration to become a landscape architect and was taken on as an unpaid apprentice in the practice of a leading professional, Warren Manning, in 1932. From his father, who worked in the building industry, he learned about construction. From Manning he absorbed a great deal about plants, and useful business knowledge such as site surveying and dealing with clients. Kiley wanted to advance further, and despite Manning's advice, was accepted as a special (non-graduate) case for the postgraduate course at Harvard; throughout his study he continued to work thirty hours per week for Manning. In 1938 he went to Concord, New Hampshire, to work for the National Park Service, which led to his preparation of a Masterplan (a projected town plan) for Concord. Moving on to Washington, D.C., he made useful contacts which led him to progress to the post of Associate Town Planner working on low-cost housing for the United States Housing Authority under Elbert Peets, who had also been an early critic of Harvard's course.

In the few years before Kiley joined the armed services, his career advanced through his first major private assignment for the Collier estate in Virginia, and then by association with the architect Louis Kahn. In 1944, due to his friendship with Eero Saarinen, he became Director of Design for the Presentations Branch of the Office of Strategic Services, which led to his rehabilitation of the Palace of Justice at Nuremberg for the international war crimes tribunal. The visit to Europe also gave him a chance to see formal styles of architecture and landscaping, which had a profound influence on his work thereafter.

Kiley decided to add architecture to his qualifications of plantsman, garden designer and town planner, and on his return from the war became a registered architect. This gave him the scope for the expansion which followed in the next forty years, with offices in New England and a large staff.

Dan Kiley and his practices have completed thousands of commissions since 1951. The range is awesome, from making gardens and houses to landscaping for schools and colleges; from public sites such as Washington Mall and La Défense, Paris, to gardens and landscaping for cultural institutions including the John F. Kennedy Library in Boston and the Henry Moore Sculpture Garden in Kansas City. Green spaces have been made for the customers of the Nationsbank Plaza, in Tampa, Florida, and in the atrium of the London Standard Chartered Bank in England. Parks have been created for corporate headquarters at Corning Riverfront Centennial Park in New York, and landscaping for Dulles Airport in Virginia. To choose one subject from such diversity is almost impossible; but there are common principles in Kiley's designs which translate from large to small enterprises. Relating back to the theme of emerging self-confident America, Kiley's landscaping has succeeded as much for the efficiency of the well-run business organization, as for the appropriateness of the landscape to the lifestyle.

One of Kiley's smaller postwar landscapes is the Miller Garden, made for Irwin and Xenia Miller who had commissioned Eero Saarinen in 1953 to build

them a house on a site overlooking the floodplain of the River Flatrock outside Columbus, Indiana. Irwin Miller managed his family's Cummins Engine Company; he and his wife favoured modernity in art and architecture. Saarinen's house was long and low, suiting the flat plains on which it stood. The one-storey building with its projecting flat roof forming a canopy supported by slim pillars, and with glass walls, was clearly related to Mies van der Rohe's Barcelona Pavilion and the Prairie houses of Frank Lloyd Wright. The house was made in four wings, each having a different function, around an open centre. There was no grand entrance, in keeping with the Irwins' wishes; and they wanted the house to 'grow out of Columbus, which is flat and on a grid. A curvy design on this landscape wouldn't have looked right'.[54] The Millers employed Eliel Saarinen to design other public buildings for Columbus, including the First Christian Church, in which their house would eventually form part of the landscape. On Eliel's death in 1950, his son Eero took over, designing the Irwin Union Bank in glass and steel in 1953, and many other public buildings.

Saarinen introduced Kiley to Miller after the house was completed. He had to consider the best way of linking the four sides of the house, each with its different function, to the garden outside, and to find an overall design

Above and top
The Miller House, Columbus, Indiana
Dan Kiley made a garden for the Miller family to complement the long, low, clean lines of the house designed by Eero Saarinen in 1953. The formal allée of honey locust trees (top) runs parallel with the house. A Henry Moore sculpture reclines at the far end, and the European beeches join the house to the meadows of the Flatrock River.

strategy which would accommodate the angularity of the building with the horizontality of the site. The first question was solved by making four different gardens and linking them spatially to each other. Then the house was connected to the garden by reducing the width of the podium on which the house stood to the width of its overlying canopy, and using the same terrazzo flooring as the house as a setting for tables and chairs. Beyond, the podium joined a carpet of ivy, which separated the lawn from the house.

The second question was answered in the language of Kiley's revelations on the way from Nuremberg – an 'epiphany' which he describes in his memoir, *Dan Kiley: In His Own Words*. The landscapes of Europe appeared to be governed by a formal geometry whose vocabulary was expressed by the terms 'allée, bosque, boulevard and tapis vert',[55] and Kiley now wanted to use this vocabulary in the modern setting of the Miller Garden. Along the west side of the house, Kiley planted an allée of honey-locust trees parallel with the building. Intended to shade the sunny side of the house, the trees provided a vertical line breaking the horizontal plane of the building. A Henry Moore reclining figure was added to the northern end some twenty years after the allée was planted; it faces a relief by Jacques Lipchitz. The perimeter of the other three sides was defined by a staggered double line of trimmed arbor vitae hedges, which, as they grew, gave privacy but also glimpses of the inner garden through overlapping planes of green. Arbor vitae was used to screen the swimming pool near the drive. Outside the hedge a line of red maples was planted. The eastern inner space was divided by a row of white oaks, which separated two apple orchards, the southern one adjoining a children's play area. Another allée, of horse chestnuts, defined the drive, each tree being encased at its base by an inset square set in horizontal planes of low cut yew. At the western end of the house, widely spaced European weeping beeches were planted to reach out across the meadow towards the woodland bordering the river beyond.

The garden has undergone few changes; its overall impression of appropriate scale, harmony, and tranquil greenness remains.

The American-Japanese Garden: Isamu Noguchi (1904–88)

The landscapes of Noguchi have been described as having 'significantly influenced the vocabulary – if not the actual course – of American landscape architecture'.[56] By this was meant the blending of sculpture and architecture with which Noguchi addressed his landscapes, in a manner similar to the emerging land artists (Chapter 7). He made his small designs for children's playgrounds and snail-shaped slides as sensuous as his larger landscapes.

Noguchi, the son of a Japanese university lecturer father who refused to acknowledge him, and an American mother, was brought up in the United States. After abandoning a course in medicine, he turned to sculpture, and for a while trained in the studio of Constantin Brancusi. He became interested in dance, and designed sets for choreographer Martha Graham. Noguchi paid several visits to Japan, trying, unsuccessfully, to communicate with his father, and attempting to absorb Japanese culture. As his work became recognized, he made frequent journeys from his home in New York, and this restlessness appears to have been associated with being neither wholly American nor Japanese. There has been much discussion of Noguchi's perceived failure to resolve this dilemma within his work,[57] but as Noguchi said about his UNESCO *Jardin Japonais*, 'More truthfully, I should say I never wanted to make a purely Japanese garden'[58] and he later expressed 'delight' at its development with 'trees fully grown, nature rampant'.[59]

Chapter 2 referred to the interest shown in Japan in the nineteenth century as the country opened up to the developed world. There was a rush to make Japanese gardens, but without much understanding of the culture from which they came. Some ended as a mere collection of lanterns, stepping stones, bridges, pavilions, and clipped shrubs, others more meaningful as the result of collaboration with Japanese gardeners.

One such garden in the United States was the Tea Garden in the Golden Gate Park in San Francisco. Originating in the Japanese Village exhibit for the California Midwinter International Exposition of 1894, the garden was built with the help of landscape architect Makoto Hagiwara (1855–1925), who came over from Japan in 1893, and San Franciscan George Turner Marsh (1855–1932).[61] The traditional Tea Garden with pavilions, gateways and tea house were altered over time, as were the attributions of authorship of the garden between Hagiwara and Marsh, Japan and America, depending on the relationship of the two countries – especially at the time of Japanese internment during the Second World War.

The small gardens designed in California by Isamu Noguchi incorporated the traditional natural Japanese elements of water and stone meaningfully placed, but did not attempt to recreate the traditional Japanese garden. He added his own signature – the fountain of water issuing from rock – to the desert planting evocative of southern California. Gardens for the IBM headquarters, New York (1964), Chase Manhattan Bank Plaza, New York (1961–64) and the Beinecke Rare Book and Manuscript Library, Yale University (1960–64) display the modernist and the Japanese together in a minimalist combination which is a more personal than national style.

In Europe he is known for the UNESCO headquarters garden in Paris for which he was commissioned in 1956, and which took many years to complete, due to the difficulties of obtaining stone from Japan. Stone was a very

**Isamu Noguchi,
Japanese Garden,
UNESCO Building, Paris**
Isamu Noguchi's 1956
design not only joins
two buildings, it also
symbolizes the peaceful
linking of two cultures –
the oriental and the
occidental. Within the
garden, a bridge links a
higher terrace, which acts
as a stage set for sculpture,
with a lower level, where
informal planting
surrounds a pool.

important sculptural element for Noguchi, used to express the essence of life and nature, and to represent mountains. Japan also sent flowering camellias, cherry trees and bamboo to Paris, as well as gardeners.

There are two parts to the UNESCO design, and many layers of meaning within the garden. The higher, delegates' garden, representing culture, was regarded by Noguchi as a stage, on which sculptures could be set. The sculptures were stones for visitors to sit in contemplation or discussion, arranged as a type of Zen garden. By contrast below it,[61] are the surrealist, biomorphic shapes of the natural *Jardin Japonais* (Japanese Garden), with lakes, planted beds, and paved central area representing the 'happy land' where one arrives and departs through time, which is represented by stepping stones across the water. There is a linear canal with its waterfalls joining the two levels.

This is a stroll garden, in which the walker observes – as in life – a changing scene. At the top of the canal is the vertical stone fountain which is the source of the water in the canal. The fountain with its calligraphic sign for peace, marks the edge of a bridge or *hanamichi* between the two buildings in the Headquarters.

Noguchi joined the internment of the Japanese in the American west voluntarily, helping to design the camps. The same characteristic of identifying with the outsider made him give his work freely for the Billy Rose Sculpture Garden for the Israel National Museum in Jerusalem between 1961 and 1965.

Here, a hillside site is shaped into five tiers of semi-circular retaining walls, the sculptures placed to blend with the natural scenery on the hilltop, and facing the setting sun. Again he uses the fountain issuing from a single stone, in the central courtyard, and desert plants.

Though Noguchi represented the search for personal identity more strongly than the other American garden-makers of this era, in his use of abstract images and designs he explored the relationship between Japanese and American cultures in a way which was to be taken further by young Japanese garden and landscape designers from the 1980s, and which continues into the twenty-first century.

In opening a dialogue between cultures Noguchi differed from the other American garden designers of the period featured here who began by looking inwards rather than outwards. Their exploration of national designs and plants followed a need to find a style to suit the way they lived and the climates that they lived in, and to express a desire to shake off the lingering European colonial control. All were happy to work alongside Modernism, despite its origins in Europe. All, particularly Burle Marx and the Harvard rebels, were intent on removing what they saw as the alien Beaux-Arts culture in architecture and gardens, which preceded Modernism. Later, as Chapter Seven shows, the achievement of adulthood enabled the Americans, as well as the Europeans, to become foci of innovation for the rest of the world.

Isamu Noguchi, Japanese Garden, UNESCO Building, Paris
A fountain with a calligraphic inscription representing peace, on the upper terrace, leads water down to the garden. Stepping stones in the foreground prompt the visitor to consider his direction in life, as well as in the garden.

European Landscapes from the 1930s to the 1960s

Shortages of manpower, money and materials delayed the advance of private landscape design after the Second World War in much of Europe, though in Britain and elsewhere leading landscape architects were employed in large-scale public schemes for energy, forestry, roads, and new settlements. Governments became involved in shaping social landscapes as planning became a recognized discipline for controlling the development of town and countryside as they emerged from wartime devastation or neglect. Here the democratic element in modernism emerged, in good public housing, linked park systems, or on the smaller scale, children's playgrounds. As in the Americas, inspiration for postwar landscape design in Europe came increasingly from modern art and architecture. Sculpture became an active, instead of passive, element in outdoor design.

Following the war, European garden design found national styles of its own. The Beaux-Arts tradition retreated, as did the English Landscape movement and Arts and Crafts; the rediscovery of national identity was as important as the move towards naturalism. Scandinavian neutrality had enabled Sweden to consolidate its 'natural' gardens; whilst Denmark, though briefly occupied, avoided widespread destruction and was thereby able to continue its more architectural landscape style. Germany, a divided territory, did not come into its own until unification in 1990, but horticulture remained a key element, as in the Netherlands. France and Spain remained as sleeping giants, saving their surprises for the end of the century.

Great Britain – from public landscapes to philosophy in the garden

Michael Laurie recalls working for Sylvia Crowe whilst she was writing *Garden Design* in 1958. 'The people in the office objected to the title since we were doing everything except garden design', he claimed,[1] thus summarizing the confusion in the British understanding of the roles of garden and landscape designers. Postwar history made both professions respectable and interchangeable; the days of the architect working with the nurseryman and engineer were numbered. As larger public enterprises absorbed the activities of town planners, architects and landscape architects, all working as a team, it was no longer possible for one person to carry through a whole enterprise alone.

Amphitheatre at the University of Aarhus, Denmark
Carl Theodor Sørensen's landscaping, begun in 1933, features a distinctive sculptural element which links the building to the fall of the slope below; it is typical of the geometry of Sørensen's designs.

In 1945 the Labour election manifesto undertook to build more houses 'in relation to good town planning – pleasant surroundings, attractive layout, efficient utility services, including the necessary transport facilities.'[2] The public grew to accept state and local government intervention, town plans and regional plans. In 1946 the New Towns Act set official approval on the concept of attracting work and housing to new settlements beyond town planner Patrick Abercrombie's Green Belt round London as a way of

clearing the slums and dealing with the wreckage of wartime. Eight New Towns were designated in Greater London between 1946 and 1949; others were to follow elsewhere. There was a need for new industry, power stations, and roads. There was also a need for trained landscape architects to be involved, as Peter Shepheard argued in *Modern Gardens* in 1953.

Shepheard (who died in 2002) recorded the showplace for new design for 1951 – the Festival of Britain, in which leading landscape designers such as H. F. Clark, Maria Shephard, Peter Youngman and Shepheard himself, made small gardens in the pavilions on the south bank of the Thames. They used new materials, and set concrete planters into pebbles. Burle Marx's biomorphic shapes appeared to be borrowed for the gardens of the Regatta restaurant, and the naturalistic landscapes of the Swedish Parks Department under Holger Blom in the moat garden.[3]

Recognizing the profession's early blindness to the modern movement, Shepheard hoped it would find a new aesthetic in what lay ahead. The landscape architect should be 'more than a mere planner of gardens'. He should be involved with the integration of existing features such as trees and streams into the overall open space pattern, linking houses, shopping centres, parks, playgrounds, and 'all the planting problems involved in the building layouts, the verges, the street trees, house gardens, and so on'.[4] Starved of garden work from private commissions, garden designers became landscape designers. Sylvia Crowe worked on Basildon New Town and Harlow with Frederick Gibberd, Geoffrey Jellicoe on Hemel Hempstead, Frank Clark on Stevenage, and Peter Youngman on Cumbernauld, Peterborough and Milton Keynes. Crowe's and Jellicoe's contributions to Harlow and Hemel Hempstead have been selected for wider description, together with some of their garden designs.

The early thinking on the New Towns was influenced by Ebenezer Howard and the Garden City movement, with its aims for a balanced community which owned its own settlement and was provided with work within the town. Sir Frederick J. Osborn (1895–1980), the Estate Manager for Welwyn Garden City, carried Howard's thinking further, enshrining original principles within the work of the New Towns Committee. Howard had envisaged the association of town and countryside, with green spaces for agriculture and recreation. Gardens were to be important for growing vegetables as well as flowers; allotments were also part of Howard's blueprint.

Postwar Britain eventually saw changes to these aims; the independent corporations owning the towns were wound up, and local authorities sold off the houses. No longer was it necessary to have work in the town before renting a house, and it was difficult to encourage a complete social balance as bosses and blue collar workers often tended not to live in the same area. The widespread ownership of cars made the walking city – where all parts were within reach on foot – no longer necessary, and the later New Towns were planned on a larger scale. But landscape architects worked hard to integrate town and country and found a new aesthetic in their creations.

Opposite

Festival of Britain Gardens, London 1951
Seen from above, the Regatta Restaurant garden (top) by H. F. Clark and Maria Shephard shows an early example of freeform planting in Britain, possibly influenced by Burle Marx. Peter Shepheard's natural planting in the Moat Garden (bottom), with its water-moulded boulders and stones from Westmorland, paralleled the work of the Swedish park makers in Stockholm.

Sylvia Crowe (1901–97)

Sylvia Crowe was the daughter of an engineer who took up fruit farming for his health. The Sussex countryside and family visits to France and Corsica appear to have been important influences in her decision to work with plants. As a girl she contracted tuberculosis, which prevented her from going to school, and she was educated at home by her mother, who had been one of the first women to go to Oxford University. In 1920 she took a practical, 'outside' course – as was usual for those who had had TB – at Swanley Horticultural College where she met Brenda Colvin. But her decision to design gardens came following a later visit to Italy, and in 1926 she was taken on by landscape gardener Edward Milner White, one of the small band who had been invited to become members of the Institute of Landscape Architects (ILA). Here she made plasticene models of gardens as a way of understanding how site affected design, and learned surveying and drawing techniques.

Crowe went on to work with Cutbush Nurseries. In 1937 she won a gold medal at the Chelsea Flower Show for a natural rock garden overlooking a pool, with a small cascade. The reception by the general public was cool, but she won the approval of Geoffrey Jellicoe. As with so many others in the field, work was cut short by the war, in which she drove an ambulance for a Polish brigade in France and then lorries for the Auxiliary Territorial Service (ATS), somehow managing to get to ILA council meetings whilst on leave. She decided to set up her own practice at the end of the war, beginning in a room in Brenda Colvin's Baker Street office; and it was at this point that the New Town programme began to get off the ground. Both Colvin and Crowe worked on the ILA's contribution to the government's New Towns Committee.

Sylvia Crowe and Frederick Gibberd (1908–84) at Harlow

Sylvia Crowe worked on Harlow as landscape consultant from 1947 to 1973, for Basildon from 1949 to 1962, for Washington in County Durham between 1964 and 1966, and for Warrington in Cheshire from 1965 to 1967. Harlow's Master Plan was drawn up by Frederick Gibberd as consultant architect planner from 1947 to 1980 (and also a landscape architect). Crowe felt Gibberd 'really cared about the landscape and was easy to work with'.[4] Gibberd and Crowe were sensitive to the site; as Gibberd said, 'the design seeks to preserve and develop the natural features which give the area its particular character: the valleys, brooks, woods, clumps of trees, are all therefore retained as "pegs" on which the design is hung'.[5] Gibberd was a collector of modern paintings, many of which were later housed for the public to view in the town hall gallery. Geoffrey and Susan Jellicoe were to suggest that the original plan for Harlow was based on a cubist interpretation of the pattern of pre-existing field boundaries, similar to that in Ben Nicholson's picture *Mousehole 1947*.[6]

After a complete survey of the land, neighbourhood units, themselves to be little communities with a shop and school, were separated by landscaped belts with roads and recreation areas. The neighbourhoods had different designers, and it was the purpose of the landscaping to hold them together. Crowe saw the countryside spilling into the neighbourhoods down stream courses and footpaths; Gibberd preserved the valley of the Netteswell Cross stream as a town park. Crowe chose indigenous tree species such as oak, birch, holly and hawthorn, and planted pleached limes (as did Jellicoe) along some greenways or main paths. She encouraged the concept of linked park systems, where sports grounds, parks, and footpaths could thread their way through built-up areas – a concept which is widely encouraged today. Old gravel pits were drained to form playgrounds. Excavated material was used to form planted mounds which screened industry and roads from housing.

Harlow's pedestrianized town centre was enlivened by modern sculpture, including a piece by Willy Soukop, and Gibberd created a formal water garden

Top
Plan of Harlow, England
Geoffrey Jellicoe asserted that Frederick Gibberd's plan for Harlow was a cubist interpretation of the field boundaries, influenced by Ben Nicholson's painting *Mousehole 1947* (below).

(now undergoing a change of location) adjoining the town hall. Here terraces with canals and colourful wall fountains provided reflecting elements for the tall buildings behind, and also a setting for Elisabeth Frink sculptures. Below the canals were geometrically shaped beds with yew hedges and square pools; at the lowest level was a lawn. Henrietta Barnett had encouraged the working classes to look at art in galleries in her ventures towards a Garden Suburb in Hampstead; Harlow took artistic provision further.

At his house at nearby Marsh Green, Frederick Gibberd bound together existing elements of a landscape – a lime avenue, a gazebo – with new planting. From 1956 he turned the existing wilderness into a series of open grassy glades surrounded by trees, each space flowing into the next and making different pictures and vistas from one glade to another. As Gibberd said: 'The garden design then becomes landscape architecture'.[7]

Over time the growth of vegetation has made unobtrusive the structure of shallow terraces and steps taking the garden down to the Pincey Brook. Spoil from the new pool sculpted in the brook has been used to build a hill now crowned by a fort for children's play; to the west of the garden, pillars from Gibberd's remodelling of Coutts Bank in the Strand, London, make a connection with Roman Harlow. Perennial plants appropriate to the soil appear as part of the surrounding green structure; there are no herbaceous borders or annuals to be bedded out. Gibberd and his wife shared a love of sculpture, often buying from rising artists, and then seeking the right space for it at Marsh Green. 'Sometimes the right site does not exist and so I make a garden for it', he claimed. '"Visioning" is what it all comes down to in the end.'[8]

Sylvia Crowe and the landscapes of tomorrow

A shared empathy with landscape gave Crowe and Gibberd a long working relationship at Harlow. Crowe applied this ability to link the manmade to the natural in other spheres than housing and gardens. Her book *Tomorrow's Landscape* (1956) surveyed the landscapes of town and countryside, pinpointing the problems caused by the imposition of man's activities on the natural landscape, and his inability to solve the conflicts.[9] Crowe was dealing with a countryside scarred by the extraction of minerals, a Forestry Commission which planted conifers in bleak rows up to the hilltops, and by

Frederick Gibberd's Garden, Marsh Lane
Rescued from the remodelling of Coutt's Bank in the Strand, London, Doric columns and Coade-stone urns stand in a glade (above), alluding to Roman Harlow. The lime avenue (far left), a pre-existing feature, leads down to the Pincey Brook. Rodin's *Eve* was moved from Harlow Water Garden. The fort in the meadow with its moat (left) was made by Gibberd for his family.

Bewl Water, Lamberhurst, Kent, 1965–83

Sylvia Crowe wanted her landscape designs to look 'almost inevitable', planting the reservoir so that no ugly expanse was exposed at low water. Sphagnum moss covered the bank foot, and indigenous trees and shrubs leading to the water's edge included willow, hawthorn and oak. A trail for walkers and horse riders follows the boundary of the reservoir.

heavy industry contaminating countryside, waterfronts and townscapes. *The Landscape of Power* (1958), *The Landscape of Roads* (1960) and *Forestry in the Landscape* (1966) gave specific examples and solutions. 'Nothing can be done unless it is recognized that that the appearance of our surroundings matters, that without good landscape and townscape our pretensions to a civilized life are futile. Once we have regained our sense of values sufficiently to realize this the necessary steps to save the landscape are technically relatively simple', she claimed.[10] She had a clear mind and a confident ability to organize answers which made her books standard texts. Yet there existed an appreciation of landscape which was akin to that of the artist; she was a regular visitor to exhibitions and enjoyed modern art.[11]

Crowe was impressed by Alwin Seifert's 1930s planting on the autobahn in Germany, and advocated natural planting with indigenous species along British main routes. She equally urged the American concept that the shaping of roads should follow the lie of the land – as rivers – to avoid monotony and for more sympathetic landscaping.

As consultant to the Southern and South West Water Boards, Crowe's work on reservoirs such as Rutland Water and Bewl Water involved tree-planting with some colourful exotics placed among the indigenous species for good composition; trees were to screen, dress the lake edges when the water level fell, and encourage wildlife. At Bewl Water in Kent, fingers of planting including willow, hawthorn, and oak extend to the water's edge, and sphagnum moss covers the draw-down zone which is exposed at low water. A trail for those on foot or horseback threads its way through the trees around the lake; there are wooden benches discreetly placed round the circuit.

Trees were again used as an important part in setting massive compositions such as power stations into their wild backgrounds. Crowe was appointed consultant to the Central Electricity Generating Board in 1968 'with a view to civilizing nuclear power stations at Trawsfynnyd and Wylfa in Wales'.[12] The raw outline of Trawsfynnyd was eased by massed planting of conifers and broadleaved trees around its feet and extending the green flow into the adjoining hillside. As first landscape consultant to the Forestry Commission in 1964 she helped to improve the visual and ecological impact of tree-planting; her aim here, as with large constructions, was to remove the perceived imposition of man on the landscape. Large-scale commercial tree-planting was to follow the contours. There should be a mix of trees to give a seasonal variation of colour, and tongues of planting could follow river valleys. Three plant layers – tree, shrub and ground flora – should be encouraged to give a vertical as well as a horizontal interest. She advised the 'ragging' of planting edges, to avoid the look of the drawing board. Lines of movement such as trails and forest roads were to be incorporated, to enhance public enjoyment. Often these suggestions were made in the field with the aid of sketches showing simple planes created by the colour of different tree masses. Crowe's ideas spread from the public sector to the private, as tree-planting grants were taken up by landowners. The American Forestry Service took notice of her work.

Crowe's *Garden Design* of 1958, with its survey of the elements of good design from gardens throughout the world, remains a substantial record of the thinking of her time. Yet Crowe moved away from private garden work, and is better known for larger commissions such as the Commonwealth Institute, London (1962–64), Magdalen College Oxford's Penicillin Rose Garden (1952–53), and the roof garden she made for the Scottish Widows Fund and Life Assurance Society headquarters building, Edinburgh (1971–76). She welcomed the use of machinery including earth-moving equipment, electric pumps for pools and fountains, and electric trimmers. She deplored the imitation of old materials for hard landscaping, and encouraged the use of new metals, concrete and glass; she introduced concrete planters, still in use today.

There are few remaining small gardens made by Sylvia Crowe, and her designs for Cutbush were destroyed in the war. Like Jellicoe, she was sometimes asked to connect an older, established garden to new work being implemented by the owner. At Barford Park in Enmore, near Bridgwater, Somerset, Crowe was asked in the 1950s to link an eighteenth century house to a walled garden which sat, in isolation, immediately behind it. The solution

Above

Barford Park, Somerset, 1950s

Crowe linked an eighteenth-century house to its separate walled garden, with a double hedge of hornbeam and an inner hedge of yew, seen on the left. Beyond is the walled garden, whose later planting by Roy Cheek, a colleague of Crowe's, echoed many of her colours and choices of plants.

was simple but effective; green walls continued the line of the house, divided by a lawn. The outer wall was made from a double row of square-trimmed hornbeam on stilts, with a low inner hedge of round-clipped yew, an arched 'doorway' being cut through both hedges leading from the outside to the lawn. On the outside, the straight hedges link two rounded features – the end of the walled garden, and the low, curved stone steps near the house.

Similar connecting work was undertaken at Hailey House, Ipsden, in Oxfordshire (1977–87) where she advised on the landscaping for new buildings, a swimming pool, squash court and stables, which were being added to the grounds of an Arts and Crafts house. Here again, clipped yew walls divided spaces; through one large opening can be seen a startling lifesize sculpture of a horse by Elisabeth Frink.

Sylvia Crowe's influence has been as much on the way of thinking of the landscape architects whom she helped to train, as the landscaping itself. In her practice worked Michael Laurie, who later taught landscape architecture at the University of California, and international garden designer John Brookes. Her visits to Australia, where she designed a park for Canberra, helped the growing profession there. Part of the brave new world which emerged after the war, she taught her followers to blend the manmade into the natural, whether for the power station or the forest.[13] At a smaller scale, simplicity was the principle she employed in the garden – the design was to look 'inevitable'. On her travels round the world, she met others who were moving in the same direction – Thomas Church and Garrett Eckbo, for instance, in California. She helped to

Right

Hailey House, Ipsden, Oxfordshire, 1977–87

Sylvia Crowe worked with Anthony Blee at Hailey House. Here, her hedges open to show the sculpture of a horse by Elisabeth Frink.

create the profession of landscape architecture in Britain, was instrumental in starting the International Federation of Landscape Architects (IFLA) from 1948, and was President of the Landscape Institute between 1957 and 1959.

Geoffrey Alan Jellicoe (1900–96)

Sylvia Crowe and Geoffrey Jellicoe experienced the same postwar change of direction towards the built environment, moved in the same circles (he was President of the Institute of Landscape Architects from 1939 to 1949 and a founder member of IFLA), admired each other's work, and often used the same features of design. Both valued the natural landscape. But where Crowe saw landscape design as a visual process whereby manmade images emerged from the landscape itself, Jellicoe eventually saw his landscapes possessing additional dimensions, with meaning deriving from modern art, classical literature and philosophy, and binding it all together, the subconscious mind. He was returning to something approaching a programme in the landscape which had been developed in the gardens of the Italian Renaissance and was played out once again in the eighteenth century. It was to emerge strongly in his *Landscape of Man* in 1975 which he wrote with his wife Susan, who self-effacingly planned much of his planting.

Jellicoe was born in London to a publisher father and a mother who had been taught to paint at the Slade School of Art. His parents moved to Sussex, where the countryside made an early impression, though he formed no love for gardening. The choice to become a landscape architect was a late one. Jellicoe claimed he could just as easily have chosen theatre design.[14] A chance meeting with architect C. F. A. Voysey in 1918 led him towards architecture. He took up a place at the Architectural Association in London in 1919, where he was to be a Studio Master and eventually Principal between 1939 and 1942. In the early 1920s the AA was deeply traditional in its teaching; its revolution, like the ones at Harvard and the Royal Academy School of Fine Arts in Copenhagen, was soon to follow.

Jellicoe absorbed the ideal classical background in the summer of 1924, when he travelled through Italy, and then southern Sweden with his friend and later business partner, J. C. Shepherd. But the purpose of the journey, enabled by an award, was to make measured drawings of the gardens, not the architecture, of the Italian villas. These were published in 1925 as *The Italian Gardens of the Renaissance*. (*The Baroque Gardens of Austria* followed in 1932 after further travel in Europe.) Jellicoe embraced landscape architecture as the most important of the visual arts after visiting Italy. He indicated the significant stages in the evolution of his ideas in the outline *Soundings*, which was written in 1993 to introduce the four volumes of his life's work, *The Studies of a Landscape Designer*.

Jellicoe described his progression through classical architecture and early rejection of modern art in his studies at the AA, and his gradual understanding of the diverse aims of the cubist offshoot Constructivism in the period before the Second World War. The Russian sculptor Naum Gabo (1890–1977) explained the concept of the invisible interior (content) amalgamating with the visible exterior (form). This was similar to Corbusier's equation of the inside of the building with the outside (which has been explored in the Villa Savoye in Chapter 3). For Jellicoe, Constructivism showed a lack of understanding of human nature; Corbusier's houses were impractical and his landscapes 'a kind of abstract pseudo-romantic carpet upon which his buildings were to float'.[15]

At Cheddar Gorge, Somerset, however, Jellicoe was able to display a sympathy for modern forms in his restaurant (1934–36) which was described by landscape architect Russell Page (1906–85) as 'long and low in order to dramatize the cave-mouth'[16] with a flat roof and white walls. Page, who introduced Jellicoe to the job, had responsibility for the landscape. This was the beginning of a working relationship which began with a commission for Ditchley Park in Oxfordshire (1935–39) and ended in 1939; as Jellicoe was said to have remarked, '"the Russell Page world" collapsed with the coming of war'.[17] For the moment, however, Jellicoe claimed that his country house garden practice consisted of placing new gardens into old settings, which he did with 'technical and academic efficiency'.[18]

New gardens in old settings was his self-deprecating way of describing, for instance, his sensitive adjustment of the gardens of thirteenth-century Mottisfont Abbey in Hampshire, to its surroundings (1936–39), or of his long association with the eighteenth-century house and gardens of St Pauls, Walden Bury in Hertfordshire (1936–92). At Mottisfont a simple plan of small, hedged enclosures leading to a double line of pleached limes opens to the fields, joining the many-roomed Abbey to the wider landscape beyond. He used the same technique at Sandringham in 1947.

At the end of the war Jellicoe went with his wife Susan to Sweden, where they drew inspiration from the architecture and landscaping of Erik Gunnar Asplund (1885–1940), whom Jellicoe described as having recreated classicism in a new language. Also at about this time Jellicoe met Frederick Gibberd, who introduced him to the paintings of Paul Klee (1879–1940) and the work of painter and sculptor Ben Nicholson (1894–1981). He had already interviewed Henry Moore (1898–1986), and had been puzzled by his sculptures. In time Jellicoe was to claim that Klee, Moore and Nicholson had the most significant influence on his work, but Nicholson was his 'greatest mentor'.[19]

Gibberd's plan for Harlow was accepted whilst Jellicoe's for the New Town of Hemel Hempstead, commissioned at the same time, was largely rejected. Jellicoe's employment as planner and advisor had ended after two years. Jellicoe was also to be excluded from designing the Battersea Pleasure Gardens for the Festival of Britain in 1951, over his refusal to allow people on to a grassy area near a lake.[20] In Hemel Hempstead there were difficulties in integrating the old town with the new, and Jellicoe later saw that his plan left insufficient scope for expansion, though the development corporation found fault with the planning of the town centre and the siting of schools.[21] The water garden, planned by Jellicoe to follow the River Gade through the middle of the town, was welcomed, and it was the first of several designs in which features in his landscape took on representational shapes. Needing to be seen from above (the main criticism of such creations) the Gade assumed the sinuous form of a water serpent, the head made by the widening of the river into a lake, and the eye marked by a fountain. Lawns spread down to the river, with footpaths through trees on one side, gardens were made (Susan Jellicoe planned the planting), and the whole was completed between 1957 and 1959.

Jellicoe made no mention of his stirring realization of subconscious influence on design whilst making the water garden, but this was a recurring theme from the 1960s. At Cliveden, Buckinghamshire, he remodelled a rose garden for the Astor family in 1962. The new pattern was based on Paul Klee's painting *The Fruit*. The circular garden's sinuous paths cross and lead out from the central figure of a Renaissance man. Each path leaves the circle through an arch fashioned as a human outline, each arch slightly offset from the next, to encourage the feeling of the spinning planet. Jellicoe appeared to be making two observations here about looking outwards at man's differing views of the world, or inwards towards a view of humanism. Landscape representing natural forms, whether human, animal or plant, paralleled the abstract works of Klee, Moore and Nicholson, and the creation of the snake-like river garden on the Gade was not the only occasion when Jellicoe sculpted a water channel into a life form. He continued to seek to understand the inspiration behind contemporary painters and sculptors, whether Picasso (1881–1973), Paul Nash (1889–1946) Jackson Pollock (1912–56), or René Magritte (1898–1967). With commissions from the United Kingdom Atomic Energy Authority to landscape the nuclear power station at Oldbury in Gloucestershire and the Rutherford High Energy Laboratories at Harwell, Berkshire, the subconscious became more insistent.

After the end of the Second World War relations between the Western Powers and the Soviet Union deteriorated into the Cold War. The possibility of a nuclear annihilation disturbed many in the late 1950s. The Campaign for Nuclear Disarmament (CND) was launched in 1958 by Canon Collins and Bertrand Russell, with marches to Aldermaston atomic weapons research establishment becoming a regular feature at Easter between 1958 and 1964. In 1964 the pacifist Henry Moore created *Atom Piece* for the landscape; a large, cold, nightmarish sculpture reminiscent of a skull and a gas-mask, which surely told mankind to be mindful of what it hoped to control. A similar piece, called *Nuclear Energy*, marks the place where the first nuclear reaction was made in a laboratory of the University of Chicago in 1942.

At Harwell Jellicoe was more philosophical, if less dramatic, than Moore. From the spoil of the excavation for the atomic particle accelerator, he sculpted three hills, which related to the gentle shapes of the chalk downs, but also to Greek mythology. The hills were named after Zeus, Themis, a wife of Zeus, and their daughter Clotho. On Clotho, one of the Fates, turned the symbolic outcome of the whole. In mythology, she spins the thread of life, and decides when to cut or break it. But because this third hill was found to be in the way of the functioning of the reactor, it was demolished, and as Jellicoe remarked, 'the fate of man is still in the balance'.[22]

The works of Carl Jung and John Bunyan's *Pilgrim's Progress* absorbed Jellicoe, and with a commission to make a memorial garden at Runnymede for US President John F. Kennedy, he moved closer to realizing a match between his perception of the power of the subconscious and landscape design. The three great gardens at Runnymede, Sutton Place in Surrey, and Shute on the Dorset–Wiltshire border, are designed as an allegory of man's journey through life.

Below
The Rose Garden at Cliveden, 1962
Inspired by the sense of movement in Paul Klee's painting *The Fruit*, Jellicoe remodelled a rose garden for the Astor family with a Renaissance man in its centre. Sinuous paths lead outwards through arches made in the human form.

The Runnymede memorial is approached through a wicket gate into a dark woodland, along a winding path of granite setts, each one representing a pilgrim. The path climbs shallow steps towards the memorial stone, a simple slab with its carved legend. Behind the stone is an American oak which is supposed to bear flaming red leaves at the time of the assassination – unfortunately the wrong species was chosen for the underlying soil, and the leaves turn brown and are usually long gone by 22 November. Nevertheless the spell remains unbroken, and turning right from the stone, there appears a path into the sunlight, representing a mark of friendship with the American people. The path is flanked by a single, pre-existing hawthorn, standing for Kennedy's Roman Catholic faith. Two wide stone stairways end this path, each descending part of the way towards the meadows beside the Thames, intended to be a place for contemplation.

During the 1970s, Geoffrey and Susan Jellicoe travelled widely in parts of the Mediterranean which they had not visited before. Jellicoe's attention was also directed towards the scale and power of water in the landscape, and it is not surprising that his designs from this time onwards incorporate related themes and incidents.

Shute is an old house with medieval roots and many later additions, near the village of Donhead St Mary in Wiltshire. There are fine views across the countryside from the back of the

Above and below

The Kennedy Memorial, Runnymede, England, 1964–65

The Kennedy stone is reached after a winding walk through a dark forest, along a path made of granite setts; each one represents the life journey of a pilgrim whose cause was upheld by Kennedy.

Figures of Ovid, Virgil and Lucretius at Shute, Wiltshire, England
Here, Jellicoe develops his theme of man's journey once again, this time following watery routes through cultural formality and informality. The figures of Ovid, Virgil and Lucretius (recently replaced for restoration), the pastoral roots of classical education, survey the canal.

house. Jellicoe was asked by the Tree family in the 1970s to make sense of a landscape of old fishponds, kitchen gardens, grass and surrounding woodland. The house stands on a ridge from which many springs rise and descend, and Jellicoe saw that the answer lay in a water garden – at Shute, water forms the centre of the allegory of life's journeys, and here, Jellicoe gives a choice of two directions.

The heart of the design lies a little way to the west of the house, in the River Nader, which rises in a clear, dark pool carrying the reflection of the surrounding greenery. By the pool, Jellicoe placed a seat on which it is possible to sit looking at it, or facing away to the lake and box-edged beds on the further bank. The two-way seat marks the point at which water coming from the source of the Nader divides and flows two ways, a symbolic moment of decision-making.

By turning westwards, the traveller moves along a grassy path at the side of a canal, enclosed between clipped green hedges. At the end of the canal are placed the busts of three pastoral poets and writers from classical history: Ovid, Virgil and Lucretius, who preside over two watery grottoes beneath which the water disappears underground. Beyond the head of the canal, water reappears, again to be shaped into a formal course which makes its way directly down the slope. But this time there is a lighter touch; the emphasis shifts to sound as well as sight, as a cascade made from differently shaped outlets creates different tones. The water sparkles downhill between flower beds and then glides along a slim, straight channel through grass shaded by trees. There are interruptions in the rill formed by bubbling fountains in different geometric shapes. The other way round the garden has no formality. A path wanders southwards through trees from the two-way seat, giving glimpses of quiet lakes which link to join the eastward flow of the stream.

It is possible to enjoy the garden's light and shade and musical stream, with its box-edged flower-beds joining the space between lakes and rill, its statuary from Mereworth, the former home of the Tree family, and its shady bog-garden down by the meadows, without any inkling of Jellicoe's underlying ideas. But it would be a pity to ignore Jellicoe's concept of man's journey through culture, with his references to the classical Mediterranean landscapes along the canal, the Islamic water-garden along the rill, and the romanticism of the woodland and grassy glades. There was a problem in joining the two routes; Jellicoe hoped to solve this by creating a temple made of arcades of ivy, meeting like a gothic window, under the sky. The temple was entered from a dark tunnel of bay; after apprehension and perhaps disorientation from the woodland approach, the resolution followed in the tall, green, sunlit temple beyond.

Sutton Place, made between 1980 and 1986 for the wealthy art-lover Stanley Seeger, is perhaps Jellicoe's finest garden, and it was created when he was in his eighties. His comments on it given in the Guelph Lecture at Guelph University, Ontario, Canada, relate to the many layers of history of the house and site, and his reflections on the influences leading to different incidents within the garden.[23] He claimed a debt of gratitude to the Villa Gamberaia, in Tuscany, Italy, whose asymmetry marked a step away from the link between villa and garden in the earlier Italian Renaissance garden. All the features are connected to the underlying theme of Creation, Life, and Aspiration.[24] The garden is a great gathering-place for the new and the old in Jellicoe's repertoire. This time, he was more certain of his theme, and he may have wanted the climax of the journey to be related to a work by Ben Nicholson before he began his plan. Jellicoe found that Seeger was a fellow admirer of Nicholson and Henry Moore. Not all of the original design was implemented – the Avenue of Fountains with its cascades and grotto were not made, the music theatre became a green theatre, and the moss garden (now the plane tree garden) to which Jellicoe made much reference in the Guelph Lecture, was unsuccessful, as the moss would not grow. That said, the garden throughout is marked by diversions and incidents to colour the journey.

The beginning, Creation, belongs to a fish-shaped lake beyond the entrance to the sixteenth-century house. By its shores are two hillocks, one representing a father, the second a mother, and between them was to be the site for a Moore sculpture reminiscent of a foetus, called *Divided Oval*; the obvious analogy is of civilization emerging from the water. Moving back towards the house, Jellicoe made additions to the original garden which help to balance the rectangle which encloses the house and west walled garden. To the east, he designed two interlocking gardens within a wall. The first, or paradise garden, lies alongside the house, and is divided from it by a moat with stepping stones; they represent the hazards which await those aspiring to reach the ultimate goal. Within the paradise garden are bubbling fountains framed by airy metal arches; the scent of flowers mingles with the murmuring of the fountains. From the paradise garden, a darker, more contemplative space under the shade of the plane tree in its centre creates a change of mood not envisaged by the original plan for the moss garden. A belvedere at the corner of the east gardens gives a view across to trees and the lawn across the back of the house. On the west side of the mansion, entry to the original walled garden leads to the pool garden. This, with its Tudor pavilions, has a setting of blue, silver and grey planting, which was originally devised by Susan Jellicoe. In the centre of the pool were stepping stones and a rounded, floating raft, designed by Jellicoe to resemble a painting by Joan Miró; on top of the sun raft were a table and chair, which reminded Jellicoe of *The Beautiful Truths*, a painting of a table on an apple suspended above water, by René Magritte.

From the kitchen gardens next to the pool, a more defined route leads, as at Runnymede and Sutton Place, to a place of disorientation and disquiet. First, the traveller finds himself in an enclosed corridor between a high brick wall and a hedge, with no exit at one end – the Magritte garden. Along the wall are large urns which originated at Mentmore, Buckinghamshire; they have been placed so that their shapes do not diminish into the distance in a manner akin to a surrealist painting. From the Magritte garden an exit is discovered through a dark, winding, evergreen tunnel; the release from uncertainty is found across the grass, where suddenly through an entrance to a hedged enclosure, a large, white relief created by Ben Nicholson appears to hang over a pool. The Carrara marble, with its simple shapes reflecting in the pool, give the perfect resolution to the earlier discord.

Jellicoe was to design several gardens in Italy which were not completed or never executed; two with historical journey themes in the United States are the Atlanta Historical Gardens (from 1992) and the ongoing Moody Gardens for Galveston, Texas, which depict the evolution of

Below

The Paradise Garden, Sutton Place, Surrey, England

Jellicoe made this garden for Stanley Seeger between 1980 and 1986. Here the theme of man's journey is more personal: he voyages through Creation, Life and Aspiration. The Paradise garden is reached from the house by stepping stones – life's hazards – across a moat.

the garden from Eden to the present day (from 1984).[25] He has been criticized for his incorporation of Jungian philosophy into his designs; but perhaps his long, active life of design made him better able to recognize retrospectively the subconscious influences from the mix of art forms and the overlay of history which make up his landscapes. This long life had seen war and hostility as recurring themes; the journey towards reconciliation was an inevitable theme for a man with a respect for humanism.

Oxford vs Cambridge in the 1960s

The 1960s were not only marked by the construction of power stations. There was also the university expansion programme, begun in 1958, following the end of restrictions in building licensing. As a building boom got under way, Oxford and Cambridge Universities sought to construct new colleges. Two, commissioned at about the same time, were bound to attract attention and comparison. St Catherine's College, Oxford, has probably received most scrutiny, though its rival, Churchill College, Cambridge, has much to offer for different reasons. Both colleges are residential, on flat sites, with St Catherine's relatively nearer to Oxford's centre; the walk back to Churchill from Cambridge is longer. St Catherine's was designed as a 'complete work' by the Danish architect, Arne Jacobsen (1902–71), who was responsible for everything from the building to the knives and forks, and importantly here, the landscaping and planting (Jacobsen's planting plan has disappeared). Churchill College was designed by the architects Richard Sheppard, Robson and Partners, and despite their agreement to produce the interior furnishings, the College authorities found fault with what was designed for them. The landscaping was done by Sheila Haywood. There are few similarities; St Catherine's is essentially Danish in construction and landscaping, and Churchill is very English.

St Catherine's College is made of precisely measured yellow brick, with a smooth pre-stressed concrete framework, flat roofs, and light and unfussy on the ground. It is a closed design, spaciously set within a rectangular site, with a river flowing across landscaped gardens by the Master's house and bisecting the grounds. A moat or canal crosses the entrance, and the nearby grass accommodates sculpture. A large, circular courtyard with a cedar tree asymmetrically placed marks the heart of the complex, behind and to the side of which small, enclosed gardens for the staff and students are divided by geometric devices – short planes of green yew, echoed by similar slim, short brick walls. Within the sheltered geometry the planting is varied and colourful, with flowers, flowering shrubs and trees. Outside the framework of the college, small courtyards are planted with flowering trees; there is good quality planting by the offices and the discreet car park. The round walled bicycle store and the grass amphitheatre by the main buildings reminds us of the circular designs of Jacobsen's contemporary, C. Theodor Sørensen.

Churchill, by comparison, is more robustly built from dark brick, an open design on spacious grounds which lend themselves to expansion. Richard Sheppard has designed the college as a series of interlinked squares, based on staircases within – as is the traditional older university system – around cool green courtyards. These are not quite extended spaces, as no student rooms open directly on to them. The courtyards are contemplative places, with sunk lawns edged with stone chippings, a tree asymmetrically placed, or a

sculpture. There is much green lawn for relaxation around the buildings. A Barbara Hepworth (1903–75) sculpture, *Four-Square Walk-Through*, is a friendly object round which students gather and sprawl on the grass. Sculpture in Churchill is not a collection of museum pieces, but invite recognition and familiarity.

Beyond the buildings of the 1960s, an addition built by the Danish architect Henning Larsen in 1992 invites the jibe that Cambridge has finally caught up. The Maersk McKinney Møller Centre, a long, slim, 'inhabited wall' with its curved roof, banded brick and foursquare windows, links the staff accommodation and the chapel at the top of the grounds.[26] In no respect does this resemble the original buildings; the attention is drawn to an octagonal tower with its common room below and viewing terrace above. The living wall is pierced by a dramatic diagonal corridor which reinforces the perception of the Danish taste for geometry; outside, the planting does not seek to draw attention from the building.

Denmark – geometry in the landscape

Denmark has a mild climate, endowed by the warm North Atlantic Drift which washes its coastline. The low-lying peninsula of Jutland has a backbone of low hills, nowhere higher than 550 feet (170 metres), formed by the end-moraines of the departing European ice-sheet. Landscapes and gardens are therefore enclosed, with hedges forming shields against the wind; though Thorbjörn Andersson considers that enclosure was a way of re-establishing boundaries in a landscape that had been cleared for cultivation.[27] The country's present boundaries date only from 1920, when Germany handed back northern Schleswig, whose territorial seizure had been one of the reasons which led Jens Jensen to emigrate to the USA in the nineteenth century. Denmark was occupied by the Germans in the Second World War, without resistance, thus escaping destruction. It emerged after 1945 strongly committed to social welfare, in which functional design found its place.

Above left

St Catherine's College, Oxford

Danish architect Arne Jacobsen designed the garden to complement his college building (begun in 1961); his original planting plan has been lost. The garden was made on two levels: the upper one, which is formal, plays with planes in alternate slim, yellow brick walls and trim, green yew hedges. An amphitheatre links this level with the informality of the one below.

Above right

Churchill College, Cambridge

Begun at the same time as St Catherine's, Oxford, Churchill's green courtyards are enclosed and play host to sculpture and spare planting.

As in most European countries, concern for the conservation of nature has grown because so little of the country's surface has remained undisturbed. On the larger scale, planning of environments became acceptable after the Second World War. Cities needed to expand, and Copenhagen's equivalent to Abercrombie's London Green Belt appeared in architect and town planner Steen Eiler Rasmussen's (1898–1990) Finger Plan in 1948, where expansion was to take place along the fingers of an outstretched hand drawn across the town, and the interstices would be left for recreational purposes, farming and forestry.

Twentieth-century design has been closely associated with geometry. The revolt against the teaching of style, seen later in England and the USA, began amongst the architects at the Royal Academy of Fine Arts School in Copenhagen. A search for a styleless aesthetic was to follow.[28] Gudmund Nyeland Brandt (1878–1945), an experienced gardener and designer, chief Parks Officer for a Copenhagen suburb, writer, and lecturer at the Fine Arts School of Architecture, set the tone. At Hellerup near Copenhagen he laid out a rectangular Coastal Park for this pleasant middle-class marina between 1912 and 1921. Rose borders and paths make straight lines to the sea, separated from the beach by a timber frame. Adjoining and behind this garden for strolling and sitting is another, sunken, garden for perennials, with corner trellises. A lime walk separates the gardens from the tennis courts. Brandt's Mariebjerg cemetery, made between 1926 and 1936, is also based on interlocking rectangles enclosing a grid of compartments hedged with yew, each treated differently, reflecting burials for children and for different denominations. The landscape is bound together by avenues of hornbeam, Scots pine and white willow. But there are also wild areas similar to the Swedish forest cemeteries, and Danes value these green spaces as part of the country's parks.

Top
Hellerup Coastal Park, Denmark
Designed by G. N. Brandt, this Coastal Park was planned with strict formality. Straight paths bisect the colourful planting, and a rectangular frame marks the coastal end of the garden.

Bottom
Mariebjerg Cemetery, Denmark
Geometry shapes the design in this cemetery made by G. N. Brandt, whether in the ground patterns of stone and grass, or the enclosures of trimmed hedges and trees.

Carl Theodor Sørensen (1899–1979)

The landscape architect who moved beyond the stiff formality of Brandt's early modernism to the more inventive geometry of the middle of the century was 'the sculptor in Danish garden art' Carl Theodor Sørensen.[29] He worked his way up from a garden apprenticeship to a student's placing with the

landscape architect Erstad Jørgensen, before setting up his own practice in 1922. Sørensen taught at the Royal Academy in Copenhagen from 1940 where he was the first Professor of Landscape Architecture, from 1954 to 1979. His writing covered many aspects of the subject from plants and designs, parks and a compendium of historical gardens in Europe, to his autobiography *Haver: Tanker og arbejder* (Garden Thoughts and Works) of 1975. His work ranged from the landscaping of the grounds of Aarhus University between 1933 and 1947, to designing his daughter's garden shortly before he died.

The main building of Aarhus University is set at the top of a shallow valley, in which there is a stream. Sørensen won a competition to lay out the grounds, which involved binding the building to the break of slope above which it had been built, and shaping the campus space below. Bridging the change of gradient was achieved by a simple and graceful amphitheatre, a device which Sørensen was to use elsewhere at Boeslunde, Roskilde and Bellahøj, and which seems to be peculiar to modern design in Denmark. Shallow grass terraces curve to join stone steps which anchor the amphitheatre to the main building's retaining wall; trees mark the outer edge. Below the university, oak trees grown from hand-planted acorns form natural groups in the grassland round which the campus is placed. Lakes fill the widened valley bottom.

Scandinavians had pioneered work on playgrounds, and younger children's needs were recognized by Sørensen before the Second World War.

Above

Aarhus University, Denmark

The amphitheatre, by landscape architect Carl Theodor Sørensen at Aarhus University, built by a group of architects under Kay Fisker from 1931. This graceful and simple device crowns the slope below; the natural landscaping is enhanced by groups of trees including oaks from acorns sown by hand.

In 1931 he wrote the influential *Park Politics in Parish and Borough* (*Parkpolitik i sogn og kobstad*). He saw that children wanted something more adventurous than swings and pools for feeding the ducks, and suggested they should be provided with logs, old cars, wooden crates and the like, which they could use for imaginative play under supervision. In 1940 the Emdrup Junk Playground was set up in a housing development, as one of a group of linked recreational spaces, with Sørensen providing the containing landscaped earthworks. Today, children grow plants, saw up wood, make bonfires, or play in huts at Emdrup. The idea caught on in Denmark, where there are other adventure playgrounds, some with animals, and are associated with youth clubs in housing developments. Amongst others, they influenced England's Lady Allen of Hurtwood who introduced adventure playgrounds to Britain.

Flat-dwellers, lovers of the open air and those on low incomes welcomed allotments; Denmark may be unique in having them designed by landscape architects. Their provision often accompanied the making of public parks, and date back to the nineteenth century. Today they are grouped into three categories, according to their size and distance from the home. Local gardens

Below left

Emdrup Junk Playground, Denmark

In 1940 Sørensen introduced the idea of playgrounds where children could enjoy supervised creative activities with wood, metal, water, and plants, using spades, saws, and hammers. Here a group tend a bonfire with its circular bench reminiscent of Jens Jensen's Council Ring (see p. 54).

Above, right

Naerum allotments, Denmark

One of a group of forty allotments, this garden shows the rounded layout, enclosed by hedges, of Sørensen's landscaped compartments for vegetables and flowers. Begun in 1948, the huts were for summer accommodation.

include school and vegetable gardens, and there are day and recreational gardens which have summerhouses and are used for weekends and holidays.

Landscape architect Georg Georgesen designed eighty plots at Rynkevang in 1925; those at Solbakken in Elsinore were laid out by Brandt in 1935 as part of the town's public park system. However the most interesting are those designed by Sørensen at Naerum in 1948 as a swarm of some forty ovals, reminiscent of the egg-shaped drumlin hills left by the retreating ice-sheets, flowing across a sloping site. Each oval measures 81 by 48 feet (25 by 15 metres), and is enclosed by a clipped hedge of privet, hawthorn, hornbeam or roses; Sørensen suggested originally that these should be fruit-producing species. Within the oval cultivation takes place, whether vegetables or flowers for flat dwellers without gardens. Each cottage-like hut inside its oval hedge is

equipped for living in the summer months. The ovals are surrounded by a large containing hedge; the whole is set on grass, which forms a connecting lawn, play-space for the children and circulation space for the adults.

On a larger scale are the Geometric Gardens in Birk, at Herning. This is a complex resulting from Sørensen's collaboration with the textile manufacturer Aage Damgaard, part of which was constructed in a large park after Sørensen's death. The complex is a wonderful assemblage of shapes within a triangular plot made of three distinct parts, best understood as a whole from the air. One part is the re-introduced Geometric Garden which gives its name to the whole. It began life as a design for the Vitus Bering Park

The Geometric Gardens, Birk, Denmark, 1956–83
This extraordinary exercize in the use of the circle, finished after Sørensen's death, comprises sculpture park, left, the Herning Art Museum (once a shirt factory) in the foreground, and the Geometric Garden (Sørensen's Musical Garden), which names the complex, centre back.

at Horsens, and was taken up by Aage Damgaard in 1956 for his Angli IV shirt factory grounds. When the factory moved out to Birk, Sørensen designed the site in its entirety, but the Geometric Garden was left until 1981. Here Sørensen plays with the circle, the ellipse, and the square, which metamorphoses into polygons. The figures, all in clipped hornbeam, form a group set in the lee of a semi-circular hedge, all in a circle of mown grass cut out of a forest square.

First on the site was the factory, a hollowed circular machine for working in, which is now Herning Art Museum. The grass centre is surrounded by a mural by Carl-Henning Pedersen. Behind the factory is another, larger circle, 585 feet (180 metres) in diameter, entered by a path through an oak forest by which it is enclosed. This is the sculpture park, whose figures occupy the grass dais on the edge of the circle, each figure separated from its neighbour by a hawthorn hedge. A pastoral dimension is added by the grazing cattle in the centre.

Sørensen designed a garden for his daughter, Sonja Poll, herself a landscape designer, between 1972 and 1979. This small garden is set around a two-storey house as an ellipse within a triangular site. The shape of the ellipse is made by a clipped beech hedge which is also the dividing line between the informal activities behind it, and the tranquillity of the simple shape around the house. The land descends towards the house in a gentle whirlpool flowing from the living-room across the lawn and round into a sitting-space at cellar level, a grey stone path defining the spiral. The bank is planted with ivy; a single apple tree shades the lawn.

Above

Sonja Poll's Garden, Holte, Denmark
Sørensen designed this garden for his daughter, Sonja Poll, from 1972. It makes use of a hollow triangular site by inserting an ellipse which embraces the house and spirals down to the sitting room at a lower level.

Sweden – All Gardens Are Nature

The shaping of Sweden's landscape in the twentieth century has something in common with those who shook off colonialism in Latin America; but the move away from other European influences was achieved by general agreement, quietly, and without a revolt. It also involved a democratization of the landscape, as people perceived that gardens should be made for everyone, not the élite estate owner. As Thorbjörn Suneson remarked, 'in Sweden history relates to class', with its overtones of conservatism.[30] In their search for an egalitarian modernism, the Swedes appear to have returned to their 'natural' roots, and in this they may have been further encouraged by a period of isolation during the Second World War.

Sweden's vast, empty wildness in the north, stretching into the Arctic Circle with its strange and otherworldly displays of the northern lights, creates intensity and feeds the imagination. The country's physical landscape has been shaped by the ice-sheets, which have left scoured rocky outcrops and a myriad of lakes. Soil has been removed by their relentless bulldozing, and deposited in ridges and rounded hillocks on the lowlands. Thin topsoil has restricted the range of plants which will grow. The climate offers long, cold winters, and hot summers which encourage the population to make the best of a short period of outside living. The low humidity sharpens the profile of hills in the distance, and increases the clarity of light.

Landscapes are also shaped by the culture of the people. Sven Richard Bergh's (1858–1919) *Nordic Summer Evening*, painted at the turn of the century, illustrates the romanticism of the period which illuminates the nature of the Swedish psyche. A young couple stand watching from their verandah as the sunlight fades, casting a glow over the lake and forest beyond, the painting emphasizing the importance of the landscape over that of the two people watching. Elements stressed by landscape architect Sven Hermelin (1900–84) as key features in Sweden's landscapes – the forest edges, the lake inlets, glades and meadows – are all here in the picture. Hermelin, Sweden's first chair in Landscape Gardening at the Alnarp Institute (1934–54), and founder of the Swedish Institute of Landscape Architects (1923), reintroduced these terms to landscape gardening in the 1930s. Until then, French and German terminology, imbued with their own national interpretations of landscape, had been common parlance.[31]

Below

Sven Richard Bergh,
Nordic Summer Evening,
1899–1900
A young couple watch the sun set over lake, forest and meadow, a natural scene which lies at the heart of Swedish landscape design.

Above

Above

Enskede Forest Cemetery, Sweden, 1915–40

One of the first cemeteries to abandon the formality of the previous century, Enkede was designed by Erik Gunnar Asplund and Sigurd Lewerentz as a place of burial in a forest, with graves set amongst trees, reached by woodland paths.

Norse mythology has made much of the forest. Yggdrasil, a mighty ash, was considered to be the tree of life, fed by the spring of wisdom at its roots. The forest was the element in which man could find refuge. In 1915, Swedish architects, Erik Gunnar Asplund (1885–1940) and Sigurd Lewerentz (1885–1975) won a competition for a forest cemetery, to be made in an old gravel working at Enskede. The cemetery was finished in 1940. The forest concept was German, and the Road to the Cross inspired by the street of graves at Pompeii,[32] but the intensity and drama of the use of the site were unquestionably Swedish. The cemetery is approached between high granite walls. On a hillside facing the approach stands a cross, which holds the eye as the cortège moves along the processional way; to one side grass stretches into the distance and over the horizon to planted birch groves and then the burial places amongst the pines. The informality of the layout, with its preservation of woodland paths, was a move away from the heavy geometry of the more usual neo-classical plan of the time.

Sven Hermelin and the Stockholm Parks Department

Swedish landscape design between 1950 and 1970 owed most to Baron Sven A. Hermelin. Educated in Germany, he had worked in Danish nurseries and the Stockholm Parks Department. Many Scandinavian designers trained in Germany, Austria or Denmark, and their ideas were also mixed with English infiltrations. Hermelin's early garden designs were similarly influenced. Later, he moved more closely to what could be best understood as Swedish design –

that of empathy with the site; a garden was designed by understanding and emphasizing existing qualities, not by imposing what did not belong. He disliked the importation of soil for planting in barren areas; and he always used species native to the area.

Hermelin was also close to the spirit of democracy and social reform, with its aspirations for the provision of good public health, and better working conditions to bring pleasure to employment. Part of this spirit encompassed the socialization of garden design, which involved the provision of parks for the public, to encourage general well-being and better health. Like Cadbury at Bournville, and perhaps influenced by the German *Schönheit der Arbeit* (Beauty of Work) movement, Hermelin believed in creating pleasant gardens around factories.[33] His gardens for the Marabou Chocolate Factory (1937–45) at Sundyberg were models of their kind, with rock gardens in which the workers could sit in the sun, a children's paddling pool with a sandy beach, a pergola-edged pool with a small fountain where adults could sit and talk, a lawn with sculpture and herbaceous borders, and a meadow which was open to the public in the summer.[34]

The provision of public parks during this period of optimism is most closely associated with the work of the Stockholm Parks Department, which was at its peak between 1936 and 1958. A body with power to influence local politicians to get things done, the department was also instrumental in training landscape architects such as Sven Hermelin. Between 1936 and 1938 architect Oswald Almqvist was Director of the Parks Department, whose work laid the foundation for future policy. Two men who followed, Holger Blom (b. 1906) and

Left

Marabou Chocolate Factory, Sundyberg, Sweden, 1937 and 1945
Landscape designers Sven Hermelin and Inger Wedborn demonstrated the social concerns of Swedish design in creating factory gardens for workers which were used by the whole family. At Sundyberg there were pools and beaches for children as well as sitting places for adults.

Stockholm Park, Sweden
The Stockholm Parks
Department, under Holger
Blom and Erik Glemme
between 1936 and
1958, blended the needs
of people with the
introduction of nature
into the city. At Norr
Mälarstrand, a stream has
been channelled between
stones and planted with
astilbe, petasites and
heracleum, making a
natural path and play area,
overlooked by a bench
and a pavilion.

Erik Glemme (1905–59), made the Stockholm Park System a leading example
of a 'regional landscape', of pine forest, flower meadows, groves, streams and
rocky extensions into lakes – of nature in the city.[35] This was a far cry from the
English civic park, with its delight in formal bedding and Victorian bandstands,
and the Parisian division between formality and 'English landscape'.

Holger Blom, architect and landscape architect, educated at the Technical
University of Stockholm and the Royal Academy of Fine Arts architectural
school, had worked with Corbusier and in planning in Stockholm before taking
up his position as Park Director, which he held for thirty-four years. Imbued
with immense energy and enthusiasm, a good organizer, educationalist and
publicity man, he was enough of a Corbusian to understand the meaning of
functionalism for parks, but was able to promote 'functionalism' with a human
face. 'Landscape architects must have an understanding of the needs of
individual human beings; it is for them that the recreation areas are to be
created', he told an audience of IFLA at its ninth Congress in 1964.[36] Blom's
poster of what parks could provide, expressed as the branch of a chestnut tree
with leaves about to open, was followed by the provision of mobile theatres,
supervised playgrounds for children, and display areas for art and sculpture
exhibitions, all in the context of the open air, trees, grass, water and flowers. Erik
Glemme, the Parks Department chief designer, focused his skills on creating

naturalistic areas within the park system in such a way that it was difficult to believe that in some parts there had been any human intervention at all.

Glemme's work is best seen between Norr Mälarstrand and Rålambshovsparken, in Tegnér Grove, and the Vasar Park. The first area is the mile long shoreline of Lake Mälaren which has been linked to the centre of Stockholm by the skilful blending of a varied series of incidents along a park pathway. This is wide enough for walking in comfort, but does not attempt to be a municipal boulevard. Where it widens, children can paddle amongst boulders on little patches of beachline. Narrower stretches are better for strolling along the lakeside where trees and shrubs fringe the edges. There are wooden jetties to linger and watch the fish or gaze at the view. There are huts made from hop poles clothed with hop vines, seats, bridges over inlets, a small café, and little enclosures where people can sit and chat. At Rålambshovsparken, there is a larger gathering place for concerts and plays, in an amphitheatre set amongst pines and boulders, a Nordic element reminiscent of the work of Jens Jensen and Carl Theodor Sørensen.[37]

Swedish landscape architect and writer Thorbjörn Andersson sees the landscaping of the Stockholm School as part of the very best in Swedish landscape architecture. After 1958, its work faded away, and its ideals were harder to achieve as populations rose, and large-scale development meant the sacrifice of the individual landscape with its intimate scale and its respect for the essence of the site.

By the 1960s, landscape architects were beginning to question the achievements of the brave new world. As increasing populations and higher environmental expectations created ever more new towns and settlements, the bulldozers removed the old houses with their backyards, designated as slums. In so doing they destroyed communities, rehousing them in high-rise blocks with no gardens, where there was a daily struggle to get down to the ground with push-chairs in lifts that may not be working, to playgrounds or parks – if such amenities had been built. Thorbjörn Andersson, mourning the tearing down of the Klara district of Stockholm as 'the urbanistic loss of the century',[37] blamed both architects and landscape architects who, carried away by Corbusier's teachings, had 'replaced regional sensibility'. J. T. P. Bijhouwer, speaking to the IFLA Congress in Amsterdam in 1960, wondered whether the modernist zeal had gone too far. Referring to a recent competition for an Amsterdam park, where designs were 'skilfully functional, rather austere, sometimes stark', he questioned whether landscape architects would have to reformulate a type of romanticism in which a love for living plant material could re-enter design. 'Let's not be so dead earnest', he said.[38] These were some of the considerations of some of the early postmodernists; others will emerge in the next chapter.

Into the Future

From the 1960s, the apportioning of style labels became even more difficult. 'Modern' reappeared in tandem with 'Postmodern'. Postmodernism broke old rules and did not replace them with new ones.

Style in design reflected wider concerns. In the developed world, the demise of extractive and heavy industries brought a gradual awakening to the destruction of rural and urban landscapes. Changes in technology left abandoned sites in cities, as industry sought different locations. Some nations recognized global warming, with its sinister effects on climate, water supplies, and plant and animal life. Such concerns engendered thinking about conservation, which in turn contributed to the rise of new design in the form of Land Art. Conservation became linked with regeneration, promoting imaginative uses for old industrial sites and run-down city centres in the form of parks, botanical gardens and garden festivals.

The three themes identified earlier – plantsmen's gardens, architectural gardens and social and environmental initiatives associated with the Garden City – weave in and out of private gardens, parks, and urban landscapes. There have been notable landscapes created in this way. In addition, there is an increasing use of deeper dimensions of meaning in design.

But there is a fourth theme, which takes us into the twenty-first century. Landscape and garden have discovered the fluidity with which art forms flow easily from one into the other on all scales: art becomes sculpture, sculpture becomes landscape. Land Art borrows from other arts to become a new synthesis for garden design. It highlights the importance of process in the appreciation of the garden; and it has become closely allied to the reconciliation of man with the natural world, and with regeneration.

Landscapes from the 1960s – high-rise blues

The high-rise building became a familiar part of the landscape where towns needed to house large populations quickly, where ground space in city-centre prime sites was too expensive for extensive spreading, and where business corporations needed to establish a base and demonstrate their power. Landscaping varied from site to site; in general, the richer the settlement, the better the landscaping. The 1960s, in particular, was an age of iconoclasm. In order to build high and build fast, old housing and old communities were swept away.

Opposite
Terraced roof garden, from Viaduc des Arts, Paris
Viewed from the Promenade Plantée on top of the Viaduc des Arts, the sides of the top storeys of a car park at the junction of Rue Hector Malot and the Avenue Daumesnil have been transformed into a cascade of colour by Andreas Christo-Fouroux.

The Death of Modernism?

The demolition of the Pruitt-Igoe building in St Louis, USA, in 1972 has become a symbol for the beginning of architectural Postmodernism.[1] This public housing project, built according to the best principles of Bauhaus Modernism in the early 1950s, was destroyed by the City of St Louis because it had become a warren of crime and badly vandalized. The architect, Minoru Nagasaki (1912–86), had followed the Corbusian Radiant City example of separating people from traffic by the provision of streets above the ground, high density housing in fourteen-storey ribbon blocks to replace the squalor of backstreet overcrowding on the ground, wide green community spaces below, and views from above. However, those who believed that communities could be created by placing together disadvantaged and disparate groups in theoretically idealized surroundings, found they were mistaken. Long 'streets in the sky' lent themselves to crime, and the height of the buildings to isolation. The inhabitants turned on the building, and vandalized it. In Britain, the collapse of the council-built Ronan Point block in Canning Town in 1968 following a gas explosion had an additional impact on thinking about high rise building as people began to question the quality of the work being done on social housing.

The housing made available by planning authorities to relieve postwar population pressure was inadequate.[2] Community space, where provided, was as bleak as the buildings themselves. The conservative architectural lobby equated crime with the International Style, for which it had no sympathy. Some of the architectural press described vast 'concrete canyons' with gusts of wind eddying round pillars, where corners had been cut in housing budgets so that the use of poor materials leading to crumbling concrete outside was matched by equally poor maintenance and running damp inside, where there was no community garden, and in which the socially deprived had been dumped. Research pointed to the design faults which led to crime – dark corners, entrances and tunnels, accessible balconies, lifts which could be easily vandalized, and the absence of people. In the slums, mothers watched from backyards and windows, and neighbours were alert to strangers. Housing should be designed for what it provided, not for how it looked.[3]

In America, writer Jane Jacobs had been saying much the same. Her observation of communities[4] showed that the safest environments were those in which the scale and design of the building could be matched by the ease with which its inhabitants could circulate in the streets, see who was about and contact one another. People and communities were important; they seemed to have been forgotten by architects. Low rise, however shabby, seemed preferable to Corbusier's Radiant City. Perhaps most surprising was the warning given as early as 1948 by the Associate Professor of City Planning at Yale University. Ten years after his escape from conservative England, Christopher Tunnard had begun to question his own early enthusiasm for Modernism. He warned, 'There is a dangerous fallacy in thinking that a certain kind of architecture or planning is intrinsically "better" than another'.[5]

The large-scale provision of garden space on the tops of buildings was seen to be impracticable. The combined weight of earth, rock, stone, turf, water and vegetation on the top of Selfridges store in Oxford Street came to around 1,800 tons. Watering by hose was necessary every day for plants bedded in shallow levels of soil, which dried out rapidly; this led to the blocking of gutters. Calcification eventually brought sprinkler systems to a halt. Soil, rocks, plants and manure had to be brought to the roof in the lifts, or provided via scaffolding at the time of construction. Wind made it necessary to shelter the plants, and a limited range was suitable for this type of setting.

In Britain, the climate discouraged roof-top relaxation, technology led to leaks, and some building societies would not give mortgages for flat-roofed houses. The roof garden for the tenants of Great Arthur House, in the Golden Lane development north of the Barbican in the City of London, gradually fell into decline, and has been restored only recently. Built in 1952 by Geoffrey Powell (1920–99), the modern garden on the sixteenth floor was reached by lift. Sitting under a winged, glazed canopy which hides the water tanks and other services, was a terrace with a rectangular pool, pergola, plant boxes, paving, and seats, made from concrete. Next to Great Arthur House, the much larger communal garden area of the Barbican's North Podium roof, completed in 1973, leaked through expansion joints on to the tenanted parts below, and needed attention only ten years later.[6] It appeared that technology and climatic demands had conspired to restrict the aspirations of modernist living, whether for healthy and serene roof gardens, or for the solutions to large-scale social housing.

There were attempts to create low-rise, smaller settlements such as those built by Span Estates in Greater London and elsewhere, by architects G. Paulson Townsend and Eric Lyons, with careful and sensitive landscaping by the landscape architects Preben Jakobsen (born in Denmark in 1934) and Ivor Cunningham. In 1959 a small development for Corner Green, Blackheath, of two-storey short terraces with

Below
North Podium Roof Garden, Barbican, London, 1983
A communal roof garden softens the once harsh inorganic landscape, using water features and colourful planting.

Bottom
Span Housing, London
Aiming to 'span' the postwar gap between expensive housing and dreary urban estates, architects G. Paulson Townsend and Eric Lyons set out to create landscaping reminiscent of a village green.

Above, right
**Kingo Housing
Development,
Fredensborg, Denmark**
Jørn Utzon addressed the
Danish concept of low-rise
living with community
greens in 1962–63 with
this spacious terraced
settlement near
Fredensborg.

their own back gardens round a communal central green, set the pattern for
many other Span estates and later private developments. Other small-scale
schemes were tried in Denmark, where architect Jørn Utzon designed the low-
rise Kingo terraced settlement at Fredensborg (1962–63). Its looped chain of
houses emerged from the green hillside with their courtyard gardens facing
south. Kingo was an early example of the move away from apartment blocks in
cities, though the Danes seemed not to have had the severe social problems
associated with high rise in America and other parts of Europe. This may be
because overcrowding seemed less severe in Denmark, and also because all
stages of the complexes, including recreational and green space facilities, were
completed together. Their low rise, high density complexes with shared
recreational space represented a move towards greater social interaction
than was provided for by Corbusian models.

For a while, architecture was infiltrated by self-doubt over Modernism,
as a new school of thinking emerged. As architect Leon Krier pointed out
in his robust support for the Neoclassicists, such architecture was being built
in Europe and North America.[7] Born in Luxembourg in 1946, Krier was trained
as an architect at Stuttgart University, Germany in the mid-1960s, where
he embraced Corbusian Modernism, only to reject it soon afterwards.
His disillusionment was mainly based on what he saw as collaboration by
leading modernists – naming Mies van der Rohe, Oscar Niemeyer, Le Corbusier
and Alvar Aalto – with totalitarian regimes. From this, by association, came
the rejection of the *Diktat* of the culture. 'Modernism's philosophic fallacy
is not its principles, materials and technology, but the fact that these are
upheld as a new paradigm, apparently revolutionizing, invalidating and
replacing all previous architectural traditions and knowledge,' he claimed.[8]

Krier's work was admired by Prince Charles, whose own views on Modernism were distinctly cool, and Krier provided the thinking behind the Prince's new settlement at Poundbury, adjoining Dorchester in Dorset. The Duchy of Cornwall had owned the land around the town since the fourteenth century, and Dorchester needed more housing and more varied work opportunities. Was this to be Neoclassicism in a Georgian country town?

Krier examined and rejected previous models. High rise would be out of place in rural Dorset. Garden cities, with their extensive layouts and large gardens, were too greedy for land. Garden suburbs provided no work, and were largely empty during the day. New Towns were based on the separation of work-place from living-place, entailing many wasteful crossing journeys. Poundbury would be set in an officially designated Area of Outstanding Natural Beauty, and would therefore be restricted to intensive housing.

Krier proposed a settlement with provision for small-scale clean manufacturing, small gardens, and mainly low-rise accommodation, based on the walking city. All parts of Poundbury and Dorchester, next door, were to be accessible on foot. Traffic was to be discouraged within the settlement, so children could play in some of the streets as well as their own playground. People would be about during the daytime, whose vigilance would prevent crime; neighbourliness would be encouraged by front doors opening onto the street, and small gardens.

The architectural press and public took notice of the proposed building styles, without understanding the best of the plans for community, the walking city, and work. Poundbury was not to be a Neoclassical settlement. It was variously described as 'Siena Down the Bridport Road', or 'Retrophilia', as the designs for street pictures provided by an Italianate town were then replaced by Dorset vernacular. Krier became disheartened as some of his concepts were rejected by local opinion. Dorset County Council disliked his plan for narrow roads and limited parking to counter the domination of the car.

From its inception in 1989, Poundbury has grown steadily. There is a chocolate factory, an upholstery works, offices, and workshops. As the town grows, communal facilities are being added. Poundbury has confounded its critics, and is popular with its residents who prefer conservative design.[9]

Landscapes from the 1980s

Those who believed that architectural Modernism was mortally ill – if not dead – by the 1980s, were mistaken.[10] A new version could be recognized, less utopian, less idealistic, not preoccupied with innovation, happy to borrow an idea from the past and unconcerned with the avoidance of symbolism, allusion and metaphor. Postmodernism, which apparently negated and supplanted Modernism, had been replaced by Post-postmodernism, or Modernism with a change of attitude – and several changes of clothes. But the popular perception of the architectural symbol of Modernism – the high-rise building – had returned, and with it, a wide palette of gardens, inside, outside, and on top.

Right

Water wall with planting at 1 Canada Square, Canary Wharf, London
The high value of land in the heart of London's Dockland development has limited the size of green public spaces. This little garden, with its water wall, fountain, bedding and shrubs, has been well designed, but is inadequate for the needs of the building above it.

London and the Docklands

On the River Thames in London, eight square miles of potential dereliction, threatened by the movement of dock activity downstream, was rescued by the London Dockland Development Corporation (LDDC) from 1981. Part of the so-called Docklands became an Enterprise Zone in 1982, as the Thatcher government granted fast-track planning and tax incentives to attract new business activity. Unfortunately little encouragement was given for the provision of garden landscape.

Canary Wharf on the Isle of Dogs became the new symbol of Thames development triumphant, its fifty-storey tower (No. 1 Canada Square) completed in 1991 by the North American Skidmore, Owings Merrill (Chicago), the tallest building in Britain. The Beaux-Arts skyscraper was landscaped by Hanna Olin Ltd with Sir Roy Strong as advisor. But the well executed formal gardens at its foot, with a tall central fountain, and annual planting in beds by the surrounding wall of falling water, are too small in scale for such a development.

The provision of garden space for the rest of Docklands, originally part of the remit of the developers, was largely ignored as profits to be made from high ground-values outweighed environmental improvement. Political

quarrels between local government and the LDDC left Island Gardens, a small
park surrounding the entrance to the foot tunnel between the Isle of Dogs and
Greenwich, bereft of investment. Low-rise housing with small gardens, and
hard-surface walkways by the water with some good landscaping, provided
very little green space on the Isle of Dogs for the needs of children, the walking
public, and to break the domination of the built landscape with parks.

By contrast in November 2000, the Thames Barrier Park was opened in
Silvertown, to the south of the old Royal Docks on the north of the Thames.
A spur to further housing and development, it has already been successful,
with half of the new housing on the western side sold before construction,
and the building of a primary school and retail units. The Park, designed by
Alain Provost (for Groupe Signes), one of the French landscape architects
for Parc André Citroën in Paris, is one of the most exciting public parks made
recently in Britain.

Behind a paved court with fountains, similar to Parc Citroën, there is a
formal green dock or sunken garden sheltered by grass and evergreen
embankments. Strong lines made by paths of turf and gravel lead towards the
Thames, rising via grassy ramps to the simple Pavilion of Remembrance for the
Borough of Newham's war dead. Beyond the pavilion are the silver upturned
hulls of the Thames Barrier, and a walkway at the river's edge. The dock's lines
are softened by yew which is being clipped into waves, and colour has been
introduced by gold- and purple-leaved shrubs, and block-planting of

Above
**The Green Dock, Thames
Barrier Park, 2000**
Designed by the French
landscape architect partly
responsible for Parc
Citroën in Paris, Alain
Provost, this stylish green
space provides parkland,
play areas, a fountain court,
a place for functions,
groves of trees, and
this deep 'dock' with its
lines of block planting of
perennials, evergreens and
grasses, leading to the
Thames Barrier.

flowering perennials. Rudbeckia, potentilla, Japanese anemone and Michaelmas daisy provide late summer flowers, and the scent of lavender pervades.

Bridges across the dock introduce diagonal lines which continue in paths across the surrounding parkland. The green dock is straddled by wide, grassy parkland with formally spaced trees; there is a children's play area to the east, and a zone for outdoor functions. Though not part of the park, the western boundary is made by the tiered 'white ship' apartment building which overlooks the grass and trees, with its balconies, ocean liner railings and 'funnel' formed by the tower, and other revived Art Deco features in its detailing.

Passed to the London Development Agency on the winding up of the LDDC in 1998, the Barrier Park has been built on the sealed site of old chemical, dye, and armaments works, as another stage in the regeneration of Docklands and a further addition to its planned green ribbon of parks and open spaces. Access will be improved by the planned extension of the Docklands Light Railway to London City Airport and Royal Albert Island.[11]

In London, the high-rise office tower is fast replacing its smaller predecessor, led partly by the demand for ventilation space by the new information technology. Confidence in flat roofs has been restored by better

waterproofing and more precise knowledge of the requirements of plants for soil depth and water. Lightweight planting mediums have been developed. Automatic watering and feeding can be provided by pop-up sprinklers which temporarily disappear from sight. The working environment of tall buildings can be improved by the introduction of atrium gardens and courtyard gardens within.

Above Cannon Street station office workers enjoy a restful view from their windows, and longer river views from a roof garden. Despite the planning difficulties posed by the listed Victorian towers, wind, and the permitted height of the vegetation, a 'dynamic geometric parterre' by Janet Jack has been planted with yew, beech, dwarf laurel and *Lonicera pileata* for shelter around the lawn, relieved by the colour provided by philadelphus, lavender, dianthus, low-growing roses and decorative grasses.[12]

At Number One Poultry, in the City, the horizontal pink and orange stripes of James Stirling's circular building with a roof-top promontory, houses stylish gardens by Arabella Lennox-Boyd for restaurant customers. From the circle, a triangular promontory site, entered by a metal gate as through a portcullis to a secluded castle retreat, has a geometric design based on lines and circles. Raised lawns form carpets for large stone balls, which echo the signs of the medieval money-lending Lombards. A drawbridge-like connection leads to the point of the triangle overlooking the architectural anarchy of the City; from a seat, the garden can be contemplated. Continuing the analogy, there may be allusions to sterling (Stirling) and silver in the quiet colours of the planting.

Above

The Roof Garden of the Coq d'Or restaurant, Number One Poultry, London
Designed by Arabella Lennox-Boyd, the gardens of Number One Poultry describe a planted half-circle around the restaurant, from which extends this quieter arrowhead. From the gate, the visitor is surprised by the low zig-zag hedges, and stone balls on green lawns.

Above
Promenade Plantée, Paris
On a defunct railway
viaduct conserved by
architect Patrique Berger,
it is possible to walk from
the Place de la Bastille
along a planted walkway,
landscaped by Jacques
Vergely. Now well
established, this
promenade boasts
a long canal, pergolas
with climbers, and
a wide range of grasses,
shrubs and perennial
planting, well frequented
by the public.

Parisian roof gardens

The French have discovered the most imaginative ways to make gardens on roofs, and to bring the garden into the heart of a building. In Paris, the drive to regenerate parts of the city has led to some fine examples.

The Viaduc des Arts supports a promenade which replaces part of the railway line which ran over a brick and stone viaduct from the station at the Place de la Bastille towards the Place Daumesnil. A little further on towards Vincennes was the goods station at Reuilly. With the closure of both stations, in 1968 and 1987 respectively, this viaduct could have been demolished for city redevelopment; instead it was made part of the scheme to regenerate eastern Paris. The architects Patrique Berger and Philippe Mathieux and landscape architect Jacques Vergely won the competition to refurbish and plant the viaduct, a strong axial route. Now there is a high-level walkway with shrubs, flowers, a pool and a pergola. The walkway overlooks yet another example of successful roof gardening in the stepped terracing of a seven-storey car park by the junction with the Rue Hector Malot. Further on, the viaduct walk becomes a bridge which crosses new housing and green space, before continuing to the park at the Bois de Vincennes.

To the southwest of the city the old area of Montparnasse was cleared for redevelopment in the 1960s, and the roof of the newly refurbished Maine-Montparnasse station has been crowned since 1987 by an evocation of the French Atlantic seaside. The Jardin Atlantique is surrounded by flowing planting in grasses of grey and lavender, and shades of grey mosaic pavement simulating waves. There are sandy beaches with moored boats, and polished, ragged-topped stone slab cliffs of red and grey. In the centre of the garden, a mast and framework evoke a ship's deck. The public enjoys this garden, in which there are places to sit, and it provides a space of colour and stimulation to the senses for the Parisian on his way to the office or the station.

Although criticized for design flaws in the storage of books, Dominique Perrault's Bibliothèque Nationale de France, completed as the last of President Mitterrand's *grands projets* in 1997, is full of wit. The library is stored in four glass high-rise buildings shaped like open books, which form the four corners. They stand on a silver teak deck which is vast and bleak in the rain, but shines in the sun. In between, below ground level, is a green forest garden atrium, its trees reaching to the open sky, a calming vista for those working at subterranean levels. The trees are *Pinus sylvestris*, which were transplanted from northern France. The theme appears to be 'nature controlled', with nature standing as a metaphor for knowledge. This is repeated outside, where parallel metal cages filled with clipped evergreens are placed on the deck surrounding the entrance level. The cages metaphorically double for bookshelves, and recall the French manner of containing shrubs behind wooden treillage in the eighteenth century.

Berlin and Daniel Libeskind

New architecture in cities continues to offer opportunity for garden design to follow. In Berlin, Daniel Libeskind's Museum illustrating Jewish history and culture is intended as a continuation of a museum which was closed by the Gestapo in 1938. It is also a commemoration of the Holocaust, and a source of reconciliation for two societies. Libeskind (born in Poland in 1946), Professor of Architecture at the University of California in Los Angeles, has designed a zig-zag ground plan which links two buildings, the Berlin Museum and its stark Jewish Museum extension. The design is made to jolt the mind, deliberately leading the visitor to experience the dislocation of Jewish lives in history, with intervening spaces between the violent shifts in direction. The link between buildings is made underground, with one exit leading to the E. T. A. Hoffmann Garden, which represents the emigration of German Jews and their exile. The visitor is immediately disorientated by a steep path leading past a forest of lines of pillars, which appear to be leaning at a different angle to the slope of the path, and through which sunlight can be seen at the end. There is vegetation growing on top of the pillars, but it cannot be reached. The building was open to the public in 1999, but the first exhibition was not mounted until the autumn of 2001. However, the message of the Holocaust and agony of the Jewish exile was powerfully demonstrated by the building alone, with its allusions to peace and reconciliation in a garden.

Above
Jewish Museum, Berlin, 2001
Daniel Libeskind's garden in the Jewish Museum repeats the Museum's theme of dislocation which he has used to heighten awareness of the horror of Jewish persecution and the Holocaust. Here, the path is set at a different angle from the forest of pillars which it passes, and the unattainable garden beyond.

Italy and Carlo Scarpa (1906–78)

Italian modernist architect Carlo Scarpa taught in the Istituto Universitario di Architettura of Venice where he also made gardens; two designs, one for a family tomb, the other for a rich man's palace, show imaginative and contemplative gardens of distinction.

The Brion Family Tomb (1969–78) made adjoining the cemetery of San Vito d'Altivole near Asolo, occupies a right-angled space enclosed by an inward-leaning wall. The entry followed by the cortège is by steps leading to the chapel, which has strong visual links to Frank Lloyd Wright. The square massiveness recalls Wright's 1906 Unity Church in Oak Park, Illinois, or even the 1920 Hollyhock House for Miss Barnsdall in Los Angeles, California. At Brion Scarpa appears to have hinted at the Mayan decorative theme used by Wright in the Hollyhock House. Next to it is the tomb; beyond the tomb is a pool and a pavilion, 'the propylaeum', with circular entrances which lead out into the main cemetery. The three elements are set in a garden; they have metaphorical associations. The pool's reflections link the worlds of life and death, as in a Japanese garden. A narrow channel takes water from the pool towards the lower lily pond with its stepping stones by the chapel. Scarpa called his concrete tomb an arcosolium, or bridge, beneath which are the tomb-slabs of the patron and his wife, bending towards each other in a loving relationship. The arcosolium refers to the shape of the arch beneath which early Christians were buried in the catacombs; here it also may relate to a bridge between life and death, countryside and town, or a link between Brion and the village in which he was born. The underside of the bridge, the vault, has traditional Venetian mosaic which glows green; the site is in full sun, with views out to the countryside with which the Brions were closely associated.

The Querini-Stampalia palace in Venice was built in the sixteenth century for an aristocrat, and is now a foundation which displays paintings, furniture and china to the public. The ground floor of the building adjoining the canal in the square of Santa Maria Formosa had been damaged by repeated flooding. Between 1961 and 1963 Scarpa was asked by his friend Giuseppe Mazzariol, the director of the Querini- Stampalia Foundation, to remodel this level and the adjoining garden. He raised the floor but also designed a surface which could be enhanced by the periodic flooding. Water is channelled from the canal through a Japanese-style gateway, and then is contained in a deep stone trough and led away. Should the water rise to the floor of the entrance hall, it would spread over coloured marble tiles which would shimmer beneath the flood, enhanced by lighting at this level. The hall gives access to the Venetian walled garden, its rectangular lawn and trees leading to an enclosure whose wall is decorated with a small band of Scarpa's characteristic yellow mosaic. Water is led from a fountain through a stone channel, along which are planted violets and strawberries, to a square lily pond.

Scarpa died in Japan, the country which seemed to define his work at the end of his career.

Below

Querini-Stampalia Palace Garden, Venice
Carlo Scarpa's garden in the Palace grounds was influenced by his strong feeling for Japanese architecture. Beneath trees stone channels lead to a square pond planted with lilies beside mosaic paving; the mosaic repeats in the wall above.

North American skyscraper gardens

America has invented and embraced the skyscraper, and has used the spaces outside and inside to create the illusion of gardens. Roof gardens have been used by museums for sculpture exhibitions. In New York, the Ford Foundation created an influential interior or atrium garden in 1967 by employing their architects Roche and Dinkeloo to enclose the plaza and build a garden court twelve storeys high, with light from two glass walls.[13] Some of the original trees did not thrive, due to lack of light, and the cryptomeria, eucalyptus, and camellias were replaced by *Ficus benjamina*, philodendron and pittosporum, with a few surviving magnolias and seasonal planting. The Trump Tower, at Fifth Avenue and 56th Street, has stepped set-backs planted by landscape architect Thomas Balsley with pear trees and cascading ivy, which form a green stairway up the glass walls of the building.

Above
Central Park as seen from a New York rooftop
Central Park, designed by Frederick Olmsted in 1858.

Below left
Roof Garden, Metropolitan Museum of Art, New York, 2001

Below right
Atrium Garden, World Financial Center, New York
Designed by landscape architect Diana Balmori.

The appalling act of terrorism on 11 September, 2001, destroyed the twin towers of the World Trade Centre in New York. After the shock, anger, disgust and bewilderment at the loss of life that it involved, New Yorkers are coming to terms with 'Ground Zero', the space left where the towers used to stand, and debating what should be done with it.

Opinion is divided. Some would defy the terrorists by rebuilding on the site, as high or even higher. Designs have been proposed by Daniel Libeskind and Norman Foster. Others point out that Ground Zero is also a graveyard for those bodies which were never recovered, and to build would not show suitable respect for the dead.

Another group would like the site to become a memorial garden, despite the constant shadow created by the surrounding skyscrapers. Such a garden could take the form of the Vietnam Veterans' War Memorial in Washington, in the grassy West Potomac Park, between the Capitol and the Potomac River. Here a long black granite wall, polished like glass, is engraved with the names of the dead and reflects the sky, and remains an important place of pilgrimage for relatives of the dead.

In Britain, those who wish to remember the sixty-seven British people who died in the New York attack do not have the site constraints of their American friends. The British garden has been planned by Land Use Consultants for Grosvenor Square, in front of the American Embassy. Here an oval space is partly framed by an oak pergola and pavilion, sheltering seats, looking on to flower beds and a stone recording the names of the British dead. The decisions facing the Americans will take longer to resolve.

Parks, botanical gardens, festival gardens:
Germany

Munich's Westpark, with its display of plantsmanship in discrete areas, was made in an old gravel quarry for a Federal Garden Exhibition in 1983. It achieves the remarkable feat of binding together a site cut by two motorways by means of a 'green bridge'. Tall earth banks moulded around the approach to the bridge and its edges soak up the sound of traffic, whose impact is minimized. The park was designed by Peter Kluska and some of the planting was by Rosemary Weisse (d. 2002), the Kassel-based landscape architect who specialized in the use of perennials. She was influenced by Professor Richard Hansen (1912–2001) at the Technical University of Bavaria, who extended the work on perennial planting and grasses which Karl Foerster began

Westpark, Munich, Germany, 1983
The last thirty years or so have seen a gradual change in planting practice which began in Germany and the Netherlands. In the Westpark, German landscape architect Rosemary Weisse has developed a natural appearance in public parks by using perennials and grasses where best suited to the soils, keeping weeding to a minimum.

and applied it to public parks as well as gardens.[14] Weisse used a mix of
perennials which were adapted to the hot and dry conditions at Westpark,
with its stony soil, not adding too much fertilizer to encourage strong growth.
Planting has been in loose drifts with little space between, and gravel is used
as a mulch. Weeds are removed before they set seed, but some wild grasses
and flowers are left alone. Maintenance is from paths which meander in and
out, and edged with plants which are resilient to walkers' feet such as
Geranium sanguineum 'album'. The aim is to create an all-year-round
naturalistic garden with the minimum of maintenance, similar to the meadow
or prairie, but more controlled. Different plants are encouraged which will give
colour and shape in their leaves, flowers and seed-heads, and cover levels of
other plants which are dying off. Contrasting colours such as red *Lychnis
chalcedonica* and white *Campanula lactiflora* grow amongst wild grasses. *Stipa
gigantea* and *Verbascum bombaciferum* divert attention from bearded iris that
have finished flowering. Hypericum and helianthemum, muscari and allium,
aster and euphorbia, emerge from the background of thyme and nepeta.

The Emscher park north of the Ruhr district is really a series of parks in a
regional development which is still unfolding. The end of coal mining and
steel production in the Ruhr valley created the prospect of a ribbon of some
seventy kilometres of bleak wasteland. But instead, the area surrounding
seventeen cities along the River Emscher, a tributary of the Rhine, is being
transformed into an imaginative park, where nature and art have been united
to celebrate past landscapes. Redundant gasometers, steel works, railway lines,
coking ovens, and waste tips have been joined in a series of 'incidents' which
extend from Duisburg in the west to Bergkamen in the east.

Seven wedges of green have been drawn at right angles along the line
marked by the River Emscher – described as a long green backbone with
green ribs sticking out.[15] Connecting former coal mining towns, each wedge
has developed a quality of its own, based around the industrial architecture
still standing. Garden festivals have been held to promote each region as it
has emerged.

The green pattern is connected by a cycle path and walking routes, the
River Emscher's polluted and noxious stream has been channelled into an
underground sewer and the new bed filled with clean rain water. Many tons of
contaminated soil have been dispatched to the bottom of pits where they are
covered with fresh earth and fast-growing vegetation. Where possible the
natural colonization of plants and trees has been left undisturbed – echium
and sedum, willow, birch, poplar, beech, buddleja and robinia – but some
management is necessary to control more rampant species. New woodlands
are explored by school groups and walkers, and children make dens and tree-
houses under the supervision of foresters.

The economic and social policy behind the Emscher Park is to use public subsidy to provide an improved landscape where, it is hoped, work opportunities will follow. New commercial and technology parks have been planned; the buildings of the port of Duisburg have been renovated to accommodate offices, housing, and restaurants, and Israeli artist Dani

Karavan has been engaged to design a city centre park. In Gelsenkirchen, in the late 1980s and 1990s, the new low-rise mixed social and private housing development of Küppersbusch-Siedlung has been built with its shops, day-care centres, city park and houses arranged around green spaces. On the cleaned-up site of a former coking plant, landscape designers Brigitte Schmelzer and Angela Bezzenberger designed a park, around which the new district of Prosper III Bottrop has emerged, part of which is the Beckheide Garden City, designed by Copenhagen architects Tegnestuen Vandkunsten. The older houses of the mine workers, themselves the result of garden city policies by mining paternalists, have been renovated and are much in demand.

Had there been previous recognition of the potential for

industrial skeletons to be reclothed and rejuvenated, as in the Duisburg-Nord Landscape Park? In 1967 the American Robert Smithson had recorded photographically New Jersey's territory of oil derricks, smoking chimneys, and deserted construction with attendant waste. His essay, entitled *A Tour of the Monuments of Passaic*, was a lament for man's devouring of the earth's resources, and his blindness to the scars he would leave behind. The Duisburg-Nord Landscape Park was made on land partly bought from the Thyssen company. A competition for its development rejected an historical and philosophical design from the Frenchman Bernard Lassus in favour of Peter Latz's industrial land art, which proposed the minimum intervention with natural regeneration, and the maximum celebration of the strong architectural elements formed by the Meiderich smelting works. Steel plates which lined the foundry pits have been made into a collage which is also a stage for theatre and concert performance in the Piazza Metallica. Chimneys, gantries, girders, metal tunnels and chutes are now lit up at night, the pink, green, blue and red strip lighting outlining the bones of the works and reflecting in water-filled pits below. The emphasis has been on the celebration, not demolition, of old industrial contructs. Lighting also outlines a metal tetrahedron, built on an old spoil heap now stabilized as a lookout over the Ruhr, and the top of the winding mechanism at the Zollverein Shaft XII, where a centre for design, culture and industrial history has been built. Small gardens have been made wherever the ground plan of old works allowed; there are muscari growing in industrial container bases, and waterlilies flower in tanks.

Near Gelsenkirchen, land artists have produced some striking displays,

Opposite page
Emscher Park, Germany
Mechtenberg Landscape Park, part of the Emscher complex (top). American landscape architect Martha Schwartz made shapes with coloured bales of hay, cutting the contours drawn by artist Peter Strauss and landscape architect Harmut Solmsdorf, using oilseed rape, clover, and 'hedges' made from maize. Piazza Metallica (bottom) is part of 70 km of redundant coal and steel works reinvigorated by the imaginative recycling of the infrastructure.

Above
Potsdam Federal Garden Show, Germany, 2000
An old Russian military site has been transformed by a garden festival, providing a permanent exhibition hall, and land for new housing nearby. Different zones, each with their own character, are linked by paths and bridges.

219

some temporary, some permanent. Richard Serra has placed a metal slab 14.5 metres high on a black spoil base on the top of the Schurenbach Tip. Another manmade hill, the Mechtenberg tip, became the theatre for more transitory works in the Mechtenberg Landscape Park between Bochum, Essen and Gelsenkirchen. In 1995 artist Peter F. Strauss, landscape architect Harmut Solmsdorf and an accommodating farmer, Bernhard Stricker, traced the course of the underground mines, and fields of energy made by overhead cables, in broad bands of oilseed rape and clover round the contours of the hill, leaving red soil paths cutting diagonally across. In 1999 artist and architect Martha Schwartz was commissioned to transform the Mechtenberg hill with bales of hay into lines and trapezoidal shapes. At the same time, the Bulgarian Christo and his wife Jeanne-Claude (both b. 1935), more usually concerned with wrapping buildings, were constructing a great wall of oil drums in the theatre which was once the Oberhausen gasometer.

A recent venture into urban regeneration in Germany has taken place in Potsdam, west of Berlin, which hosted the 2001 Bundesgartenschau (Federal Garden Festival) on an old Russian military site. The developing infrastructure, such as a new tram route, should stimulate further growth. The triangular site exploits geometry, with avenue axes defining the boundaries and rectangular embankments enclosing sunken arenas, one of which contains cubes full of gardens. Like a game of dice, the garden cubes contain smaller cubes tipped on edge on a grass carpet, each one full of flowering plants. Corten steel bridges join the embankments and make viewpoints; beds of red roses divide the great hall for horticultural shows from the slopes of the arena beyond.

England

Not only is the Eden Project near St Austell in Cornwall concerned with conservation and regeneration, but the shaping of its site and encircling planting demonstrates how such large-scale work can take on the mantle of Land Art. Cornwall is a historically poor county; the loss of its copper and tin, the decline of the fishing industry and recent problems in farming have accentuated difficulties created by geographic isolation. Tourism has become a mainstay of the economy.

Tim Smit, born in the Netherlands in 1954, an archaeologist turned record producer who had settled in Cornwall, had successfully recreated the gardens of Heligan, a nineteenth-century house, with earlier origins, to the south of St Austell, for the public to view. The idea of giant climatically controlled greenhouse domes ('biomes') in which plants of like environments could be grown, to attract visitors and to act as a catalyst for regeneration in Cornwall, seems to have been shared by Smit and a Cornish architect, Jonathan Ball. A large team of engineers, building contractors, architects and landscape

architects was assembled. Much employment has been created; expecting under a million visitors in the opening year, the Project in fact attracted over two million people in 2001.

The large site required for this massive venture was provided by a china clay pit which was nearing exhaustion. The Project's objective is to promote an understanding of plants and their uses, and this is achieved by housing them in domes made of plastic-like hexagons of ethyleneterafluoethylene. Two biomes have been constructed, that of the Humid Tropics tall enough to accommodate fully grown rainforest trees, and a mighty waterfall which gives both drama and a site for wetland plants. The second completed biome contains warm temperate plants; cool temperate plants can be grown on the slopes below the domes. A third biome, for arid conditions, is planned. There is space enough to create an impression of the living environment and surprises at every turn; plant museum it is not.

Outside, the hollow of the pit has been sculpted around the two biomes, circling around a central lake above which terraces of planting form swathes of colour. This is a developing project which will attract people back, and already claims international importance.

France

There is a spectacular group of modern parks in Paris, all based on the regeneration of industrial sites. To the northeast is Parc de la Villette, once an abattoir. To the southwest is Parc André Citroën, on the site of the former automobile works, whilst to the southeast just across the Seine from the Bibliothèque Nationale de France is Bercy, created from the old Paris wine market. The three sites present the formal design tradition in a manner which accommodates Postmodernism, and in the case of Parc de la Villette, some

The Eden Project, Cornwall, England
This remarkable piece of Land Art occupies the hollow formed in a Cornish china-clay pit, now exhausted. Moon-like biomes containing plants in natural groups reflect, with colourful flags, in a lake, and are circled by terraces of planting.

Parc de la Villette, Paris
Built on the site of an old abattoir, the park provides a science park, space for varied activities and an underlying philosophical theme. A brilliantly coloured folly (top) is a point on an imaginary grid. A wavy roof beside a straight path (middle) joins galleries and gardens. Alexandre Chemetoff's bamboo garden (bottom) leads to an enclosed *cylindre sonore* with thrumming wall cascades.

philosophical undertones. Throughout, there is humour, colour, and surprises.

La Villette was the first of the three, one of President François Mitterrand's *grands projets*, set rolling for the second time in 1983 after he had defeated Valéry Giscard d'Estaing for the Presidency in 1981. Mitterrand held two separate competitions, one for the public park and another for the conversion of the abattoir into a Science Museum. Parc de la Villette was to integrate town and park, be fluid in design to accept different impromptu activities, and appeal to a wide range of people including the immigrant population of Paris. Yet it was also to have an organized structure.[16]

Much has been written about the connection between French-Swiss landscape architect Bernard Tschumi's (b. 1944) successful design for the park and the deconstructionist texts (not themes) which underpin it.[17] Meanings are different for different users: a park can mean dogwalking, tree-climbing, plant spotting, playing football, listening to the band, or sunbathing on the grass. The word 'park', therefore, has to be deconstructed into separate elements. Philosopher Jacques Derrida was consulted by Tschumi, and he advised that it would be possible to put back the elements using a structural solution. For this 'structural solution' Tschumi chose points, lines, and surfaces.

'Points' were a series of bright red follies on legs on an imaginary grid which, superimposed on the ground, absorbed existing structures. The follies were to represent variety and mechanization in the twenty-first century, and each red cube could be a café, a place to marvel at astronomy, or a play centre from which children on bicycles hurtle down a ramp.

'Lines' are straight walks through the park which link with galleries leading to activities. One walk has a wavy roof and this threads its way through many of the follies. A canal forms another line, over which people climb bridges and survey the whole; the canal side provides grass on which people perform *t'ai chi* or gaze into the water. 'Surfaces' are large spaces in which people kick balls, picnic on the grass, and sunbathe, oblivious of the wedge, circle, and lines of the ground plan.

A sinuous walk links themed gardens. A sunken bosquet leads down to an enclosed, circular Moghul garden with its water-organ cascades. From the gateway out, a deep path leads up through Alexandre Chermetoff's Bamboo Garden, whose feathery fronds rise above a striped grey and white pavement. There is a geometrical vine garden in tiers up a slope, the grey stone slabs relieved by pots of scarlet pelargoniums.

The Science Museum, designed by Frenchman Adrian Fainsilber, forms the main mass closing the northeast corner, from which the focus falls on his great silver Geode, a globe which houses a cinema. Parc de la Villette is at its best full of people on a hot day, enjoying the interaction of park and town. Theories of

Left
Parc Citroën, Paris
New planting by one of the axial paths of the park, created on the site left by the old Citroën car factory in southwest Paris.

Parc Citroën, Paris
Gilles Clément's gardens
are enclosed on the south
side of the park, with rich
themes entwined in the
colours of the planting.
Each colour has reference
to a metal, a day of the
week, a sense, and
a season.

The Jardin argenté (top)
is one of the most
successfully colour-
themed gardens, its cool
silvery-grey impeccable
in all seasons.

One of the best-known
images of the park is its
parterre of fountains
(bottom), in which children
delight in summer, and
which are left to their
more dignified formal
role in winter.

deconstruction do not appear either to interest or deter users of the park.

Parc André Citroën was begun after a competition in 1985 resulted in the commissioning of two teams under the co-ordination of Alain Provost (landscape architect). One team comprised Gilles Clément (landscape architect) and Patrique Berger (architect), and the other Provost with his architect partner, Jean-Paul Viguier. The park was viewed as a mechanism for stimulating urban regeneration in that part of Paris, working through one of the series of urban development areas called *Zones d'Aménagement Concertées* (Joint Management Zones). Ultimately management is in the hands of the City of Paris.

The park design, though strongly formal, is less abstract than at Parc de la Villette. Instead, the park rises in a series of shallow tiers, from the Seine quay via wide steps, to a central green area of rectangular lawn. To the left is a series of themed gardens under the direction of Berger and Clément; to the right are a canal and cascades. At the head of the lawn is a water parterre with fountains flanked by greenhouses. A diagonal axis follows a line through *Magnolia grandifloras* trimmed like tubes, cuts the base of the water parterre, and makes its way across hornbeam hedges round grass enclosures, ending in the black garden of the Provost team, who are responsible for the canal, lawn and fountains.

There is much to engage the eye and the intellect in the walled gardens of Berger and Clément. Each has a theme around a colour which refers to a metal, the garden metals being arranged according to the laws of alchemy; there are additional references to the days of the week, the senses, and the seasons. The 'Jardin argenté', or silvery garden, is planted with species such as *Pyrus salicifolia, Salix purpurea, Santolina neapolitana, Festuca glauca, Euphorbia seguleriana*, and *Salvia argentea*. Silvery gravel mulches the planting and floors the garden, through which silver-grey stepping stones move from low plants towards trees and shrubs. There is a garden of movement, whose massed planting refers to changes over time, underlining the concept of garden being process rather than fixture.

There is also a great deal of fun. The water parterre has jets of variable height spouting suddenly from flat stone slabs, in which children (and their parents) disport themselves. The canal moves with serenity towards a water wall and cascades in which there is much illicit paddling; and the heads of the fountains in the canal, clustering together, have the appearance of a flock of long-necked geese. A hot-air balloon is constantly tethered, offering rides; there are simpler pleasures, such as ice-cream, relaxing on the grass, jogging, or riding a bicycle.

Parc de la Villette and Parc Citroën have been criticized for being too stylish and too formally horticultural, with few ecological considerations. But Paris can be applauded for making parks for people; the hot May of 2001 proved how popular they were.

Barcelona and the resurgence of Spain

Spain's emergence as an innovator in landscape design is relatively recent. Although there was much innovation in art and architecture, albeit intermittently, Spain's turbulent political history in the twentieth century kept it looking inwards. Spain remained neutral during the First World War, and many creative people were drawn to cities such as Barcelona. Tensions between the Republican left and the Nationalist right led to the Civil War (1936–39), and victory for the Nationalists under Franco (1892–1975) who was effectively Spain's dictator until his death. Franco's conservatism, repression, and refusal to modernize had a stultifying effect on Spanish culture, and provoked unrest amongst Basques, Catalans and Andalucians. After Franco's death, there was a resurgence in the arts; Spain's membership of the European community in 1985, and its hosting of the Olympic Games in 1992, were two steps towards prosperity and a new outward approach to the world.

Catalonia has been a cradle for creativity throughout the twentieth century. Barcelona, its capital, likes to think of itself as more forward-looking than Madrid. In 1929, it played host to an International Exhibition, and the site now holds the re-created pavilion of Mies van der Rohe, which has had immense influence amongst architects and landscape architects worldwide. Repressed after it fell to Franco in 1939, twenty years were to pass before Spain was opened to foreign investment and tourism, and Barcelona developed in a mindless, unplanned scramble of property speculation and immigration. There was no concern for parks and green spaces.

Population grew fast. In 1900 it was about 500,000. By 1990 the Barcelona region had expanded to four million people, and the city proposed a green belt, limiting urban development and linking open spaces in the mountain ranges running parallel with the coast. Green corridors including woodland and nature parks were planned to link up around Barcelona – the Parque de Collserola and Montjuïc on the west, the Parque de la Serralada de Marina on the east.

But within the city, changes had already begun. The Parque Juan Miró, approved in 1983 and built on the site of an old slaughterhouse, was planned

Above, left

**Parque Joan Miró,
Barcelona, 1983**

The *Dona I Ocell*, Miró's
tubular sculpture in bright
colours, admires itself in a
pool, or surprises the visitor
by its appearance between
trees in the park below.

Above right

**Parque l'Espanya
Industriel, Barcelona**

Luis Peña Ganchegui's park
draws in the towers of a
railway to make them
a part of this city park,
relating them to the lake
below like so many
warships.

Right

Barcelona Pier, 1997

This park has enlivened
a dreary part of the
waterfront, with its grid
planting of *Gleditsia* and
palms vying for attention
with the inanimate arms of
the lighting elements.

by Solana, Galí, Arriola and Quintana as four large, sandy squares, shaped by
the planting of *Washingtonia robusta* palms. This is a hard surface park for
people to play petanque or laze on shaded benches. Behind the squares is a
large pool, in which is reflected the red, yellow, blue and green *Dona I Ocell*, a
tall tubular sculpture made by Miró. Redundant textile works, lorry works and
railway land have also been turned into parks.

In 1992, the Olympic Games brought new investment to the site of the
1929 Exhibition on Montjuïc. More recently, attention has focused on the
coastline. The Parque de l'Espanya Industriel has been designed by the Basque
architect Luis Peña Ganchegui with towers seemingly belonging to warships
circling menacingly around a lake; there are sculptures by British sculptor
Anthony Caro and Andrés Nagel. One of the most jaunty parks is Barcelona

Pier, where architects Jordi Henrich and Olga Tarrasó have worked with Barcelona City Urban Projects Service from 1997. Instead of a bleak stretch pointing to the sea, there is now a display of *Gleditsia triacanthos*, *Phoenix dactilifera* and *Washingtonia robusta* palms, and *Casuarina equisetifolia* planted in a grid. Beside them, and masquerading as trees planted in their own grid, are brushed steel lighting elements with three arms capable of throwing light in different directions, and looking remarkably like a forest of mobiles which could have been made by American George Rickey (b. 1907).

Barcelona's Botanical Gardens, commissioned by the City Council to transform a waste dump on Montjuïc facing the Olympic site, opened in 1999. Most of the funding was provided by the European Union, with the remaining twenty per cent coming from the City.

The landscape architect Bet Figueras and the architect Carlos Ferrater designed a network of large, triangular beds in the amphitheatre left by the tip set in the red hillside, separated by wide, white, angular paths made in horizontals. The beds are broken by flights of steps or paths which join lower horizontal paths. There are long views across Barcelona. The purpose of the Botanic Garden is to conserve the Mediterranean vegetation of the Levant, the Iberian Peninsula, North Africa, Chile, Australia, California and the Canary Islands, grouping some two thousand species by ecological principles in their geographical settings. Plants are therefore placed in communities as they would be in their own habitats, and are not displayed as museums of taxonomic groups. Water plants have not been forgotten in this dry landscape;

a pool greets the visitor moving from the entrance buildings. Rainwater is stored underground, and the irrigation system works on solar power. Waste is recycled as compost; no pesticides are used.

The initial rawness has receded, with vegetation acclimatizing on the red triangular beds and green slopes behind their equally red triangular corten steel supports. This is a remarkable landscape, a mix of land art, regeneration and sustainable botany, which engages all the senses.

Plantsmanship in Europe and the USA

From the start of the century, greater attention has been directed towards styles of planting which derive from continental Europe. With its origins in Germany and the Netherlands, the use of perennials, wild flowers, and grasses in the places which suit them, has become widespread across the Atlantic. With each plantsman comes a different approach, so that one will favour making a 'cottage' garden, while another will attempt an introduction of a 'wild' meadow. Cultivation methods include selective weeding, so that invasive species are kept in check and ground cover is maintained until seeding is imminent. The reasons for this change from the traditional orderly flower bed, apart from its intrinsic beauty when done properly, include the misguided belief that the garden demands little maintenance, and the wide availability of perennials and grasses. With a few exceptions, Europeans have continued to lead the field in plantsmanship and plant-led design.

The Netherlands – Mien Ruys (1904–99) and Piet Oudolf

It is not surprising that Mien Ruys became a landscape architect, as her father, Bonne Ruys, had founded a nursery at Moerheim, Dedemsvaart, which is still

Mien Ruys's Garden and Nursery, the Netherlands
At Moerheim is the nursery established by Bonne Ruys, Mien Ruys's father, which became her home and an international centre for plants. This water garden is part of the living display of plant ecology which demonstrates the suitability of the subject for the setting.

run by his grandson, Theo, and has an international reputation for its plants.
Neither is it surprising that Mien Ruys worked with hardy perennials, as part
of her education on garden architecture was acquired at the Berlin-Dahlem
gardens, not far from Karl Foerster. With German influence strong, perennials
remain a leading feature of the Moerheim nursery. From beginnings in the
family's garden architecture department, and working experience in England
(where she assimilated ideas on cottage garden planting), Mien Ruys's
clients first included country houses. But she became interested in
Modernism and the functional approach to garden space, with its dislike of
over-ornamentation. A garden design in *De 8 en Opbouw* in 1942 (the journal
of the Dutch branch of CIAM of which she was a member) shows a very simple
layout for a house in a polder. A pool with its rounded end looks towards the
flat landscape beyond, reached by a low terrace from the house. The boundary
is partly lined with low shrubs, and there is a small border on the eastern side.
Later she designed gardens for social housing, such as at Frankendael in 1949,
where terraced houses surround a communal central green and children's play
areas, each house having its own garden and allotment as well.[18]

Ruys lectured at the Technical University of Delft, founded a garden
magazine, wrote about perennials, and had a wide practice from gardens to
industrial landscapes. Her home and garden at Moerheim for over seventy
years was a showcase for testing plants in a great variety of conditions, from
marsh to dry garden. It was planned with a strong architectural shape, and
architectural planting.

Piet Oudolf (b. 1936) is equally well known in the Netherlands and in
Britain, where his commissions have included a nursery garden in Surrey, and
twin borders for the Royal Horticultural Society at Wisley. But his Millennium
Garden for the Pensthorpe Waterfowl Park by the River Wensum in Norfolk
displays his flair for plantsmanship on a large scale, and his ability to give
landscape interest in early autumn by the use of grasses and perennials which,
when they finish flowering, retain colour and shape. The continental aim to
create a version of the natural garden, treating the space as a flowing whole, is
well displayed here. There is no hard landscaping at Pensthorpe, just meadow-
like drifts of colour in which plants are repeated with different associations.
The overwhelming colour theme is variations on purple, with loosestrife,
Monarda 'Balance', *Foeniculum vulgare* 'Giant Bronze', *Echinacea* 'Rubinstern'
and *Astilbe* 'Purpurlanze' set off by grasses including deschampsia, miscanthus
and stipa, and the intervention of blue *Nepeta racemosa* 'Walker's Low' and
occasional white and yellow coneflowers.[19]

Oudolf's nursery at Hummelo in the Netherlands was begun in 1992 to
expand supplies of perennials suitable for his designs, and his garden behind
it displays the asymmetrical grouping developed elsewhere. Variations of

Above left
**ABN/AMRO Bank,
Amsterdam, 2000**
Piet Oudolf uses blocks of
perennials in an abstract
linear form.

Above right
Bury Court, Surrey
Piet Oudolf's garden for
the owners of Green Plants
Nursery displays seven
plant borders with
perennials, around
a centre of grasses.

Below
**Washington Federal
Reserve Garden, 1979**
Wolfgang Oehme and
James van Sweden have
followed the European
trend for block planting
of perennials; this early
commission over a car park
in Washington requested
green shade for sitting
areas in the summer.

colour – pink/mauve astrantia, astilbe and monarda – are relieved by pale lemon foxgloves. Grasses spread before the boundary hedges whose tops are cut in wavy lines.

At Bury Court in Surrey, Oudolf has shown in the garden he made with Marina Christopher and John Coke how a style seemingly best adapted to large areas can be refined to small gardens. In the old walled farmyard, Oudolf has avoided planting in 'rooms', and has surrounded an irregularly-shaped lawn with seven borders filled with perennials. These have been carefully selected, like Foerster, for a long flowering season and long life, sturdy stems (to avoid staking), resistance to disease and the ability to survive bad weather. Varieties best suited to the wetter climate in Britain are bred in the nursery attached to the garden. In the autumn, grasses transform and redefine the spaces between the few trees in the garden. Bury Court displays Oudolf's preferred colour range including rust, madder, lilac and indigo with surprise bursts of red, orange and yellow.[20]

North America – Wolfgang Oehme and James van Sweden

Private gardens on the eastern side of the USA have traditionally been associated with annuals and lawns, or instant creations by landscape designers told to make low maintenance a priority. The Washington-based partnership of German-born Wolfgang Oehme (b. 1930) and American James

van Sweden (b. 1935) has sought to introduce German and Dutch ideas in what they promote in their *Bold Romantic Gardens* as a new American style.[21] Oehme began his career in a German horticultural school, and took a course in Landscape Architecture at the University of Berlin before going to America in 1965. Van Sweden studied architecture and landscape architecture in America, then urban planning in the

Netherlands. Introduced by the Dutch landscape architect and university lecturer Jan Bijhouwer (1898–1974), their 1977 professional partnership, based on complementary skills, has attracted commissions from private gardens, public and corporation parks and landscapes, in the United States and abroad.

Oehme and van Sweden see their New American Garden as 'a metaphor for the American meadow' – perhaps the prairie garden without the emphasis on native plants. They follow the broad principles of layers of perennial planting with year-round interest, with a narrower palette for corporate bodies and public parks. For such clients, the emphasis on low maintenance, with limited watering, no dead-heading or use of pesticides, must be attractive. Flowering trees and grasses form taller layers of interest.

Washington's Federal Reserve Garden was an early commission, and the constraints posed by the site, which lies over an underground garage, are not obvious. The commission specified green shade for the hot summer in a noisy city, and sitting areas with sculpture. Eighteen inches of soil provides a sufficient planting medium for blue *Liriope muscari* and *Epimedium x versicolour* to blend into taller grasses such as *Calamagrostis acutiflora stricta*. A greater allowance of four feet of soil around the edge of the garden allows flowering trees such as *Sophora japonica* and varieties of oak. In spring, tulips, hyacinths and daffodils bloom under *Pyrus calleryana* 'Bradford'. A favourite late-flowering combination is the orange coneflower *Rudbeckia fulgida* 'Goldsturm' set against *Miscanthus sinensis gracillimus*. Scent has not been omitted, with a raised bed of roses adjacent to the entrance.

Britain

From the 1960s, British plantsmen and women moved towards using subjects ecologically suited to their gardens. Beth Chatto has long been a pioneer of this approach at her garden and nursery at Elmstead Market near Colchester in Essex, as has John Brookes. His garden at Denmans in Sussex, itself a classic design of its time, accommodates subjects well suited to sun, light soils, and the pebbly 'river' which flows into the lake. By the end of the twentieth century the new continental planting style had begun to be adopted in Britain.

Some park authorities see the benefit from low maintenance perennials in run-down areas, which suffered from disastrous local authority financial policies forced on them by central government, including compulsory competitive tendering, which lost men skilled in plants and plant maintenance to the strimmers and mowers. The value of vigilant park keepers also disappeared with the 1980 Right to Buy Act, under which many keepers' cottages were sold by park authorities. Recently low maintenance regimes, with wildflowers and grasses, have been tried by Gloucester City Council and Sheffield's Concorde and Bole Hills parks.[22]

Private gardens have adopted some semblance of the German and Dutch ideas. Penelope Hobhouse's courtyard garden at her Bettiscombe home in Dorset is a fine blend of English 'cottage' garden and perennial colour. Dan Pearson has demonstrated a similar approach in Frances Mossman's garden at Home Farm in Northamptonshire, with a greater use of grasses. But the English country garden still holds great sway, as successive Chelsea and Hampton Court Shows demonstrate; this may be partly English conservatism, although wet winters encourage mildew and rot rather than the interesting shapes in grasses and seed heads of the drier and colder mid-continent.

However, the first International Garden Festival to be held at Westonbirt, Gloucestershire, in the summer of 2002 at last displayed innovative land art approaches in design and plantsmanship, in Neil Wilkin's sparkling glass Suncatcher trees, in Nicholas Pearson Associates' spiral mount Primeval, Medieval, Modern, and in Ricardo Walker and Guillermo Acuna's garden representation of the colours and weave of a poncho.

Geometry in plantsmanship

Another school of European plantsmen creates formal designs in gardens using evergreen trees and shrubs. The Belgian Jacques Wirtz (b. 1924) and two of his sons have undertaken work on all scales from country estates to small courtyards, in Belgium and in several European countries. Wirtz's French projects range from the garden at Chaumont, home to the permanent garden festival, to the redesigned Carrousel garden in the Tuileries in Paris.

The proposed marriage of Wirtz's 1991 design to the existing Le Nôtre plan for the Tuileries posed problems. Though Paris had shown itself to be a leader in modern park design, many felt that formality and historical precedent should be observed.[23] The burning of the Palace of the Tuileries by the Commune in 1871 had left a space between the Louvre and the Tuileries which had never been landscaped satisfactorily. This was further accentuated by the pyramid in front of the Louvre (1989), by architect I. M. Pei. Also to be considered was the relationship of the Tuileries to the longer axis westwards, towards the Arc de Triomphe. Wirtz's design did not draw on any one period, and blended in old elements such as the nineteenth-century chestnut trees and park furniture. Bosquets which flank the smaller Arc de Triomphe du Carrousel (1805) have been joined by Wirtz's lines of green yew hedges fanning westwards into a shape reminiscent of the rays of light emanating from the Sun King himself, retaining their visual emphasis by increasing in width as they recede towards the larger Arc de Triomphe.

Wirtz and his son Peter are the planners for a garden for the Duchess of Northumberland at Alnwick. This is a blend of historical precedent with forms of land art, which aims to attract the public and present educational themes.

The Duchess described her concept as a 'classically designed garden' with 'water in every possible space' which would 'come alive' using lighting and tricks of technology.[24] Pavilion walls designed by Belgian architect Paul Robbrecht will have curtains of water, with a pool and fountains inside a contemporary glasshouse. Outside the pavilion are ambitious projects for a water labyrinth, lakes, a grotto, an ornamental vegetable garden, a serpent garden and spiral of clipped evergreens. The plan, drawn by the Wirtz team, displays a wealth of green structural shaping and parterres which borrow from French seventeenth-century design but incorporate the present, including the use of lighting in water and vegetation, ice sculpture, and a combination of fire and water features. The first phase was completed in September 2002.

Spain – Fernando Caruncho

Because many of his commissions have been for private gardens, the work of Fernando Caruncho in Spain is not as well known as it should be. Before deciding to become a gardener, Caruncho studied philosophy at university, absorbing ideas from classical Greek writers; and later he moved towards the culture, teaching, and designs of Moorish Spain, Renaissance Italy, and Japan. In this he resembles many modern practitioners of garden making. This background, enriched by childhood summer holidays with grandparents in their Catalonian home overlooking the mountains, has been reflected in the making of strong designs. Caruncho regards the straight line as man's intervention in nature; he claims he is obsessed with the grid, on which his gardens are based, and that his designs unconsciously adopted the formula of the golden section, whose proportions are pleasing to the eye. In his gardens he tries to capture the qualities of light and the mysteries of enclosure, and to approach the 'mythological, symbolic and religious origins of the garden'.[25] It is not surprising that he feels an affinity with the work of Luis Barragán, on whose ideas he has based his own house in northwest Madrid (1988–89). The low, single-storey building and its surrounding plain stucco walls are coloured warm orange by the application of iron sulphate, a tone used in many Caruncho buildings, which reflects in the long raised trough at the base of the wall. His courtyard garden is sheltered by a metal lattice on which climb scented roses, jasmine, and wisteria. Descending to the garden, the attention is drawn to an angular pool partly surrounded by a pillared pergola covered with wisteria, with a deep red sun pavilion made of metal. Layers of smooth green leaves roll towards the pool, giving it colour. Ivy cascades from the pavilion, to join low hills of trimmed escallonia – pavilion and hedge-pruning evoke the Japanese garden.

At Mas de Les Voltes, Castel de Ampurdán (1995–97), Caruncho has designed a garden of many elements for the owner of a large Catalan

Mas de Les Voltes, Spain, 1995–97

Catalonian philosopher and garden-maker Fernando Caruncho has made a garden at Castel de Ampurdán which uniquely combines formality with agriculture. Using his preferred grid in which to design, and making reference to ancient Mediterranean culture, he has turned wheat fields into gardens by spacing olive trees and cypresses along the paths and edging the fields with stone.

farmhouse. Here the grid is obvious, but it is formed by a water terrace with delicate brick edging, reached by steps descending from the farmhouse. There are thin, ivy-covered walls making terraces on which vines have been planted, and olive trees flank the brick steps. The outline of the four quarters of the water parterre is marked by slim cypresses. Beyond the water, angular golden fields of wheat make their own parterre, held in place by neat stone edging, with alternate pencil cypresses and ancient olives growing in the mown grass allées between the fields. The historic references in this garden are numerous, but combine in a novel manner. No other formal designer has 'combined agricultural crops to create a formal design'.[26]

Land Art

Land art, environmental art or earth works, are terms which have been applied to a form of land sculpture which emerged in the United States in the late 1960s. The concept has been accepted in a variety of forms and scales in landscapes and gardens. Some are temporary, when there is an underlying theme of process, others are permanent. Many of these forms have arisen from concern for man's carelessness in stripping the planet and leaving behind ugly scars. In some there is simplicity, in others, complicated messages to be interpreted.

Michael Heizer (b. 1944) may have been the first proponent of a new art form in the western deserts of the USA, but he raised controversy by expressing his anti-art establishment policies by damaging the earth's surface with his early creation *Double Negative* (1969–70) which displayed his two deep gashes excavated in a Nevada mesa. Robert Smithson's (1938–73) *Spiral Jetty* of 1970 made in the Great Salt Lake, Utah, became one of the best-known works in silent protest at 'manmade systems mired in abandoned hopes' where the wreckage of vehicles and detritus of oil working had violated the lake. Here Smithson created a spiral form in the water using local rock, the shape reflecting the shape of the salt crystals growing in the lake, and the mythological connection of the Great Salt Lake with a whirlpool.[27] Using stones from his sites, England's Richard Long (b. 1945) created circles and lines in the landscape, representing journeys. These were recorded and the process of journeying and recording were regarded as the landscape. Circles and lines represent shared knowledge; one of his most recent circles has been made from slate and is eight metres wide. Suggesting the shared historical experience of many centuries, *Orcadian Circle* is set on a grassy terrace in the middle of oak saplings in a three-acre garden overlooking the sea near Dublin, as part of the landscaping by Jonnie Bell for a private art gallery.[28]

Ian Hamilton Finlay has claimed that 'A garden is not an object but a process';[29] no other art form is more subject to change over time. Thus some recent land artists have chosen to focus on the process of making and the process of change. Andy Goldsworthy (b. 1956) makes beautiful, ephemeral collages, and photographs them as they disintegrate. Of this genre is a chandelier of green and brown sycamore leaf sections, pinned together with pine needles and hung from a tree[30] and shards of ice forming fish, bridges and columns.[31] More semi-permanent structures include his serpentine earthworks along a disused railway track at Lambton, County Durham (1988), and the beechwood arch over an entrance to the Hooke estate, Dorset (1986).

Goldsworthy is attempting to engage with natural forms, and the transitory character of what he produces is immaterial to him.[32] Similarly, artist Chris Parsons creates patterns in the dew on lawns in the early autumn mornings by sweeping the shapes with a broom; the pattern disappears as the sun burns off the dew.

Kathryn Gustafson (b. 1952)

Following Heizer and Smithson, America has produced many land artists who are also landscape architects. Kathryn Gustafson is one of the most creative of today's landscape makers, with an ability to design on small and large scales with equal originality and thoughtfulness. Brought up in Washington, Gustafson originally worked in fashion in America. She then studied landscape at the Ecole Supérieure du Paysagisme in Versailles until 1979. She is skilled at thinking in three dimensions and expressing her designs as models and sections.

Gustafson finds her concepts within the 'dreams and aspirations of the client', but they are also firmly based on the client's cultural background. A park design for Beirut

Above

Richard Long, Orcadian Circle, 2000
Set against the tranquil background of Dublin Bay, Richard Long's slate circle makes reference to shared history. Like Jens Jensen's council rings in America, the circle can signify the sharing of understanding between different cultures, and the healing of rifts.

Below

National Botanic Garden of Wales, 2001
The great Water Wall forms the climax to Kathryn Gustafson's design for the Welsh Botanic Garden. Set under a soaring glass dome, the dazzling colours of the Mediterranean plants descend in tiers towards the Water Wall at the heart of the dome.

encompasses a garden of reconciliation, with a table containing a channel of drinking water under the shade of trees, where all faiths can share a meal. The Westergasfabriek park in the making in Amsterdam is very similar in aim to the Emscher Park in Germany, translating an old gas works into a series of water gardens, canals, plazas and performance areas.

Gustafson has had a series of commissions in France, where she completed a simple garden for the Aulnay L'Oréal Centre in 1992. Based on the shape of a woman's body, the garden lies within a space enclosed by offices, whose windows look on to a lake, grass, and ivy-clad ridges dividing channels of water. Water lilies blooming in the lake, roses and yellow and white potentilla add touches of colour to the green ground cover under the windows, and soften the design. A larger project at Terrasson in the Dordogne uses aluminium and gold leaf ribbon threaded through a grove of oaks as a reference to time through the elements.

In 2001 the National Botanic Garden of Wales opened to the public. On a windy hillside near Carmarthen, British architect Norman Foster's glass dome encloses a garden designed by Gustafson. Inside, there is drama created by the sun streaming through the roof, which becomes the sky. A descent between tiered beds, which support brilliantly coloured plants from the Mediterranean regions of the world, leads towards a sandstone ravine with its wall of water descending nearly six metres into a pool.

Gustafson's most recent commission in Britain is for a fountain garden in Hyde Park to commemorate Diana, Princess of Wales. Described as a double cascade in a grove of flowering trees, the restrained design is bounded by an oval, and concentrates on a metaphorical representation of the nature of the Princess. The speed of the water as it rushes down slopes and the stillness of the rest of the channel is intended to evoke the life of Diana. The accessibility of the garden, with children and adults encouraged to play in the water, underlines Gustafson's theme of 'Reaching Out – Letting In', which she also equates with Diana's ability to espouse people and causes.

Patricia Johanson (b. 1940)

Johanson sometimes refers to her work simply as 'sculpture', though this belies the scale of a remarkable synthesis of solutions to the problems of the environment, expressed as landscape parks.

Johanson has degrees in arts subjects, and architecture, which she felt compelled to study in order to deal with the 'man's world' of engineers she had entered with her structural designs. Her work has been influenced by the art of Georgia O'Keeffe (1887–1986), who painted plants and other forms from nature in New Mexico. Johanson also has a wide grasp of the interrelationship of trees, plants, insects, birds, animals, the soil and the sea in a way which goes beyond the scientific term 'ecology'. She seeks to engage in this relationship by creating landscapes which can erase the scars caused by human activity, putting in place a design which not only pleases the eye but teaches about a better relationship between man and the land. Her landscapes are public ones, as she feels that 'it's better to approach everything as art, and make it available to everyone'.[33]

Johanson's exploration of man and the land began in 1970, noting natural changes around a line sculpture she had made in a woodland called Cyrus Field near her home in north New York State. She built up a body of thought through drawings based on plant forms for functional purposes. There were municipal water gardens in which lakes, shaped like the petals of a water lily, performed varied activities from reclamation to boating; and a park inspired by a piece of lichen, with its curling edges forming benches. Johanson's first completed commission was begun in 1981 for the degraded and eroding lagoon at Fair Park in Dallas, Texas, in which life had been killed by nitrogen from lawn fertilizer. After research into how to regenerate the ecosystem, she chose two plants on which she based designs for water sculptures. One was the Delta Duck-Potato, *Saggitaria Platyphylla*, whose knotty roots would help to combat erosion. The sculpture made up in gunite (cement, sand and water) mimicked the shape of its natural model which was already doing its work in the water. Gunite roots became paths, the stems and leaves were for birds to perch on or people to find seats. The second plant was the Texas Fern, *Pteris Multifida*, which when made as a large sculpture, provided not only bridges and islands but lagoons and habitats for aquatic plants and animals needed to complete the food chain in the lagoon.

Johanson's 'Endangered Garden' was made for the Department of Public Works in San Francisco from 1988, to disguise a sewer pipe around Candlestick Cove, to provide a habitat for many species of wildlife losing the battle with the expanding town, and to give access for the public to appreciate their environment. Shaped like an endangered San Francisco garter snake, the garden runs along the top of the buried sewer pipe. Its head is shaped from mounds which are planted with flowers to attract butterflies which have all but disappeared locally, and its body becomes a walk around the Bay. There are steps down to the beach in the shape of the Ribbon Worm, whose loops fill with water when the tide returns forming a habitat for the real creature. An arbor for resting along the walk plays with snake images and butterfly images, and acts as a habitat for birds; there are references to the Ohlone Indians whose artefacts are found in the region, and the shapes and colours of the scales and stripes of the snake. Rare salt marsh plants are being encouraged such as *Cordylanthus maritimus* subsp. *palustris*.[34] Outside America Patricia Johanson has similar large environmentally protective projects such as her

**Rainforest Park,
Ibidos, Brazil, 1992**
This drawing by American
Patricia Johanson defines
the way in which she sees
her landscape parks,
designed in order to
restore ecologies upset
by man's activities. Here a
rainforest plant becomes
a model for trails and
high walkways through
trees for visitors.

1992 Amazon Rainforest Park, sculpture which filters
waste from water in the 1995 Nairobi River Park, and the
1996 Ulsan Dragon Park in South Korea which combines
flood control with restoring wetlands.

In Seoul, South Korea, Johanson adopted a *haetae*
(a mythical creature which wards off evil near buildings)
as a shape for the Millennium Park which is being built
on a reclaimed landfill site on an island in the Han River.
In order to stabilize the site, terraces similar to those for rice paddy farming are
planned for the slope, defining the shape of the *haetae* and acting as paths
and access roads to the top, with waterfalls issuing from its paws.

Contemporary Japanese Design

Japan has continued to influence occidental gardens and their makers since
the country was opened up to the West following the Meiji restoration in 1868.
The model of the Japanese temple at the Chicago Exhibition of 1893 may have
introduced Frank Lloyd Wright to the black beams and deep-roofed style of
building which he adopted in the Robie House and others, and Wright shared
the Japanese concern for the interrelationship of nature with buildings.

Monet at Giverny (Chapter One) and the makers of the Japanese Tea
Garden at the Golden Gate Park (Chapter Five) were representative of many
who were fascinated by the pictures created by the traditional Japanese
garden, but unable to understand its history or the significance of the forms
in the picture. The pastiche Japanese garden soon joined the collection of
style revivals in the West during the early twentieth century, though Japanese
gardeners were often employed. Significant gardens were made in the
twentieth century as well as those of Paris and San Francisco, including Tully,
Kildare, Republic of Ireland; Tatton Park, Cheshire, UK; Westfalen Park,
Dortmund, Germany; Clingendael, the Hague, Netherlands; and the Nitobe
Gardens, British Columbia, Canada.

The Japanese garden evolved, as did all Western gardens, from centuries of
history, and an importation of ideas from China, through Korea. A reverence for
natural objects came from Shinto and Buddhist influences, and stone, water
and plant material took on symbolic references of religious, mythical and
historical significance. Zen gardens, made of raked stones, were places in
which priests meditated. Each object in a garden was to be placed in a set
manner to achieve harmony and good luck. Only recently have these
principles been translated into English from the eleventh-century *Sakuteiki* or
Records of Garden-Making.

In Japan the Second World War only interrupted a period of absorption of
Western landscape and garden features. Shrubs were not tightly pruned as

before, exotic plants and grass lawns were introduced instead of national plants and moss beneath trees, and large fountains, waterfalls and pools replaced their more discrete traditional Japanese counterparts. Such examples could be seen in the gardens of the late 1960s. Western garden-makers such as John Brookes opened schools of design in Japan.

Today's Japanese garden designers have often been educated in both Tokyo and the West, have a comfortable relationship with both cultures, and have evolved a new Japanese style which refers to the past and looks to the present. Their gardens in Japan are often constructed for Western-style houses. The space constraint relevant to traditional Japanese courtyard gardens (in this mountainous country, with its rugged coastline, nearly three quarters of the population live on five per cent of its ground surface) is appropriate to many houses outside Japan, and in such situations designers such as Robert Murase (with Japanese and American parents) have created small gravel gardens perhaps punctuated with stepping stones between azaleas and maples, with a focal point such as a waterfall quietly coursing down a rocky wall in view of the house windows.

Other notable Japanese designers of the 1980s and 1990s include Motoo Yoshimura and Shodo Suzuki, equally well known in the United States. Suzuki's designs have a traditionally narrow palette of plants, which might include bamboo, camellia, prunus, azalea and maple. His Japanese gardens include a contemplative example in Chichibu, to the northwest of Tokyo, where a stream divides a centrally placed stone terrace in an angular course, overlooked by stone benches.

The Fakuda Garden in Kyoto was designed by Yoshimura with the emphasis on water. There is a winding stream which has four ponds with waterfalls; smooth stepping stones in the stream contrast with unworked stone boulders on the banks; and maple and mahonia reflect in the water.[35]

Japanese designers have been willing to adopt the avant-garde, including mysterious steam gardens evoking misty Japan, the vapour dispensed by devices hidden in vegetation or among rocks. Lighting adds an extra dimension at night, whether in parks or private gardens; architect Makoto Wei Watanabe's installation of four-metre-high fibre-optic rods wave like grasses at the foot of a mountain setting.

Below
Steam Garden, Chaumont Garden Festival, France, 1998
Peter Latz's Nebelgarten demonstrates the Japanese influence on European garden-makers: stone sets the design, and steam adds mystery.

Bottom
Musashino City, Tokyo, 1999
In front of a research and development centre near Tokyo, Japanese landscape architect Yoji Sasaki has designed a grid of water and grass squares; cherry trees allude to the traditional garden.

Yoji Sasaki, born in Japan in 1947, educated at Kobe and Osaka Universities in Japan and Berkeley and Harvard Universities in the USA, university lecturer, writer and practising landscape architect, represents an emerging group of first generation designers who have observed the proliferation of high-rise buildings with their harsh materials and styles which accompanied the business boom of the 1980s (and its subsequent collapse in the 1990s). He is perhaps pulling back from Western Internationalism, finding the wholesale adoption of European styles both shallow and meaningless, and the modern city, without space for parks and nature, lonely and unfulfilling.

Through the 1990s he sought to recover a Japanese identity in his work. His 1994 NTT Plaza and 1996 Enko River Art Promenade for Hiroshima are two schemes where he has used spaces imaginatively and metaphorically, offering the public connecting green corridors where there are no parks. The Plaza, raised above the street by an office block, has a dynamic floor pattern of black and white, using polished granite, pebbles, concrete and sawn stone, and with trees placed where paths cross. The Promenade, a terrace of cherry trees, leads into the city by the river, with contrasting shapes and colours of decking, grass and water which form a grid overlooked by offices in Musashino City.[36]

Ian Hamilton Finlay (b. 1925)

The 'stone poems' of the gardens of the Scotsman Ian Hamilton Finlay have been described as Land Art, and they also convey messages to the visitor who will persist in unravelling their meaning. He presented his philosophy of life as short poems with a terse simplicity in his Wild Hawthorn Press from 1961, and then as lettering on stone tablets placed in grass, on plinths and plaques in trees as 'living poetry', in walls or by the wayside. These convey pastoral, maritime and philosophical themes or arguments, depending upon their sites, and introduce an interface with nature, war and death.

Below

Stockwood Park, Luton, England

Ian Hamilton Finlay designed a garden for Stockwood Park in the 1990s, which is open to the public. The pastoral theme of the garden is set by the lettering 'I Sing for the Muses' carved into the stone plaque which hangs from a tree, overlooking a flock of stone sheep.

Finlay's best-known garden is at his home of Little Sparta, in the Pentland Hills southwest of Edinburgh. The 4-acre (1.5 hectare) estate was named after his acrimonious battles (which he dubbed 'The Spartan Wars') with the Scottish Arts Council and the Strathclyde Regional Council over what he could and could not do on his land. He has placed references to war, which are all the sharper because of the surrounding beauty of the landscape. Stones by the loch are carved with the name of the French Revolutionary Saint-Just, in a reference to the local men (the 'Saint-Just Vigilantes') who helped him against the council. By the door of his house a statue of Apollo stands in a lararium – a small temple containing the household gods – but he holds a gun, not a lyre. Grenades are set as finials on the gate-posts.

Using the theme of the Wartime Garden, Hamilton Finlay made drawings of weapons in association with gardens: a tank with camouflage as a pergola, a battleship with blazing guns as a fountain. These were engraved on Portland stone by John Andrews for Battersea Park in 1977. The reference could be about earth, air, fire and water, abhorrence of war, or alternatively, turning weapons of destruction into peaceful gardens.

The pastoral scene with classical associations is also a frequent theme, expressed as a programme in an eighteenth-century landscape. At Stockwood Park in Luton, there are six pieces of sculpture; the first, a plaque set high in a tree, evokes the classical landscape of Claude and Poussin where shepherds tell stories and play their flutes. Nearby is a group of large stones representing sheep, underlining the message. A curved wall resembling the Temple of the British Worthies at Stowe bears a line of inscriptions relating to Ovid – a storyteller who told about deception. 'For Daphne Read Laurel' says one, referring to Daphne's transformation into a laurel to avoid the attentions of Apollo.

Finlay has had attention abroad earlier than in Britain. Gardens have been made for the Max Planck Institute in Stuttgart, Germany (1975), where he makes play with the Latin word 'unda' (wave) on five concrete screens, and the German word 'Schiff' (ship) on two more concrete screens divided by water. Here the curved inscription reflects in the water as a boat with sails. At the Kröller-Müller Museum, in the Netherlands (1980–82), the names of Rousseau, Corot, Robespierre, Michelet and Lycurgus are carved into neoclassical plinths surrounding mature trees in a rhododendron glade, as in an ancient sacred grove. Each name has a connection with the French Revolution. Perhaps Lycurgus, the ninth-century Spartan lawmaker who wanted to expel the evils of crime, want and arrogance from the State, and advocated the wealthy giving up their property, makes the most significant political impact amongst the five.

 The stone poems are not for the under-educated, nor those unversed in Greek and Latin, and the message can become esoteric, particularly in the many public parks for which he has had commissions – perhaps not the 'contemporary Arcadia for "everyone"' to which he may have aspired.[37] This is a pity, for Finlay has much to say.

Charles Jencks

Two recent gardens in Scotland have raised the profile of Land Art because of their powerful visual impact, which can satisfy the senses before any questioning begins. Charles Jencks, born in 1939 in Baltimore, USA, studied architecture and literature at Harvard before taking his doctorate in architecture at London University. In recent years he has explored the

The Garden of Cosmic Speculation, Borders, Scotland

Charles Jencks and his wife Maggie Keswick together developed a highly individual landscape in Scotland from 1988: sadly she did not live to see it finished. Both were intrigued by the forces of energy in the making of the universe, and this spiral with its curved lake below, represents cosmic energy displayed as Land Art.

relationship between architecture and language, and has become fascinated by the patterns created by the universe – whether in moving water or spinning meteorological systems. This has led him to demonstrate these interrelationships as a 'language of landscape' expressed in large formations of earth and water.

Landform Ueda, a spiral mound with crescent-shaped lakes, was opened to the public in the grounds of the National Gallery of Modern Art in Edinburgh in 2002, providing a view across the Edinburgh skyline and announcing the presence of a Scottish sculpture park around it. The dramatic landform, seven metres high, is named after a Japanese scientist who discovered patterns of overlapping but non-repeating curves. Jencks is still working on the Garden of Cosmic Speculation, made on his late wife Maggie Keswick's estate in the Scottish Borders. Both contributed to the garden. Maggie was interested in Chinese gardens, constructing the waves of *chi* (energy) which emanate from the house and combine with Jencks's concept of the energy of the expanding universe. There are wavy ha-ha walls and clipped hedges, and a curving Chinese red board-walk, which represents a fractal bridge, that jumps over two brooks before penetrating the ground.

Jencks prefers to consider his landscape in terms of metaphor rather than abstraction. Below the house is a Garden of Senses set in the old kitchen garden, which expresses sight, hearing, touch, DNA and other themes in a series of small incidents framed in planting. 'Touch' has nettles and lambs' ears (*Stachys lanata*) growing around it. 'Smell' is a pair of upturned noses set in a shallow depression with thyme planted so that an aroma is released as one approaches. There are plays on words set in the paving, which read the same from either direction. Humour is important, as pun and metaphor.

Beyond the Garden of Senses is the larger landscape, an immensely still, tranquil water parterre, with curving lakes set between turf ridge and conical hill some fifty feet high, made from the spoil from excavating the lakes. From the top of the hill, reached by a winding path, the whole garden is revealed. Landscape and sky reflect in the lakes below. A narrow turf path divides the lakes and takes you into the woodland beyond.

At one level, the three elements mirror the nineteenth-century 'big house' garden: the formal landscape near the house, the parterre, and the wilderness beyond. But on the return to the house from the woodland there are features which place the landscape within a much more interesting framework. The Symmetry Break terrace, depicted by stripes of gravel and turf which tilt and twist, represents four jumps by which the universe has developed. Here energy begins in straight lines, matter (represented by curved lines of grass) emerges to bend space and time, life emerges from matter (an egg shape), and consciousness (a hedge) springs out of life and grows. Further on, hanging aluminium spirals represent the plasma stream of particles that are emitted from the centre of a Black Hole. This burst of energy has been seen several times by the Hubble Telescope.

The theme of the developing universe is repeated in a water feature on a slope below the house. To a certain extent the bigger picture had been hinted at by the gates to the kitchen garden, displaying soliton waves – waves which run on and do not join, similar to a tidal bore, or a *tsunami* (the Japanese name for a wave created by an earthquake on the sea bed). On the top of the glasshouses and walls in front of the kitchen garden are metal globes representing the Atom, the Universe and Gaia theory where the world can be regarded as a self-regulating system, just as the universe self-organizes and expands in a series of jumps. More daunting are the 'Equations which Generate the World' – on top of the greenhouses.

Jencks has equated architecture with the laws of physics in *The Architecture of the Jumping Universe* and his garden has to be seen as an extension of his theorizing.[38] But at a simple level the garden can be read as an expression of the waves of energy emitted by all these movements in space and time, combined in a landscape of beauty. This is an immensely forward-looking garden, where the great magician-architect-astrologer weaves his interpretation of the emerging history of the cosmos.

Below
Garden of the Senses
The more usual planted parterre with statues has been replaced by an ear, an eye, noses, DNA structures and more, all surrounded by appropriate planting.

Bottom
The Black Hole Terrace
The twisting chequerboard represents space and time warp; aluminium spirals represent the plasma stream of particles emitted from the centre of a black hole.

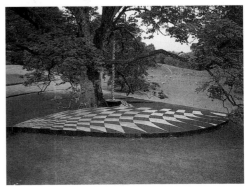

Endnote

This book has followed the movement of new styles of garden design through the twentieth century, underlining the fact that they can be led by new methods of planting as well as by architectural form. National styles have emerged in countries which have moved away from colonial control, and have been re-invented in others during wartime isolation, or for political reasons. Two world wars and the flight of talent from one part of the world to another shifted the focus of innovation away from England and continental Europe. At the beginning of the twenty-first century the world has become an even smaller place with ideas moving between countries with increasing rapidity. There are now many centres of innovation.

At the beginning of the century, styles were borrowed and parodied, ending as pastiche – sometimes beautiful, sometimes meaningless. At the end of the century, they were borrowed and re-invented with a new confidence in a Postmodern manner, sometimes absorbing aspects of other cultures and disciplines to become vital new styles of their own. The lag between innovation in art and introduction in the garden has closed dramatically. The distinctions between art forms has narrowed as the concern for conservation has combined artist, sculptor, architect, and garden designer in large-scale projects which often blend the talents of more than one country. Though it could be said that innovation – and some styles – have become international, in the end it is the cultural and physical contexts which shape the implementation of the style, and will save us all from some bland, all-embracing garden of the future.

Notes

Introduction

1. David Cannadine, 'How do you Write the Nineteenth Century?' Seminar at the Institute of Historical Research, London, 30 November 2000

Chapter One

1. 'Country Gardens Old and New' in *Gardens in Edwardian England*, Antique Collectors' Club, Woodbridge, Suffolk, England, 1985, pp. 43, 81
2. Edith Wharton, *Italian Villas and their Gardens*, The Century Company, New York, 1904, p. 6
3. Betty Radice, 'Letter to Domitius Apollinaris', *The Letters of the Younger Pliny*, Penguin Books, Harmondsworth, 1963, pp. 139–44
4. Robin Whalley (ed.), *The Boke of Iford*, Libanus Press, Marlborough, England, 1993, pp. 6, 7
5. Ibid. p. 37
6. Ibid. p. 32
7. Buscot Park Archive, New Stairway design: plan and elevation 1912, signed H. A. Peto
8. John House, 'Monet: The Last Impressionist?' in Paul Hayes Tucker, George T. M. Shackleford, Mary Anne Stevens (eds), *Monet in the 20th Century*, Royal Academy of Arts and Yale University Press, London and New York, 1998, p. 2
9. Despite the fact that Monet's youngest son, who inherited the property, allowed it to fall into neglect, the garden was rescued by the State in 1966 on Michel's death.
10. Geneviève Aitken and Marianne Delafond, *La Collection d'Estampes Japonaises de Claude Monet à Giverny*, La Bibliothèque des Arts, n.d.
11. Isabelle Van Groeningen, *The Development of Herbaceous Planting in Britain and Germany from the Nineteenth to Early Twentieth Century*, unpublished DPhil, University of York Institute of Advanced Architectural Studies, 1996
12. Beatrix Farrand saved Gertrude Jekyll's archives when they were put on the market after Jekyll's death by her executors in a disinterested Britain. She took them to her home at Reef Point in Maine, and bequeathed them to the University of California at Berkeley in 1955.
13. Rosamund Wallinger, 'In Miss Jekyll's Footsteps', *Historic Gardens Review*, Autumn 1999, p. 18
14. Somerset Record Office, Hestercombe Collection C/FB 18; see also Janet Waymark, 'Hestercombe', in *Historic Gardens Review*, Spring/Summer 2002, pp. 8–11
15. Mac Griswold and Eleanor Weller, *The Golden Age of American Gardens*, Harry N. Abrams and the Garden Club of America, New York, 1992, p. 18
16. Dumbarton Oaks Archive, Beatrix Farrand to Mildred Bliss, 24 and 25 June 1922
17. Dumbarton Oaks Archive, Mildred Bliss to Beatrix Farrand, 13 July 1922; Beatrix Farrand to Mildred Bliss, 7 July 1922
18. Gertrude Jekyll, preface, in Wilhelm Miller, *The Charm of English Gardens*, Hodder and Stoughton, London and New York, n.d., c. 1900
19. Thomas H. Mawson, *The Life and Work of an English Landscape Architect*, Richards, England, 1927. See also Harriet Jordan, *Thomas Hayton Mawson: The English Garden Designs of an Edwardian Landscape Architect*, unpublished PhD thesis, Wye College,

University of London, 1988.
20. Jordan, *Thomas Hayton Mawson*, p. 20
21. Edward Kemp, *How to Lay Out a Garden*, Bradbury and Evans, London, 3rd edition, 1864
22. Thomas H. Mawson and E. Prentice Mawson, *The Art and Craft of Garden Making*, Batsford, London, 5th edition, 1926, pp. 7, 8
23. Studio Yearbook, *Studio*, London, 1907
24. Mawson, *The Art and Craft of Garden Making*, p. 386
25. Ibid. p. 387
26. David Ottewill, *The Edwardian Garden*, Yale University Press, New Haven and London, 1989, p. 175
27. Mawson, *The Art and Craft of Garden Making*, p. 374; *The Life and Work of an English Landscape Architect*, pp. 129–30

Chapter Two

1. William Robinson, Preface to *Gravetye Manor, or Twenty Years' Work round an Old Manor House*, John Murray, London, 1911; Saga Press, New York, 1984, p. xxii. Mea Allan, *William Robinson 1838–1935. Father of the English Flower Garden*, Faber and Faber, London, 1982, provides good background on Robinson.
2. Van Groeningen, *The Development of Herbaceous Planting*, pp. 302, 305
3. William Robinson, *The Wild Garden*, John Murray, London, 1870; Century Hutchinson and the National Trust, 1986, p. 9
4. Ibid. p. 7
5. Ibid. p. 10
6. Ibid. p. 15
7. Ibid. p. 16
8. Nicole Milette, *Landscape Painter as Landscape Gardener: The Case of Alfred Parsons RA*, unpublished DPhil, University of York, IAAS, 1997
9. Elizabeth C. MacPhail, *Kate Sessions: Pioneer Horticulturist*, San Diego Historical Society, 1976
10. Ibid. pp. 49–50
11. Ibid. pp. 68–69
12. Ibid. pp. 69–71
13. Ibid. pp. 113–16
14. T. D. A. Cockerell, 'K. O. S. and California Floriculture', in *Bios* vol. XIV no. 4, December 1943, p. 172
15. *California Garden*, July 1909
16. Cockerell in *Bios*, vol. XIV no. 4, p. 172
17. *California Garden*, May 1923
18. Victoria Padilla, *Southern Californian Gardens*, University of California Press, Berkeley and Los Angeles, 1961, p. 169
19. *Bios*, vol. XIV no. 4, p. 174
20. MacPhail, *Kate Sessions*, p. 65
21. David C. Streatfield, *California Gardens. Creating a New Eden*, Abbeville Press, New York, 1984, pp. 71–72. The E. F. Chase house is also known as Katherine Teats house.
22. Ibid. p. 68
23. *Bios*, vol. XIV no. 4, p. 178
24. Wilhelm Miller, of the Department of Horticulture of the University of Illinois's College of Agriculture at Urbana, 1915; see Christopher Vernon, 'Wilhelm Miller and the Prairie Spirit in Landscape Gardening', in Therese O'Malley and Marc Treib (eds), *Regional Garden Design in the United States*,

Dumbarton Oaks Colloquium XV, Washington, USA, 1995, pp. 271–75.
25. Robert E. Grese, 'Prairie Gardens of O. C. Simonds and Jens Jensen', in O'Malley and Treib (eds), *Regional Garden Design*, p. 104
26. Grese, 'Prairie Gardens of O. C. Simonds and Jens Jensen', p. 6
27. Jens Jensen, *Siftings*, Ralph Fletcher Seymour, Chicago, 1939; Johns Hopkins University Press, 1990, p. 34
28. Ibid. p. 63
29. Ibid. p. 28
30. Robert E. Grese, *Jens Jensen. Maker of Natural Parks and Gardens*, Johns Hopkins University Press, 1992, p. 8
31. Ibid. p. 80
32. Ibid. p. 93
33. Ibid. p. 88
34. Jensen, *Siftings*, p. 66
35. Ibid. pp. 86–87
36. Grese, *Jens Jensen*, plan pp. 116–17
37. Jensen, *Siftings*, p. 71
38. Miller in Vernon, 'Wilhelm Miller and the Prairie Spirit in Landscape Gardening', (appendix) p. 13
39. Mac Griswold and Eleanor Weller, *The Golden Age of American Gardens: Proud Owners, Private Estates, 1890–1940*, Harry N. Abrams, Inc. and Garden Club of America, New York, 1991, p. 266
40. Ibid.
41. Jan Woudstra, 'Jacobus P. Thijsse's Influence on Dutch Landscape Architecture', in Joachim Wolschke-Bulmahn (ed.), *Nature and Ideology*, Dumbarton Oaks Colloquium XVIII, Washington, USA, 1997, pp. 168–69
42. Jan Woudstra, *Landscape for Living: Garden Theory and Design of the Modern Movement*, unpublished PhD thesis, University of London, 1997, p. 107
43. Woudstra, 'Jacobus P. Thijsse's Influence…', p. 170
44. Ibid. p. 171
45. Ibid. p. 175
46. Marie Luise Gothein, *Geschichte der Gartenkunst*, 1913; translated into English as *A History of Garden Art*, J. M. Dent and Sons, London, 2 vols, 1928
47. Gothein, quoting Ferdinand Avenarius (1856–1923), *A History of Garden Art*, p. 357
48. J. Wolschke-Bulmahn, 'Wild Garden and Nature Garden', in *Journal of Garden History*, vol. 12 no. 3, p. 189
49. Gothein, *A History of Garden Art*, vol. II, p. 358
50. Ibid. p. 360
51. Van Groeningen, *The Development of Herbaceous Planting*
52. Gert Gröning and Joachim Wolschke-Bulmahn, 'Changes in the Philosophy of Garden Architecture in the 20th Century and their Impact upon the Social and Spatial Environment', in *Journal of Garden History* vol. 9 no. 2, April–June 1989, p. 64
53. Willy Lange and Otto Stahn, *Gartengestaltung der Neuzeit*, J. J. Weber, Leipzig, 1907
54. Gröning and Wolschke-Bulmahn, 'Changes in the Philosophy of Garden Architecture', p. 55
55. Woudstra, *Landscape for Living*, p. 293
56. Joachim Wolschke-Bulmahn and Gert Gröning, 'The Ideology of the Nature Garden: Nationalistic Trends in Garden Design in Germany during the

Early Twentieth Century', in *Journal of Garden History* vol. 12 no. 1, 1992, p. 75

57. Ibid. p. 75

58. Sylvia Crowe, *The Landscape of Roads*, Architectural Press, London, 1960

59. Van Groeningen, *The Development of Herbaceous Planting*

60. Ibid. p. 448

61. Isabelle Van Groeningen, 'Gifts from a Giant', in *The Garden*, vol. 123, part 5, May 1998, pp. 367–71

62. Karl Foerster, *Vom Blütengarten der Zukunft*, Furche-Verlag, Berlin, 1917

63. Van Groeningen, 'Gifts from a Giant', p. 369

64. Foerster, *Vom Blütengarten der Zukunft*, p. 82

65. Van Groeningen, *The Development of Herbaceous Planting*, p. 440

66. Jost Hermand, 'Rousseau, Goethe, Humboldt: Their Influence on Later Advocates of the Nature Garden', in Wolschke-Bulmahn (ed.), *Nature and Ideology*, p. 54

67. Van Groeningen, *The Development of Herbaceous Planting*, p. 448. See also Julia Sniderman Bachrach, *The City in a Garden. A Photographic History of Chicago's Parks*, Centre for American Places in association with Chicago Park District, 2002.

Chapter Three

1. *1900: Art at the Crossroads* (exhibition), Royal Academy of Arts, London, 2000

2. H. H. Arnason, preface to *A History of Modern Art*, Thames & Hudson, London, 4th Edition, 2000, p. 12

3. Woudstra, *Landscape for Living*, 151, fig. 83

4. Helene Damen and Anne-Mie Devolder (eds), *Lotte Stam-Beese 1903–88*, De Hef, Rotterdam, 1993, pp. 104–13 (Dutch with English commentary)

5. 'To Read and Respect a Place', in *Topos*, 29, December 1999, pp. 55–60

6. Paul Greenhalgh, 'The Style and the Age', in Paul Greenhalgh (ed.), *Art Nouveau 1890–1914*, V&A Publications, London, 2000, p. 19

7. Birgit Wahmann, 'The Jugendstil Garden in Germany and Austria', in Monique Mosser and Georges Teyssot (eds), *The Architecture of Western Gardens*, MIT Press, Cambridge Massachusetts, 1991, pp. 454–56

8. Kurt Hoppe, *Gärten und Garten-Architekturen*, Westdeutsche Verlagsgesellschaft, 1909

9. Leberecht Migge, *Die Gartenkultur Des 20. Jahrhunderts*, Eugen Diederichs, Jena, 1913

10. I am grateful to Pamela Robertson of the Hunterian Museum, University of Glasgow, for drawing my attention to this point.

11. Anne Hustache, *Victor Horta. Maisons de Campagne*, Le Musée Horta, 1994, pp. 62–65

12. Juan Bassegoda Nonell, 'The Labyrinth and the Güell Park', in *Jardins et Sites Historiques*, ICOMOS, 1993, pp. 281–85

13. Josep M. Carandell, *Park Güell. Gaudí's Utopia*, Triangle Postals, 1998

14. Dorothée Imbert, *The Modernist Garden in France*, Yale University Press, New Haven and London, 1993, p. 233

15. Ibid. p. 46

16. Ibid. p. 136

17. Catherine Royer, 'Art Deco Gardens in France', in Mosser and Teyssot (eds), *The Architecture of Western Gardens*, pp. 460–62

18. Albaicín/Sadea (eds), *El Carmen de la Fondacion Rodríguez-Acosta de Granada*, n.d.

19. Richard Sudell, *Landscape Gardening*, Ward Lock and Co., London, 1933, pp. 375–77, 381, 383, unattributed to Selfridges store.

20. Gordon Honeycombe, *Selfridges*, Selfridges, London, 1984, pp. 161–64

21. Robert McGregor, *The Art Deco City, Napier, New Zealand*, The Art Deco Trust, 1998

22. I am grateful to Elisabeth Whittle, of CADW – Welsh Historic Monuments' Register of Parks and Gardens in Wales, for information here.

23. Charles Jencks, *Modern Movements in Architecture*, Penguin Books, Harmondsworth, 1973, 2nd edition 1987, p. 143

24. Peter Blake, *Le Corbusier*, Pelican Books, Harmondsworth, 1960, pp. 21–22

25. Translated by Frederick Etchells as *Towards a New Architecture*, The Architectural Press, London, 1927

26. Ibid. paperback edition, London, 1970, p. 166

27. Le Corbusier, *Précisions sur un état présent de l'architecture et de l'urbanisme*, Vincent Fréal, Paris, 1960, pp. 136–39

28. Ibid.

29. Ibid. p. 138

30. Le Corbusier et Pierre Jeanneret, *Œuvres Complètes de 1929–1934*, Les Editions d'Architecture Erlenbach, Zurich, 1947, p. 24

31. Imbert, *The Modernist Garden in France*, pp. 147–183, and Jan Woudstra, 'The Corbusian Landscape: Arcadia or No Man's Land?' in *Garden History* 28, 1, 2000, pp. 135–52

32. Russell Page, *The Education of a Gardener*, Penguin, London 1985, p. 266

33. Le Corbusier, *Vers Une Architecture*, pp. 211–47

34. Frank Lloyd Wright, *An Autobiography*, Quartet Books, London, 1977, pp. 192, 194

35. Anne Whiston Spirn, 'Frank Lloyd Wright: Architect of Landscape', in David G. De Long (ed.), *Frank Lloyd Wright. Designs for an American Landscape 1922–1932*, Harry N. Abrams Inc., New York, 1996, pp. 135–70

36. According to Peter Blake, 'International Style' was a term first used by Alfred H. Barr Jr, in his catalogue to Henry-Russell Hitchcock's and Philip Johnson's *Modern Architecture* exhibition of 1932 in New York, referring to 'the architecture of the Bauhaus and its allies in Europe since the end of World War I' (Peter Blake, *No Place Like Utopia*, W. W. Norton, New York, 1996, p. 106).

37. Christian Hubert and Lindsay Stamm Shapiro, *William Lescaze*, Institute for Architectural and Urban Studies and Rizzoli International Publications Inc., New York, 1982, pp. 72–74

38. Christopher Hussey, *Country Life*, 11 February 1933, pp. 144–49

39. Laurence Fricker, 'Dartington Hall, Devonshire, England', in *Beatrix Jones Farrand: Fifty Years of American Landscape Architecture*, Dumbarton Oaks, Washington, D.C., 1982, pp. 77–96. Reginald Snell, *From the Bare Stem*, Devon Books, Exeter, 1989

40. Dartington Archives, unclassified garden designs attributed to Beatrix Farrand. Fridy Duterloo, 'William Lescaze and the Modern Landscape', in the *Dutch Yearbook for the History of Garden and Landscape Architecture*, 1997, no. 3, pp. 176–205

41. Duterloo, 'William Lescaze and the Modern Landscape', pp. 180–81

42. Hussey, *Country Life*, 11 February 1933, p. 146

43. Duterloo, 'William Lescaze and the Modern Landscape', p. 197

44. G. C. Taylor, *Modern Gardens*, Country Life, 1936, p. 15

45. Christopher Tunnard, 'Garden Design at Chelsea Show, 1936', in *Landscape and Garden*, summer 1936, pp. 90–94

46. Christopher Tunnard, 'Modern Gardens for Modern Houses', in *Landscape Architecture*, January 1942, reprinted in Marc Treib (ed.), *Modern Landscape Architecture: A Critical Review*, MIT Press, Cambridge Massachusetts, 1993, p. 162

47. Ibid. p. 160

48. Ibid. p. 163

49. Christopher Tunnard, *Gardens in the Modern Landscape*, The Architectural Press, London, 1938, p. 72, quoting Le Corbusier *Towards a New Architecture*, p. 9

50. Tunnard, in Treib (ed.), *Modern Landscape Architecture*, p. 162

51. Lance M. Neckar, 'Christopher Tunnard: The Garden in the Modern Landscape' in Treib (ed.), *Modern Landscape Architecture*, p. 146

52. Tunnard, *Gardens in the Modern Landscape*, pp. 69–99

53. Christopher Tunnard, television broadcast of Garden Planning, in *Landscape and Garden*, summer 1938, p. 118

54. Tunnard, in Treib (ed.), *Modern Landscape Architecture*, pp. 162–65

55. Ibid. p. 163

56. Ibid. p. 164

57. Tunnard, *Gardens in the Modern Landscape*, pp. 129–32

58. Ibid. p. 137

59. Ibid. p. 136

60. Alan Powers, *Serge Chermayeff: Designer Architect Teacher*, RIBA Publications, London, 2001, pp. 118–41

61. Ibid. p. 129

62. Ibid. p. 132

63. Christopher Tunnard, 'Planning a Modern Garden: An Experience in Collaboration', in *Landscape and Garden*, spring 1939, p. 25

64. Ibid.

65. Powers, *Serge Chermayeff*, p. 136

66. Tunnard, 'Planning a Modern Garden', pp. 25–27

67. Tunnard, *Gardens in the Modern Landscape*, pp. 139–40

68. Christopher Tunnard, *City of Man: A New Approach to the Recovery of Beauty in American Cities*, Charles Scribner's Sons, 1953, p. 225

69. Neckar, 'Christopher Tunnard', p. 144

Chapter Four

1. Henry Mayhew, *London Labour and the London Poor*, Griffin, Bohn and Company, 1861; Dover Publications 1968 vol. I, p. 140

2. Gustave Doré and Blanche Jerrold, *London: a Pilgrimage*, Grant and Co., London, 1872; Wordsworth Editions Ltd, Ware, 1987

3. *Illustrated London News*, 5 September 1846

4. Stewart Dick and Helen Allingham, *The Cottage Homes of England*, Edward Arnold, 1909; Bracken Books 1991, p. 92

5. Gertrude Jekyll, *Old West Surrey*, London, 1904; Phillimore, Chichester, 1999, p. 208

6. Milette, *The Case of Alfred Parsons*, p. 153

7. Andrew Mearns, *The Bitter Cry of Outcast London:*

An Inquiry into the Conditions of the Abject Poor, James Clarke, London, 1883

8. Royal Commission on the Housing of the Working Classes, 1885, vol. I, First Report, vol. II, Minutes and Evidence and Appendices (C 4402), British Parliamentary Papers 1884–85

9. John Bateman, *The Great Landowners of Britain and Ireland,* Harrison, London, 4th Edition, 1883

10. Public Record Office Cres 5/538, Portman Papers, Bryanston Farm Labour Journal 1903–1906

11. Royal Commission 1885, Reports of the Commissioners

12. H. Rider Haggard, *Rural England,* vol. I, Longmans, London, 1902, pp. 258, 260–62

13. Janet Waymark, *Dorset Landed Estates, 1870–1990, their Survival and Influence,* unpublished PhD thesis, University of London, 1995, pp. 125–37

14. John Nelson Tarn, *Five Per Cent Philanthropy,* Cambridge University Press, 1973, p. 158

15. J. H. Whitehouse, 'Bournville. A Study in Housing Reform', *Studio,* London, 1901–2 pp. 162–172

16. Ibid. p. 168

17. Walter L. Creese, *The Search for Environment: the Garden City, Before and After,* Yale University Press, New Haven, 1966, pp. 114–16

18. 'Industrial Gardens', in *Landscape and Garden,* winter 1936, pp. 230–32

19. Raymond Unwin, *Cottage Homes and Common Sense,* Fabian Tract no. 109, Fabian Society, 1902

20. Raymond Unwin, *Nothing Gained by Overcrowding! How the Garden City Type of Development may benefit both Owner and Occupier,* P. S. King, London, 1912

21. Peter Hall, *Cities of Tomorrow,* Basil Blackwell, Oxford, 1988; 1990, p. 89

22. Dennis Hardy, *From Garden Cities to New Towns,* E. & F. Spon, London, 1991, p. 24

23. Ebenezer Howard, *Garden Cities of To-morrow,* reprinted Attic Books, Wales, 1985, p. 118

24. Ibid. p. 92

25. Ibid. p. 11

26. Hall, *Cities of Tomorrow,* p. 100

27. Mervyn Miller, *Heritage Garden City Trails,* Letchworth Garden City Corporation, n.d.

28. Ibid. The Stone House, 212 Nevells Road

29. Ibid. 158 Wilbury Road

30. Stephen Ward, *The Garden City Past, Present and Future,* E. & F. Spon, London, 1992, p. 6

31. M. H. Baillie Scott, *Houses and Gardens. Arts and Crafts Interiors,* George Newnes Ltd, 1906; Antique Collectors' Club Ltd, Woodbridge, Suffolk, 1995, p. 122–23

32. Robert Lancaster, *Letchworth Garden City,* Alan Sutton Publishing Co., Stroud, Gloucester, England, 1995, p. 5

33. Tarn, *Five Per Cent Philanthropy,* p. 118

34. Mervyn Miller and A. Stuart Gray, *Hampstead Garden Suburb,* Phillimore and Co. Ltd, Chichester, 1992, pp. 19–21

35. J. S. Nettlefold, *Practical Housing,* Garden City Press, Letchworth, 1908

36. Ibid. pp. 149–50

37. Camillo Sitte, *City Planning according to Artistic Principles,* trans. G. R. and C. C. Collins, Random House, New York, 1965

38. Raymond Unwin, *Town Planning in Practice,* Fisher Unwin, 1909; Princeton Architectural Press, New York, 1994, illus. no. 104, p. 155

39. Ibid. illus. nos. 112, 113, p. 165; no. 195 p. 263

40. Peter Waymark, *A History of Petts Wood,* Petts Wood and District Residents' Association, 4th edition, 2000

41. David Lambert, *Detached Town Gardens,* Theme Study for English Heritage, July 1994

42. David Crouch and Colin Ward, *The Allotment: its Landscape and Culture,* Faber and Faber, London, 1988, pp. 66–67

43. Royal Commission on the Employment of Children, Young Persons and Women, 1868–69, 101(3)

44. *The Land: The Report of the Land Enquiry Committee,* vol. I, Hodder and Stoughton, London, 1913, pp. 171, 179

45. Waymark, *Dorset Landed Estates,* pp. 75–76

46. Ruth Duthie, *Florists' Flowers and Societies,* Shire Books, Princes Risborough, 1988

47. Crouch and Ward, *The Allotment,* pp. 66–69

48. A. Richmond, 'Land Settlement in England', in *Journal of the Royal Agricultural Society of England,* vol. 106, 1945, pp. 114–15

49. Jane Addams, *Twenty Years at Hull-House,* 1910; Signet Classic, New York, 1961, pp. 219, 172

50. Ibid. pp. 278–79

51. Ibid. p. 170

52. Daniel Schaffer, 'The American Garden City: Lost Ideals', in Ward (ed.), *The Garden City,* p. 128

53. A. Miller, 'Radburn and its Validity Today', in *Architect and Building News,* vol. 2 (6) 27 March, 1969, pp. 30–35

54. David Myrha, 'Rexford Guy Tugwell: Initiator of America's Greenbelt New Towns, 1935–6', in Donald A. Krueckeberg (ed.), *The American Planner, Biographies and Reflections,* Methuen, New York, 1983, pp. 225–49

55. Ibid. pp. 237–38

56. Christian Zapatka, 'Greenbelt, Maryland', in Mosser and Teyssot (eds), *The Architecture of Western Gardens,* pp. 451–52

57. Krueckeberg (ed.), *The American Planner,* p. 245

58. Birgit Wahmann, 'Allotments and Schrebergärten in Germany', in Mosser and Teyssot (eds), *The Architecture of Western Gardens,* pp. 451–52

59. Georg Metzendorf, *Kleinwohnungs-bauten und Siedlungen,* Alexander Koch, Darmstadt, 1920

60. Franziska Bollerey and Kristiana Hartmann, 'A Patriarchal Utopia: the Garden City and Housing Reform in Germany at the turn of the Century', in Anthony Sutcliffe (ed.), *The Rise of Modern Urban Planning 1800–1914,* Mansell, London, 1980, pp. 151–54

61. Hall, *Cities of Tomorrow,* pp. 117–19

62. Gerhard Fehl, 'The Nazi Garden City' in Ward (ed.), *The Garden City,* p. 102

63. Catherine Cooke, 'Russian Responses to the Garden City Idea', in *Architectural Review,* June 1978, pp. 353–63

64. Howard, *Garden Cities of To-morrow,* pp. 103–4

65. Shun-ichi Watanabe, 'The Japanese Garden City' in Ward (ed.), *The Garden City,* pp. 70–71

Chapter Five

1. Sima Eliovson, *The Gardens of Roberto Burle Marx,* Harry N. Abrams Inc./Sagapress Inc., New York, 1991, p. 22. See also Marta Iris Montero, *Burle Marx: The Lyrical Landscape,* Thames & Hudson, London, 2001.

2. David Underwood, *Oscar Niemeyer and Brazilian Free-form Modernism,* George Braziller, Inc. New York, 1994, pp. 19, 17

3. Silvio Soares Macedo, 'Roberto Burle Marx and the Founding of Modern Brazilian Landscape Architecture', in Rossana Vaccarino (ed.), *Roberto Burle Marx: Landscapes Reflected,* Princeton Architectural Press and Harvard University Graduate School of Design, 2000, p. 17

4. Vaccarino, *Roberto Burle Marx,* p. 11

5. Lélia Coelho Frota, 'A Painter and Visual Artist in the Brazilian Modernist Movement', in Vaccarino (ed.), *Roberto Burle Marx,* p. 30

6. P. M. Bardi, *The Tropical Gardens of Burle Marx,* Colibris Editora Ltda., Brazil, 1964

7. Luis Barragán, 'Escrito de New York: Ideas Sobre Jardines', 1931

8. Lawrence Joseph, 'The Garden of Ulysses: Ferdinand Bac, Modernism and the Afterlife of Myth', in *Studies in the History of Gardens and Designed Landscapes,* vol. 20 no. 1 January–March 2000, pp. 6–24

9. Antonio Riggen Martínez, *Luis Barragán: Mexico's Modern Master 1902–1988,* Monacelli Press, New York, 1996, p. 92

10. Joseph, 'The Garden of Ulysses', p. 8

11. Ibid. p. 13

12. Martinez, *Luis Barragán,* p. 87

13. Marc Treib, 'A Setting for Solitude: The Landscape of Luis Barragán', in Federica Zanco, (ed.), *Luis Barragán: The Quiet Revolution,* Skira Editores, Milan, 2001, pp. 114–46

14. Ibid. p. 126

15. Martinez, *Luis Barragán,* pp. 276–82

16. James Y. Yoch, *Landscaping the American Dream: The Gardens and Film Sets of Florence Yoch 1890–1972,* Harry N. Abrams Inc./Sagapress Inc., New York 1989

17. Michael Laurie, 'Thomas Church, California Gardens, and Public Landscapes', in Treib (ed.), *Modern Landscape Architecture,* pp. 166–79

18. Thomas Church, *Gardens Are for People,* University of California Press, Berkeley, 3rd edition, 1995, p. 174

19. Ibid. p. 212

20. Daniel Gregory, 'Just Add Water: the Productive Partnership between Thomas Church and Sunset Magazine', in *Studies in the History of Gardens and Designed Landscapes,* vol. 20, no. 2, April–June 2000, pp. 120–29

21. Diane Harris, 'Thomas Church as Author: Publicity and the Professional at Mid-century', in *Studies in the History of Gardens...,* vol. 20, no. 2, p. 164

22. Dorothée Imbert, 'Thomas Church: Defining Styles – the Early Years' in *Studies in the History of Gardens...,* vol. 20, no. 2, pp. 96–120

23. Church, *Gardens Are for People,* p. 115

24. Göran Schildt, *Alvar Aalto: The Complete Catalogue of Architecture, Design and Art,* Rizzoli, New York, 1994, pp. 185–87

25. Powers, *Serge Chermayeff,* p. 146

26. Peter Shepheard, *Modern Gardens,* The Architectural Press, London, 1953

27. Church, *Gardens Are for People,* p. 184

28. Marc Treib, 'Thomas Church: The Modernist Years', in *Studies in the History of Gardens...,* vol. 20, no. 2, figs. 6, 7

29. Michael Laurie, 'Thomas Church: California Gardens and Public Landscapes', in Treib (ed.), *Modern Landscape Architecture,* pp. 173, 176

30. James C. Rose, 'Freedom in the Garden', in *Pencil Points,* October 1938

31. Dan Kiley and Jane Amidon, *Dan Kiley: In his Own*

Words, Thames & Hudson, London and New York, 1999, p. 12

32. Marc Snow, *Modern American Gardens Designed by James C. Rose*, Reinhold Publishing Corp. 1967, p. 17. 'Marc Snow' is a pseudonym for James Rose, who, as folklore has it, upset his publishers so much that he had to present his work under a different name.

33. Kiley and Amidon, *Dan Kiley*, p. 11

34. *Landscape Design Architectural Record*, 1939–40

35. Marc Treib and Dorothée Imbert, *Garrett Eckbo*, University of California Press, Berkeley, 1997, p. 97, note 4

36. Garrett Eckbo, 'Small Gardens in the City', in *Pencil Points*, September 1938

37. Garrett Eckbo, 'Pilgrim's Progress', in Treib (ed.), *Modern Landscape Architecture*, p. 209

38. Treib and Imbert, *Garrett Eckbo*, pp. 36–39

39. Ibid. pp. 20, 36

40. Lawrence Halprin, *The Franklin Delano Roosevelt Memorial*, Chronicle Books, San Francisco, 1997

41. Treib and Imbert, *Garrett Eckbo*, pp. 106–79

42. Ibid. p. 135

43. Ibid. p. 141

44. Powers, *Serge Chermayeff*, p. 146. MARS (Modern Architectural Research Association) was the British branch of the Congrès International d'Architecture Moderne (CIAM) which was formed in 1933. MARS and Telesis sought to involve architects and associated planners and designers with a search for solutions to the social implications of urban advance.

45. Eckbo, 'Pilgrim's Progress', p. 207

46. Garrett Eckbo, *Landscape for Living*, Duell, Sloan and Pearce, New York, 1950, pp. 12–19

47. Treib and Imbert, *Garrett Eckbo*, pp. 62–63

48. James C. Rose, 'Freedom in the Garden', in *Pencil Points*, October 1938

49. James C. Rose, 'Articulate Form in Garden Design', in *Pencil Points*, February 1939

50. Treib and Imbert, *Garrett Eckbo*, pp. 26–27

51. James C. Rose, 'Plants Dictate Garden Form', in *Pencil Points*, November 1938

52. Rose, 'Articulate Form'

53. Amidon and Kiley, *Dan Kiley*, p. 11

54. Gary R. Hildebrand, *The Miller House: Icon of Modernism*, Spacemaker Press, Washington, 1999, p. 16

55. Amidon and Kiley, *Dan Kiley*, p. 18

56. Marc Treib, 'A Sculpting of Space', in *Landscape Design*, February 1998, p. 21

57. Ibid.; Charles Jencks, seminar, Design Museum, London, 15 October 2001

58. Isamu Noguchi, *A Sculptor's World*, Harper and Row, New York, 1968, p. 167

59. Isamu Noguchi, *The Isamu Noguchi Garden Museum*, Harry N. Abrams, New York, 1999, p. 37

60. Kendal H. Brown, 'Rashômon: The Multiple Histories of the Japanese Tea Garden at Golden Gate Park', in *Studies in the History of Gardens...*, vol. 18, no. 2 April–June 1998, pp. 93–119

61. Ana Maria Torres, *Isamu Noguchi: A Study of Space*, The Monacelli Press, New York, 2000, p. 106

Chapter Six

1. Michael Laurie, foreword to Sylvia Crowe, *Garden Design*, Garden Art Press, Woodbridge, Suffolk, 1958, 3rd edition 1994, p. vii

2. Dennis Hardy, *From New Towns to Green Politics: Campaigning for Town and Country Planning 1946–1990*, E. & F. N. Spon, London, 1991, p. 24

3. Shepheard, *Modern Gardens*, illustrations pp. 73–79

4. Geoffrey Collens and Wendy Powell (eds), *Sylvia Crowe*, Landscape Design Trust Monograph no. 2, 1999, p. 54

5. Sir Frederick Osborn and Arnold Whittick, *The New Towns: The Answer to Megalopolis*, Leonard Hill, London, 1963, p. 197

6. Geoffrey and Susan Jellicoe, *The Landscape of Man*, Thames & Hudson, London, 1975, revised edition 1987, pp. 346–47

7. Frederick Gibberd, 'The Design of a Garden', in *The Garden*, vol. 104, part 4, April 1979, p. 135

8. Ibid. p. 136

9. Sylvia Crowe, *Tomorrow's Landscape*, Architectural Press, London, 1956

10. Sylvia Crowe, *Landscape of Power*, Architectural Press, London, 1958, p. 105

11. Collens and Powell, *Sylvia Crowe*, p. 163

12. Obituary for Sylvia Crowe, *The Times* 10 July 1997

13. Sylvia Crowe influenced others who were later concerned with landscaping and ecology, such as Nan Fairbrother (1913–71), *New Lives, New Landscapes*, The Architectural Press, London, 1970. Ian L. McHarg's *Design with Nature*, John Wiley and Sons Inc., 1969, expressed a parallel philosophy in the USA.

14. Geoffrey Jellicoe, 'Soundings', in *Geoffrey Jellicoe: Studies of a Landscape Designer Over 80 Years*, vol. I, Garden Art Press, Woodbridge, Suffolk, 1993, p. 16

15. Jellicoe, 'Soundings', p. 24

16. Russell Page, *The Education of a Gardener*, William Collins, 1962; Penguin Books, Harmondsworth, 1985, p. 29

17. Michael Spens, *Gardens of the Mind*, Antique Collectors' Club, Woodbridge, Suffolk, 1992, p. 67

18. Jellicoe, 'Soundings', p. 26

19. Ibid., p. 40

20. Spens, *Gardens of the Mind*, pp. 70–71

21. Osborn and Whittick, *The New Towns*

22. Jellicoe, quoted in Spens, *Gardens of the Mind*, p. 101

23. Given to Guelph University in Ontario, Canada, in 1983.

24. Geoffrey Jellicoe, 'Towards a Landscape of Humanism', in *Guelph Lectures on Landscape Design* IV, pp. 149–95

25. Michael Spens, *The Complete Landscape Designs and Gardens of Geoffrey Jellicoe*, Thames & Hudson, London, 1994

26. David Wild, *Architecture Today*, October 1992

27. Thorbjörn Andersson, 'Appearances and beyond: time and change in Swedish landscape architecture', in *Journal of Garden History*, vol. 17, no. 4, 1997, p. 238

28. Lulu Salto Stephensen, 'The Danish landscape and landscape gardening: on the visualization of the aesthetic potential for nature in cultivation in the twentieth century' in *Journal of Garden History* vol. 17, no. 4, 1997, p. 299

29. Ibid. p. 303. See also Sven-Ingvar Andersson and Steen Høyer, *C. Th. Sørensen: Landscape Modernist*, The Danish Architectural Press, Copenhagen, 2001.

30. London Historic Parks and Gardens Conference, 1999

31. Thorbjörn Andersson, 'Appearances and beyond', p. 292

32. Hakon Ahlberg's essay in Gustave Holmdahl, Sven Ivar Lind and Kjell Ödeen (eds), *Gunnar Asplund, Architect, 1885–1940*, National Association of Swedish Architects, Stockholm, 1950; reprinted 1981 by Byggförlaget, pp. 31–32

33. Thorbjörn Andersson, 'Appearances and beyond', p. 292

34. Shepheard, *Modern Gardens*, pp. 114–15

35. Thorbjörn Andersson, 'Erik Glemme and the Stockholm Park System', in Treib (ed.), *Modern Landscape Architecture*, p. 118

36. Holger Blom, 'Planning for Recreation', in Clifford R. V. Tandy (ed.), *Landscape and Human Life*, Djambatan, Amsterdam, 1966, p. 38

37. Andersson, 'Erik Glemme and the Stockholm Park System', pp. 122–27

38. Ibid. p. 132

39. J. T. P. Bijhouwer, 'The Landscape Architect and the Artist: Where are we going in Design?', in Sylvia Crowe (ed.), *Space for Living*, Djambatan, Amsterdam, 1961, pp. 81–82

Chapter Seven

1. Charles Jencks, *The Language of Post-modern Architecture*, Academy Editions, London, 1977, p. 9

2. Alice Coleman, *Utopia on Trial: Vision and Reality in Planned Housing*, Hilary Shipman, London, 1985, 2nd edition 1990. Based on research done at King's College, London.

3. Ibid. p. 173

4. Jane Jacobs, *The Death and Life of Great American Cities*, Jonathan Cape, London, 1962

5. Tunnard, *Gardens in the Modern Landscape*, 2nd. revised edition 1950, p. 7

6. Janet Jack, 'On a Podium', in *Landscape Design*, September 1992, pp. 24–25

7. Leon Krier, foreword in Andreas Papadakis and Harriet Watson (eds), *New Classicism*, Academy Editions, London, 1990, pp. 6–13

8. Ibid. p. 7

9. Waymark, *Dorset Landed Estates*, pp. 375–97

10. Juhani Pallasmaa, 'Tradition and Modernity', in Michael Spens (ed.), *The Recovery of the Modern*, Architectural Review, Oxford, 1996

11. 'Thames Barrier Park', in *Landlines*, December 2000/January 2001, pp. 4–5; and Kathryn Firth and Richard Burdett, 'Thames Barrier Park – a Catalyst for Urban Regeneration', in *Topos*, vol. 35, June 2001, pp. 54–62

12. Janet Jack, 'A Bridge with a View', in *Landscape Design*, September 1992, pp. 27–28

13. Janet Jack, 'Shaping Interior Landscape', in *Landscape Design*, August 1985, p. 27

14. Brita von Schoenaich, 'The End of the Border?', in *Landscape Design*, April 1994, pp. 9–14

15. *Topos*, vol. 26, March 1999, devoted its entire edition to Emscher Park.

16. Peter Neal, 'Parc de la Villette', in *Landscape Design*, February 1988, pp. 30–34

17. Tom Turner, *City as Landscape. A Post Post-modern View of Design and Planning*, E. & F. Spon, London, 1996, pp. 208–14; Lodewijk Baljon, *Designing Parks*, Architectura & Natura Press, Amsterdam, 1992, Garden Art Press, Woodbridge, England, 1995

18. Woudstra, *Landscape for Living*, pp. 125, 151

19. Lisa Buckland, 'Call of the Wild', in *Gardeners' World*, July 2001, pp. 56–60; Sue Seddon, 'A Plan for All Seasons', in *Gardens Illustrated*, November 2001, pp. 36–43
20. Marina Christopher, *Bury Court*, Green Plants
21. Wolfgang Oehme and James van Sweden, *Bold Romantic Gardens*, Spacemaker Press, Washington, 1990, 1998
22. Report of the British Association Science Festival, *The Times* 9 September 2000
23. Catherine Laroze, 'Tuileries: Le Jardin du Carrousel', in *Les Jardins de Jacques Wirtz*, Fondation Pour L'Architecture, Paris, 1993, pp. 165–73
24. *Garden Design Journal*, late Spring, 2000, p. 2
25. Guy Cooper and Gordon Taylor, *Mirrors of Paradise: The Gardens of Fernando Caruncho*, The Monacelli Press, New York, 2000, p. 23
26. Cooper and Taylor, Mirrors of Paradise, p. 155
27. John Beardsley, *Earthworks and Beyond*.

Contemporary Art in the Landscape, Abbeville Press, New York, 1984, 3rd. edition 1998, pp. 20–22
28. Jonathan Bell, 'Orcadian Circle', in *Gardens Illustrated*, October 2001, p. 102
29. Ian Hamilton Finlay, *Nature Again After Poussin*, Wild Hawthorn Press, 1979, pp. 21–22
30. Centre d'Art Contemporain, Castres, France, 1988
31. *Ice Fish* and *Ice Column*, Dumfriesshire, 1987; *Snowballs*, London, Summer 2000
32. Terry Friedman and Andy Goldsworthy (eds), *Hand to Earth: Andy Goldsworthy Sculpture 1976–1990*, W. S. Maney, Yorkshire, 1990
33. Patricia Johanson, *Art and Survival: Creative Solutions of Environmental Problems*, Gallerie, March 1992, p. 25
34. Patricia Johanson, 'Public Landscapes', booklet accompanying Johanson exhibition at The Painted Bride Art Centre, Philadelphia, USA, 1991

35. Guy Cooper and Gordon Taylor, *Paradise Transformed*, The Monacelli Press, New York, 1996
36. David N. Buck, *Responding to Chaos. Tradition, Technology, Society and Order in Japanese Design*, Spon Press, London and New York, 2000, pp. 182–91
37. Patrick Eyres, 'Ian Hamilton Finlay and the Cultural Politics of Neo-classical Gardening', in *Garden History*, vol. 28, no. 1, Summer 2000, p. 164. Felix von Zdenek and Pia Simig (eds), *Ian Hamilton Finlay. Works in Europe 1972–1995*, Cantz Verlag, 1995. Yves Abrioux, *Ian Hamilton Finlay: A Visual Primer*, Reaktion Books, London, 1985, 1992
38. Charles Jencks, *The Architecture of the Jumping Universe*, Academy Editions, London, 1995

Bibliography

Abrioux, Yves, *Ian Hamilton Finlay: A Visual Primer*, Reaktion Books, London, 1985, 1992
Addams, Jane, *Twenty Years at Hull-House*, 1910; Signet Classic, New York, 1961
Aitken, Geneviève, and Marianne Delafond, *La Collection d'Estampes Japonaises de Claude Monet à Giverny*, La Bibliothèque des Arts, n.d.
Albaicín/Sadea (eds), *El Carmen de la Fondacion Rodriguez-Acosta de Granada*, n.d.
Allan, Mea, *William Robinson 1838–1935: Father of the English Flower Garden*, Faber and Faber, London, 1982
Andersson, Thorbjörn, 'Erik Glemme and the Stockholm Park System', in Marc Treib (ed.), *Modern Landscape Design: A Critical Review*, MIT Press, Cambridge, Massachusetts, 1993, pp. 114–33
———, 'Appearances and Beyond: Time and Change in Swedish Landscape Architecture', in *Journal of Garden History* vol. 17, no. 4, 1997, pp. 278–94
Andersson, Sven-Ingvar, and Steen Høyer, *C. Th. Sørensen, Landscape Modernist*, The Danish Architectural Press, Copenhagen, 2001
Arnason, H. H. and Marla F. Prather, *A History of Modern Art*, Thames and Hudson Ltd, London, 4th edition, reprinted 2001
Bachrach, Julia Sniderman, *The City in a Garden: A Photographic History of Chicago's Parks*, Centre for American Places in association with Chicago Park District, 2002
Baillie Scott, Mackay Hugh, *Houses and Gardens: Arts and Crafts Interiors*, George Newnes Ltd 1906; reprinted by Antique Collectors' Club Ltd, Woodbridge, Suffolk, 1995
Baljon, Lodewijk, *Designing Parks*, Architectura & Natura Press, Amsterdam, 1992; Garden Art Press, England, 1995
Bardi, P. M., *The Tropical Gardens of Burle Marx*, Colibris Editora Ltda, Brazil, 1964
Bateman, John, *The Great Landowners of Britain and Ireland*, Harrison, London, 4th edition, 1883
Bell, Jonathan, 'Orcadian Circle', in *Gardens Illustrated*, October 2001, pp. 100–6
Bijhouwer, J. P. T., 'The Landscape Architect and the

Artist: Where are we Going in Design?' in Sylvia Crowe (ed.), *Space for Living*, Djambatan, Amsterdam, 1961, pp. 78–82
Blake, Peter, *Le Corbusier*, Pelican Books, Harmondsworth, 1960
———, *No Place Like Utopia*, W. W. Norton, New York, 1996
Blom, Holger, 'Planning for Recreation', in Clifford R. V. Tandy (ed.), *Landscape and Human Life*, Djambatan, Amsterdam, 1966, pp. 35–38
Bollerey, Franziska, and Kristiana Hartmann: 'A Patriarchal Utopia: The Garden City and Housing Reform in Germany at the Turn of the Century', in Anthony Sutcliffe (ed.), *The Rise of Modern Urban Planning 1800–1914*, Mansell, London, 1980, pp. 151–54
Brown, Jane, *Gardens of a Golden Afternoon, The Story of a Partnership: Edwin Lutyens and Gertrude Jekyll*, Allen Lane, London, 1982
Brown, Kendal H., 'Rashōmon: The Multiple Histories of the Japanese Tea Garden at Golden Gate Park', in *Studies in the History of Gardens and Designed Landscapes*, vol. 18, no. 2, April–June 1998, pp. 93–118
Buck, David N., *Responding to Chaos: Tradition, Technology, Society and Order in Japanese Design*, Spon Press, London and New York, 2000
Buckland, Lisa, 'Call of the Wild', in *Gardeners' World*, July 2001, pp. 56–60
CADW, Welsh Historic Monuments, Register of Parks and Gardens in Wales
Carandell, Josep M. *Park Güell: Gaudí's Utopia*, Triangle Postals, 1998
Chicago Department of Cultural Affairs, *A Force for Nature: The Life and Work of Jens Jensen* (exh. cat.), Chicago, 2002
Christopher, Marina, *Bury Court*, Green Plants, 2000
Church, Thomas, *Gardens Are for People*, University of California Press, Berkeley, 3rd edition, 1995
Cockerell, T. D. A., 'Kate Olivia Sessions and California Floriculture', in *Bios*, vol. XIV, no. 4, December 1943
Coleman, Alice, *Utopia on Trial: Vision and Reality in Planned Housing*, Hilary Shipman,

London, 1985, 2nd edition 1990
Collens, Geoffrey, and Wendy Powell (eds), *Sylvia Crowe*, Landscape Design Trust Monograph no. 2 1999
Cooke, Catherine, 'Russian Responses to the Garden City Idea', in *Architectural Review*, June 1978, pp. 353–63
Cooper, Guy, and Gordon Taylor, *Paradise Transformed: The Private Garden for the Twenty-First Century*, The Monacelli Press, New York, 1996
———, *Mirrors of Paradise: The Gardens of Fernando Caruncho*, The Monacelli Press, New York, 2000
Creese, Walter L., *The Search for Environment: The Garden City, Before and After*, Yale University Press, New Haven, 1966
Crouch, David, and Colin Ward, *The Allotment: its Landscape and Culture*, Faber and Faber, London, 1988
Crowe, Sylvia, *Garden Design*, Garden Art Press, Woodbridge, Suffolk, 1958; 3rd edition, 1994
———, *Tomorrow's Landscape*, Architectural Press, London, 1956
———, *Landscape of Power*, Architectural Press, London, 1958
———, *The Landscape of Roads*, Architectural Press, London, 1960
——— (ed.), *Space for Living*, Djambatan, Amsterdam, 1961
Damen, Helene, and Anne-Mie Devolder (eds), *Lotte Stam-Beese 1903–1988*, De Hef, Rotterdam, 1993 (Dutch with English summary)
De Long, David G. (ed.), *Frank Lloyd Wright: Designs for an American Landscape 1922–1932*, Harry N. Abrams Inc, New York, 1996
Descaisne and Naudin, *Manuel de l'Amateur de Jardin*, 1864
Dick, Stewart, and Helen Allingham, *The Cottage Homes of England*, Edward Arnold, 1909; Bracken Books 1991
Doré, Gustave, and Blanche Jerrold, *London: a Pilgrimage*, Grant and Co, London, 1872;

Wordsworth Editions Ltd, Ware, 1987

Duterloo, Fridy, 'William Lescaze and the Modern Landscape' in the *Dutch Yearbook for the History of Garden and Landscape Architecture*, 1997, no. 3

Duthie, Ruth, *Florists' Flowers and Societies*, Shire Books, Princes Risborough, 1988

Dumbarton Oaks Colloquium VIII, *Beatrix Jones Farrand (1872–1959), Fifty Years of American Landscape Architecture*, Washington, USA, 1982

Eckbo, Garrett, 'Small Gardens in the City: A Study of their Design Possibilities', in *Pencil Points*, vol. 18, September 1937, pp. 573–86

———, 'Pilgrim's Progress', in Marc Treib (ed.), *Modern Landscape Architecture: A Critical Review*, MIT Press, Cambridge, Massachusetts, 1993, pp. 206–19

Eliovson, Sima, *The Gardens of Roberto Burle Marx*, Harry N. Abrams Inc./Sagapress Inc., New York, 1991

Elliott, Brent, *Victorian Gardens*, Batsford, London, 1986

Fairbrother, Nan, *New Lives, New Landscapes*, Architectural Press, London, 1970

Fehl, Gerhard, 'The Nazi Garden City', in Stephen V. Ward (ed.), *The Garden City*, E. and F. N. Spon, London, 1992, pp. 88–103

Foerster, Karl, *Vom Blütengarten der Zukunft*, Furche-Verlag, 1917

Gothein, Marie Luise, *Geschichte der Gartenkunst*, 1913, English trans. *A History of Garden Art*, J. M. Dent and Sons Ltd, 1928

Fricker, Laurence, 'Dartington Hall, Devonshire, England,' in Diane Kostial McGuire and Lois Fern (eds.) *Beatrix Jones Farrand (1872–1959): Fifty Years of American Landscape Architecture*, Dumbarton Oaks Colloquium VIII, Washington, USA, 1982

Firth, Kathryn, and Richard Burdett, 'Thames Barrier Park – a Catalyst for Urban Regeneration', in *Topos*, vol. 35, June 2001, pp. 54–62

Friedman, Terry, and Andy Goldsworthy (eds), *Hand to Earth: Andy Goldsworthy Sculpture 1976–1990*, W. S. Maney, Yorkshire, 1990

Frota, Lélia Coelho, 'A Painter and Visual Artist in the Brazilian Modernist Movement', in Rossana Vaccarino (ed.), *Roberto Burle Marx: Landscapes Reflected*, Princeton Architectural Press and Harvard University Graduate School of Design, 2000, pp. 25–40

Gardens in Edwardian England (facsimile of *Country Life's Gardens Old and New*), Antique Collectors' Club, Woodbridge, Suffolk, 1985

Gibberd, Frederick, 'The Design of a Garden', in *The Garden*, vol. 104, part 4, April 1979, pp. 131–36

Greenhalgh, Paul (ed.), *Art Nouveau 1890–1914*, V&A Publications, London, 2000

Gregory, Daniel, 'Just Add Water: The Productive Partnership between Thomas Church and Sunset Magazine', in *Studies in the History of Gardens and Designed Landscapes*, vol. 20, no. 2, April–June 2000, pp. 120–29

Grese, Robert E., *Jens Jensen: Maker of Natural Parks and Gardens*, Johns Hopkins University Press, 1992

———, 'Prairie Gardens of O.C. Simonds and Jens Jensen' in Therese O'Malley and Marc Treib (eds), *Regional Garden Design in the United States*, Dumbarton Oaks Colloquium XV, Washington, USA, 1995, pp. 99–124

Griswold, Mac, and Eleanor Weller, *The Golden Age of American Gardens*, Harry N. Abrams and the Garden Club of America, New York, 1992

Gröning, Gert, and Joachim Wolschke-Bulmahn, 'Changes in the Philosophy of Garden

Architecture in the 20th Century and their Impact upon the Social and Spatial Environment', in *Journal of Garden History*, vol. 9, no. 2, April–June 1989, pp. 53–70

Haggard, Henry Rider, *Rural England*, Longmans, 1902

Hall, Peter, *Cities of Tomorrow*, Basil Blackwell, Oxford, 1990

Halprin, Lawrence, *The Franklin Delano Roosevelt Memorial*, Chronicle Books, San Francisco, 1997

Hampel, W. *Teppichgärtnerei*, Paul Parey, Berlin, 1891

Hardy, Dennis, *From Garden Cities to New Towns*, E. and F. N. Spon, London, 1991

———, *From New Towns to Green Politics: Campaigning for Town and Country Planning 1946–1990*, E. and F. N. Spon, London, 1991

Harris, Diane, 'Thomas Church as Author: Publicity and the Professional at Mid-century', in *Studies in the History of Gardens and Designed Landscapes*, vol. 20, no. 2, April–June 2000, pp. 157–70

Hermand, Jost, 'Rousseau, Goethe, Humboldt: Their Influence on Later Advocates of the Nature Garden', in Joachim Wolschke-Bulmahn (ed.), *Nature and Ideology*, Dumbarton Oaks Colloquium XVIII, Washington, USA, 1997

Hildebrand, Gary R., *The Miller House: Icon of Modernism*, Spacemaker Press, Washington, 1999

Holmdahl, Gustave, Sven Ivar Lind and Kjell Ödeen (eds), *Gunnar Asplund, Architect, 1885–1940*, National Association of Swedish Architects, 1950; reprinted by Byggförlaget, 1981

Honeycombe, Gordon, *Selfridges*, Selfridges, London, 1984

Hoppe, Kurt, *Gärten und Garten-Architekturen*, Westdeutsche Verlagsgesellschaft, 1909

Howard, Ebenezer, *Garden Cities of To-morrow*, 1902; reprinted by Attic Books, Wales, 1985

Hubert, Christian, and Lindsay Stamm Shapiro, *William Lescaze*, Institute for Architectural and Urban Studies and Rizzoli, New York, 1982

Hustache, Anne, *Victor Horta: Maisons de Campagne*, Le Musée Horta, 1994

ICOMOS, *Jardins et Sites Historiques*, 1993

Imbert, Dorothée, *The Modernist Garden in France*, Yale University Press, New Haven and London, 1993

———, 'Thomas Church: Defining Styles – the Early Years' in *Studies in the History of Gardens and Designed Landscapes*, vol. 20, no. 2, April–June 2000, pp. 96–120

'Industrial Gardens' in *Landscape and Garden*, winter 1936, pp. 230–33

Jack, Janet, 'Shaping Interior Landscape', in *Landscape Design*, August 1985, pp. 27–29

———, 'On a Podium', in *Landscape Design*, September 1992, pp. 24–25

———, 'A Bridge with a View', in *Landscape Design*, September 1992, pp. 27–28

Jacobs, Jane, *The Death and Life of Great American Cities*, Jonathan Cape, London, 1962

Jekyll, Gertrude, *Old West Surrey*, London, 1904; reprinted by Phillimore, Chichester, 1999

Jellicoe, Geoffrey, 'Towards a Landscape of Humanism', in *Guelph Lectures on Landscape Design IV*, 1983, pp. 149–95

———, *Studies of a Landscape Designer Over Eighty Years*, vol. I, Garden Art Press, Woodbridge, Suffolk, 1993

——— and Susan Jellicoe, *The Landscape of Man*, Thames and Hudson, London, 1975; new edition 1987

Jencks, Charles, *The Language of Post-modern

Architecture*, Academy Editions, London, 1977

———, *Modern Movements in Architecture*, Penguin Books, Harmondsworth, 2nd edition, 1987

———, *The Architecture of the Jumping Universe*, Academy Editions, London, 1995

Jensen, Jens, *Siftings*, Ralph Fletcher Seymour, Chicago, 1939; reprinted Johns Hopkins University Press, 1990

Johanson, Patricia, *Public Landscapes* (exhibition booklet), The Painted Bride Art Centre, Philadelphia, Pennsylvania, 1991

———, *Art and Survival: Creative Solutions of Environmental Problems*, Gallerie, 1992

Joseph, Lawrence, 'The Garden of Ulysses: Ferdinand Bac, Modernism and the Afterlife of Myth', in *Studies in the History of Gardens and Designed Landscapes*, vol. 20, no. 1, January–March 2000, pp. 6–24

Kemp, Edward, *How to Lay Out a Garden*, Bradbury and Evans, London, 3rd edition, 1864

Kiley, Dan, and Jane Amidon, *Dan Kiley: In His Own Words*, Thames and Hudson, London, 1999

Krueckeberg, Donald A. (ed.), *The American Planner, Biographies and Reflections*, Methuen, New York, 1983

Lancaster, Robert, *Letchworth Garden City*, Alan Sutton Publishing Co., Stroud, Gloucestershire, 1995

Lange, Willy, and Otto Stahn, *Gartengestaltung der Neuzeit*, J. J. Weber, Leipzig, 1907

Laroze, Catherine, 'Tuileries: Le Jardin du Carrousel', in *Les Jardins de Jacques Wirtz*, Fondation Pour L'Architecture, 1993, pp. 165–73

Laurie, Michael, 'Thomas Church, California Gardens, and Public Landscapes', in Marc Treib (ed.), *Modern Landscape Architecture: A Critical Review*, MIT Press, Cambridge, Massachusetts, 1993, pp. 166–79

Le Corbusier (trans. Frederick Etchells) *Towards a New Architecture*, The Architectural Press, London, 1927 (first published as *Vers une Architecture*, Paris, 1923)

———, *Précisions sur un état présent de l'architecture et de l'urbanisme*, Les Editions G. Crès et Cie, Paris, 1930, Vincent Fréal, Paris, 1960

——— and Pierre Jeanneret, *Œuvre Complète de 1929–1934*, Les Editions d'Architecture, Erlenbach, Zurich, 1947

Les Jardins de Jacques Wirtz, Fondation Pour l'Architecture, 1993

London Historic Parks and Gardens Trust, *City Parks in the Next Millennium* (proceedings of the 1999 Conference)

Macedo, Silvio Soares, 'Roberto Burle Marx and the Founding of Modern Brazilian Landscape Architecture', in Rossana Vaccarino (ed.), *Roberto Burle Marx: Landscapes Reflected*, Princeton Architectural Press and Harvard University Graduate School of Design, 2000, pp. 13–24

MacPhail, Elizabeth C., *Kate Sessions: Pioneer Horticulturist*, San Diego Historical Society, 1976

McGregor, Robert, *The Art Deco City, Napier, New Zealand*, The Art Deco Trust, 1998

McHarg, Ian L., *Design With Nature*, John Wiley and Sons, Inc., New York 1967

Martínez, Antonio Riggen, *Luis Barragán: Mexico's Modern Master 1902–1988*, The Monacelli Press, New York, 1996

Mawson, Thomas H., and E. Prentice Mawson, *The Art and Craft of Garden Making*, 5th edition, B. T. Batsford Ltd, London, and Charles Scribner's Sons, New York, 1926

———, *The Life and Work of an English Landscape Architect*, Richards, 1927

Mayhew, Henry, *London Labour and the London Poor*, Griffin, Bohn and Company, 1861; reprinted by Dover Publications 1968

Mearns, Andrew, *The Bitter Cry of Outcast London: An Inquiry into the Conditions of the Abject Poor*, James Clarke, London, 1883

Metzendorf, Georg, *Kleinwohnungs-bauten und Siedlungen*, Alexander Koch, Darmstadt, 1920

Migge, Leberecht, *Die Gartenkultur Des 20. Jahrhunderts*, Eugen Diederichs, Jena, 1913

Miller, A., 'Radburn and its Validity Today', in *Architect and Building News*, vol. 2 (6), 27 March, 1969, pp. 30–35

Miller, Mervyn, and A. Stuart Gray, *Hampstead Garden Suburb*, Phillimore and Co. Ltd, Chichester, 1992

Miller, Wilhelm, *The Charm of English Gardens*, Hodder and Stoughton, London and New York, c. 1900

Montero, Marta Iris, *Burle Marx: The Lyrical Landscape*, Thames & Hudson, London 2001

Mosser, Monique, and Georges Teyssot (eds), *The Architecture of Western Gardens*, MIT Press, Cambridge Massachusetts, 1991

Myrha, David, 'Rexford Guy Tugwell: Initiator of America's Greenbelt New Towns, 1935–36', in Donald A. Krueckberg (ed.), *The American Planner, Biographies and Reflections*, Methuen, New York, 1983, pp. 225–49

Neal, Peter, 'Parc de la Villette', in *Landscape Design*, February 1988, pp. 30–34

Neckar, Lance M., 'Christopher Tunnard: The Garden in the Modern Landscape', in Marc Treib (ed.), *Modern Landscape Architecture: A Critical Review*, MIT Press, Cambridge Massachusetts, 1993, pp. 159–66

Nettlefold, J. S., *Practical Housing*, Garden City Press, Letchworth, 1908

Noguchi, Isamu, *A Sculptor's World*, Harper and Row, New York, 1968

———, *The Isamu Noguchi Garden Museum*, Harry N. Abrams, New York, 1999

Nonell, Juan Bassegoda, 'The Labyrinth and the Güell Park', in *Jardins et Sites Historiques*, ICOMOS, 1993

Oehme, Wolfgang, and James van Sweden, *Bold Romantic Gardens*, Spacemaker Press, Washington, 1990

O'Malley, Therese, and Marc Treib (eds), *Regional Garden Design in the United States*, Dumbarton Oaks Colloquium XV, Washington, 1995

Osborn, Frederick, and Arnold Whittick, *The New Towns: The Answer to Megalopolis*, Leonard Hill, London, 1963

Ottewill, David, *The Edwardian Garden*, Yale University Press, New Haven and London, 1989

Pallasmaa, Juhani, 'Tradition and Modernity', in Michael Spens (ed.), *The Recovery of the Modern*, Architectural Review, Oxford, 1996, pp. 132–46

Papadakis, Andreas, and Harriet Watson (eds), *New Classicism*, Academy Editions, London, 1990

Padilla, Victoria, *Southern Californian Gardens*, University of California Press, Berkeley and Los Angeles, 1961

Page, Russell, *The Education of a Gardener*, William Collins Sons & Co. Ltd 1962; Penguin Books, 1985

Powers, Alan, *Serge Chermayeff: Designer Architect Teacher*, RIBA Publications, London, 2001

Radice, Betty, *The Letters of the Younger Pliny*, Penguin Books, Harmondsworth, 1963

Richmond, A., 'Land Settlement in England' in *Journal of the Royal Agricultural Society of England*, vol. 106, 1945, pp. 114–15

Robinson, William, *The Wild Garden*, John Murray, London, 1870; Century-Hutchinson and the National Trust 1986

———, *Gravetye Manor or Twenty Years' Work Round an Old Manor House*, J. Murray, London, 1911; Sagapress, New York, 1984

Rose, James C., 'Freedom in the Garden: A Contemporary Approach in Landscape Design', in *Pencil Points*, vol. 19, October 1938, pp. 639–43

———, 'Plants Dictate Garden Forms: Each has a Place as Material in Landscape Design', in *Pencil Points*, vol. 19, November 1938, pp. 695–97

———, 'Articulate Form in Garden Design', in *Pencil Points*, vol. 20, February 1939, pp. 98–100

———, *Creative Gardens*, Reinhold Publishing Corporation, New York, 1958

Rosenblum, Roger, MaryAnne Stevens, Ann Dumas (eds), *1900: Art at the Crossroads*, Royal Academy Publications, 2000

Royal Commission on the Housing of the Working Classes, British Parliamentary Papers, 1884–1885, vol. I: First Report; vol. II: Minutes and Evidence and Appendices (C 4402)

Royal Commission on the Employment of Children, Young Persons and Women, British Parliamentary Papers, 1868–69

Royer, Catherine, 'Art Deco Gardens in France', in Monique Mosser and Georges Teyssot (eds), *The Architecture of Western Gardens*, MIT Press, Cambridge Massachusetts, 1991

Schaffer, Daniel, 'The American Garden City: Lost Ideals', in Stephen V. Ward (ed.), *The Garden City*, E. and F. N. Spon, London, 1992, pp. 127–42

Schildt, Göran, *Alvar Aalto: The Complete Catalogue of Architecture, Design and Art*, Rizzoli, New York, 1994

Schoenaich, Brita von, 'The End of the Border?', in *Landscape Design*, September 1992, pp. 9–14

Seddon, Sue, 'A Plan for All Seasons', in *Gardens Illustrated*, November 2001, pp. 36–43

Shepheard, Peter, *Modern Gardens*, The Architectural Press, London, 1953

Sitte, Camillo (trans. G. R. and C. C. Collins), *City Planning according to Artistic Principles*, Random House, New York, 1965

Snell, Reginald, *From the Bare Stem*, Devon Books, Exeter, 1989

Snow, Marc, *Modern American Gardens Designed by James C. Rose*, Reinhold Publishing Corp. 1967

Spens, Michael, *Gardens of the Mind*, Antique Collectors' Club, Woodbridge, Suffolk, 1992

———, *The Complete Landscape Designs and Gardens of Geoffrey Jellicoe*, Thames & Hudson, London, 1994

——— (ed.), *The Recovery of the Modern*, Architectural Review, Oxford, 1996

Spirn, Anne Whiston, 'Frank Lloyd Wright: Architect of Landscape', in David G. De Long (ed.), *Frank Lloyd Wright: Designs for an American Landscape 1922–1932*, Harry N. Abrams Inc., New York, 1996

Stephensen, Lulu Salto, 'The Danish Landscape and Landscape Gardening: on the Visualization of the Aesthetic Potential for Nature in Cultivation in the Twentieth Century', in *Journal of Garden History*, vol. 17, no. 4, 1997, pp. 295–309

Streatfield, David C., *California Gardens, Creating a New Eden*, Abbeville Press, New York, 1984

Sudell, Richard, *Landscape Gardening*, Ward Lock and Co, London, 1933

Sutcliffe, Anthony (ed.), *The Rise of Modern Urban Planning 1800–1914*, Mansell, 1980

Tandy, Clifford R. V. (ed.), *Landscape and Human Life*, Djambatan, Amsterdam, 1966

Takei, Jiro (trans. Marc P. Keane), *Sakuteiki: Visions of the Japanese Garden*, Tuttle Publishing, Boston, Rutland, Vermont, Tokyo, 2001

Tarn, John Nelson, *Five Per Cent Philanthropy*, Cambridge University Press, 1973

Taylor, G. C., *Modern Gardens*, Country Life, 1936

Topos: Emscher Park, No. 26, March, 1999, Callwey, Munich

Topos: Barcelona, No. 29, December, 1999, Callwey, Munich

Topos: Landscape Architecture in Scandinavia, Callwey, Munich and Birkhäuser, Basel, 2002

Torres, Ana Maria, *Isamu Noguchi: A Study of Space*, The Monacelli Press, New York, 2000

Treib, Marc (ed.), *Modern Landscape Architecture: A Critical Review*, MIT Press, Cambridge, Massachusetts, 1993

———, 'A Sculpting of Space', in *Landscape Design*, no. 267, February 1998, pp. 21–28

———, 'Noguchi's Spiritual Quest', in *Landscape Design*, no. 269, April 1998, pp. 29–32

———, 'Thomas Church: The Modernist Years', in *Studies in the History of Gardens and Designed Landscapes*, vol. 20, no. 2, April–June 2000, pp. 130–56

———, 'A Setting for Solitude: The Landscape of Luis Barragán' in Federica Zanco (ed.), *Luis Barragán: The Quiet Revolution*, Skira Editores, Milan, 2001, pp. 114–39

——— and Dorothée Imbert, *Garrett Eckbo*, University of California Press, Berkeley, 1997

Tucker, Paul Hayes, George T. M. Shackleford, MaryAnne Stevens (eds), *Monet in the 20th Century*, Royal Academy of Arts and Yale University Press, London and New York, 1998

Tunnard, Christopher, 'Garden Design at Chelsea Show', in *Landscape and Garden*, summer 1936, pp. 90–94

———, *Gardens in the Modern Landscape*, The Architectural Press, London, 1938

———, 'Television of Garden Planning' in *Landscape and Garden*, summer 1938, p. 118

———, 'Planning a Modern Garden: An Experience in Collaboration', in *Landscape and Garden*, Spring 1939, pp. 23–27

———, 'Modern Gardens for Modern Houses' in *Landscape Architecture*, January 1942

———, *The City of Man: A New Approach to the Recovery of Beauty in American Cities*, Charles Scribner's Sons 1953

Turner, Tom, *City as Landscape: A Post Post-modern View of Design and Planning*, E. and F. Spon, London, 1996

Underwood, David, *Oscar Niemeyer and Brazilian Free-form Modernism*, George Brazillier Inc., New York, 1994

Unwin, Raymond, *Cottage Homes and Common Sense*, Fabian Tract no. 109, Fabian Society, 1902

———, *Nothing Gained by Overcrowding! How the Garden City Type of Development may Benefit both Owner and Occupier*, P. S. King, London, 1912

———, *Town Planning in Practice*, Fisher Unwin, 1909; Princeton Architectural Press, New York, 1994

Vaccarino, Rossana (ed.), *Roberto Burle Marx: Landscapes Reflected*, Princeton Architectural Press and Harvard University Graduate School of Design, 2000

Vernon, Christopher, 'Wilhelm Miller and the Prairie Spirit in Landscape Gardening' in Therese O'Malley and Marc Treib (eds), *Regional Garden Design in the United States*, Dumbarton Oaks Colloquium XV, Washington, USA, 1995

Van Groeningen, Isabelle, 'Gifts from a Giant', in *The Garden*, vol. 123, part 5, May 1998

Von Zdenek, Felix, and Pia Simig (eds), *Works in Europe 1972–1995: Ian Hamilton Finlay*, Cantz Verlag, 1995

Wahmann, Birgit, 'Allotments and Schrebergärten in Germany' in Monique Mosser and Georges Teyssot (eds), *The Architecture of Western Gardens*, MIT Press, Cambridge Massachusetts, 1991, pp. 451–53

———, 'The Jugendstil Garden in Germany and Austria' in Monique Mosser and Georges Teyssot (eds), *The Architecture of Western Gardens*, MIT Press, Cambridge Massachusetts, 1991, pp. 454–56

Wallinger, Rosamund, 'In Miss Jekyll's Footsteps', in *Historic Gardens Review*, Autumn 1999, p. 18

Ward, Stephen, (ed.), *The Garden City Past, Present and Future*, E. & F. Spon, London, 1992

Watanabe, Shun-ichi, 'The Japanese Garden City' in Stephen V. Ward (ed.), *The Garden City Past, Present and Future*, E. & F. Spon, 1992, pp. 69–83

Waymark, Peter, *A History of Petts Wood*, Petts Wood and District Residents' Association, 4th edition, 2000

Waymark, Janet, 'Hestercombe', in *Historic Gardens Review*, Spring/Summer 2002, pp. 8–11

Whalley, Robin (ed.), *The Boke of Iford*, Libanus Press, Marlborough, 1993

Wharton, Edith, *Italian Villas and their Gardens*, The Century Company, New York, 1904.

Whitehouse, J. H., 'Bournville: A Study in Housing Reform', in *Studio*, London, 1901–2, pp. 162–72

Wolschke-Bulmahn, Joachim, 'Wild Garden and Nature Garden', in *Journal of Garden History*, vol. 12, no. 3, 1992

——— and Gert Gröning, 'The Ideology of the Nature Garden: Nationalistic Trends in Garden Design in Germany during the Early Twentieth Century', in *Journal of Garden History*, vol. 12, no. 1, 1992

——— (ed.), *Nature and Ideology*, Dumbarton Oaks Colloquium XVIII, Washington, D.C., 1997

Woudstra, Jan, 'Jacobus P. Thijsse's Influence on Dutch Landscape Architecture', in Joachim Wolschke-Bulmahn (ed.), *Nature and Ideology*, Dumbarton Oaks Colloquium XVIII, Washington, 1997

———, 'The Corbusian Landscape: Arcadia or No Man's Land?', in *Garden History*, 28:1, 2000

Wright, Frank Lloyd, *An Autobiography*, 1932; Quartet Books, London, 1977

Yoch, James Y., *Landscaping the American Dream: The Gardens and Film Sets of Florence Yoch 1890–1972*, Harry N. Abrams Inc./Sagapress Inc., New York 1989

Zanco, Federica (ed.), *Luis Barragán: The Quiet Revolution*, Skira Editores, Milan, 2001

Zapatka, Christian, 'Greenbelt, Maryland', in Monique Mosser and Georges Teyssot (eds), *The Architecture of Western Gardens*, MIT Press, Cambridge, Massachusetts, 1991, pp. 513–15

Selected Journals and Newspapers

Architect and Building News
Architectural Review
Bios
California Garden
Country Life
Dutch Yearbook for the History of Garden and Landscape Architecture
Garden, the journal of the Royal Horticultural Society
Garden Design, journal of the Landscape Institute

Garden History, the journal of the Garden History Society
Historic Gardens Review
Illustrated London News
Journal of Garden History; 1998 renamed *Studies in the History of Gardens and Designed Landscapes*
Journal of the Royal Agricultural Society of England
Landscape and Garden, 1934–1939, journal of the Landscape Institute
Landscape Design, journal of the Landscape Institute
Landlines, journal of the Landscape Institute
Pencil Points
Studio
The Garden, the journal of the Royal Horticultural Society
The Times
Topos, European landscape journal

Unpublished sources

Jordan, Harriet, *Thomas Hayton Mawson: The English Garden Designs of an Edwardian Landscape Architect*, PhD thesis, Wye College, University of London, 1988

Lambert, David, *Detached Town Gardens*, Theme Study for English Heritage, July 1994

Milette, Nicole, *Landscape Painter as Landscape Gardener: The Case of Alfred Parsons RA*, DPhil thesis, University of York Institute of Advanced Architectural Studies, 1997

Van Groeningen, Isabelle, *The Development of Herbaceous Planting in Britain and Germany from the Nineteenth to Early Twentieth Century* DPhil thesis, University of York Institute of Advanced Architectural Studies, 1996

Waymark, Janet, *Dorset Landed Estates, 1870–1990, their Survival and Influence*, PhD thesis, University of London, 1995

Woudstra, Jan, *Landscape for Living: Garden Theory and Design of the Modern Movement*, PhD thesis, University of London, 1997

List of Illustrations

All photographs are by Janet Waymark unless otherwise stated.

2 © Red Cover/Hugh Palmer **8** © Country Life Picture Library **26** © Somerset Archive and Record Service **35 (top)** Courtesy of the Lindley Library **39 (top)** from W. Hampel, *Die Moderne Teppichgärtnerei*, Paul Parev, Berlin, 1891 **41, 42 (left)** Courtesy of the West Sussex Record Office **44–48** San Diego Historical Society Photograph Collection **52** Jens Jensen Drawings and Papers, Bentley Historical Library, University of Michigan **53** Courtesy of the Chicago Park District **54** Photo Ron Ackerman, courtesy of the Abraham Lincoln Memorial Garden Foundation, Illinois **55 (top)** Courtesy of the Chicago Park District **(bottom)** Jens Jensen Drawings and Papers, Bentley Historical Library, University of Michigan **60** from Willy Lange, *Gartengestaltung der Neuzeit*, J. J. Weber, 1928 **62** from *Die Land-Baufibel*, George D. W. Callwey, Munich **65** from Karl Foerster, *Vom Blütengarten der Zukunft*, Furche-Verlag, 1917 **68** Photo Robert P. Ruschak, courtesy of Western Pennsylvania Conservancy **70 (top)** Ferdinand Hart Nibbrig, *Abundance*, 1895. Oil on canvas 99 x 150 (39 x 59). Private collection, The Netherlands **70 (bottom)** Santiago Rusiñol, *The Green Wall*, 1901. Oil on canvas, 95 x 105 (37 ¾ x 41 ⅜). Centro de Art Reina Sofia, Madrid **74** from Kurt Hoppe, *Gärten und Gärten-Arkitekturen*, Wiesbaden, 1909 **75** Charles Rennie Mackintosh, *The Hill House: Perspective from the Southwest*, 1903. Ink, 33 x 55 (13 x 21 ⅝). Glasgow School of Art **76** Victor Horta, design for La Bastide à la Hulpe. Musée Horta, Brussels. © DACS 2003 **79** Antonín Brunner, The Municipal Mud Baths Bohdaneč, 1913. Colour lithograph poster, 89 x 59 (35 x 23 ¼) **80** from Michel Roux-Spitz, *Bâtiments et jardins à l'exposition des arts décoratifs*, 1925 **81** from André Lurçat, *Terrasses et Jardins* **82** Photo Man Ray. © Man Ray Trust/ADAGP, Paris and DACS, London 2003 **85** Photograph by Robert McGregor **88–89** Le Corbusier © FLC/ADAGP, Paris and DACS, London 2003 **94** © Bauhaus-Archiv, Berlin **99** © BBC **101** By courtesy of Peter Chermayeff **104** William Stephen Coleman, *A Cottage Garden in Summer*. Watercolour. Courtesy of Christopher Wood Gallery **106** Gustave Doré, *Over London – By Rail*, 1870. Engraving from Blanchard Jerrold and Gustave Doré, *London – a Pilgimage*, London 1872 **107** Cottage at East Morden, *Illustrated London News*, 5 September 1846 **108 (left)** George Elgood, *Cottage garden plants at Cleeve Prior*, from *Some English Gardens*, Longmans, London, 1904. By courtesy of the University of Liverpool Library **108 (right)** Helen Allingham, *The Clothes Basket*, from Stewart Dick, *The Cottage Homes of England*, Edward Arnold, London 1909 **110** Thomas Mawson, plan for Port Sunlight, 1910. Cumbria Record Office, Kendal. Courtesy of former partners of Thomas H. Mawson & Son **111** Courtesy Cadbury Trebor Bassett **114** Barry Parker, plan of New Earswick. Courtesy of the First Garden City Heritage Museum, Letchworth Garden City, UK **115 (top)** from Ebenezer Howard, *Garden Cities of To-morrow*, 1902 **115 (bottom)** from Ebenezer Howard, *To-morrow: A Peaceful Path to Real Reform*, 1898 **117** from M. H. Baillie Scott, *Houses and Gardens*, 1906 **124** Photos Peter Waymark **127** © Imperial War Museum, London **129** Osborn Collection, Welwyn Garden City Library **131** From Georg Metzendorf, *Kleinwohnungs-bauten und Siedlungen*, published by Alexander

Index